ENDORSEMENTS

God is looking for friends who will be part of incredible and miraculous revivals on the earth simply by giving their yes and yielding to His great love. Linda Anderson is one who courageously said yes to God with her words and her actions. Through her yes, healing rooms was birthed, transforming individual lives and their region through supernatural healings. In Mozambique, when God heals one deaf person, often hundreds in a village come to Christ. Every believer is invited into this reality of demonstrating God's love with Holy Spirit power. Whether you are in Africa or the United States or any other nation, His promise still stands. Read Ignited and allow God to stretch your faith and give you tools to step into the supernatural. Will you give God your yes and see what He will do through your life? I promise you it won't be boring!

Heidi G Baker Ph.D.
Co-founder and Executive Chairman, Iris Global

This book is an excellent read for the beginner who wants to learn about healing, as well for those who need to be reminded and refreshed on God's will to heal. Linda covers everything from our relationship with God, to His will to heal and our part to walk in faith and share the testimony. In seventeen chapters she takes you through a complete walk from the cross to the revival of healing that is coming on the earth today. You will truly be blessed and equipped as you read this book.

Cal Pierce
International Director, Healing Rooms Ministries
www.healingrooms.com

Linda's new book, Ignited, lays at our feet a clear understanding of how to step into the healing heart of God. The Bible tells us that everywhere Jesus went, He healed **all,** and then Jesus said that His followers would do even greater things. Ignited will stir your faith to believe afresh in the healing power of God. Linda leads us to see that there is an extraordinary life full of faith, that can unleash the healing power of God. Miracles are happening and Linda is a catalyst for these as she daily walks out her faith in God. You will find Ignited a faith building book from a faith filled author. I highly recommend this book!

Tom Anderson
Lead Pastor, Horizon Christian Church
www.horizonrenosparks.com

BOOKS BY LINDA ANDERSON

Where Miracles Begin
The Prayer Team Handbook
Freedom From Fear
Real Women in the Middle of Real Life
Ignited

IGNITED

GUIDE TO PERSONAL AND SHARED HEALING

Linda Anderson

authorHOUSE®

AuthorHouse™
1663 Liberty Drive
Bloomington, IN 47403
www.authorhouse.com
Phone: 1 (800) 839-8640

Published by AuthorHouse 09/05/2019

Interior Image Credit: Dawson King - dkphotographyreno.com

This book may be ordered by contacting: His Way Ministries
1995 E. Prater Way Sparks, NV 89434
www.hiswaytoday.org
1.775.787.6259

ISBN: 978-1-7283-2069-4 (sc)
ISBN: 978-1-7283-2068-7 (e)

Library of Congress Control Number: 2019910608

Print information available on the last page.

DEDICATION

To Jesus Christ:
my King and Healer
and source of life and love.

I also dedicate this book to my amazing family:
Tom, my husband, who has the most generous
and loving heart of any person I have ever known,
Tamarah, our daughter, who worships,
and leads others to worship the beautiful King
in spirit and in truth, along with her husband, Heath,
who has a heart as big as the sky;
to our son, Gregg, who walks in integrity
and loyalty before God, and his wife, Cortina, who
personifies the Proverbs 31 woman.

I also dedicate this book to my grandchildren,
who all love God and are my absolute joy:
Brayden, his wife, Emily, Gabrielle, Adrienne, and Rowan.

To the Doctors of the Cross:
Your burning passion for God and your
lifestyle of prayer has helped to create the context
for the greatest move of God, I have ever witnessed.

And finally, to our Pastors Prayer Shield pastors,
Mike and Nancy Kelly, who faithfully lead our
Pastors Prayer Shield to protect us daily through prayer.

ACKNOWLEDGEMENTS

My special thanks to Marla Dye, my faithful assistant,
who labored in love to push this book forward.
Many thanks to those who edited - especially
John Eichelberger and Petite Proutsos.

CONTENTS

INTRODUCTION

When Holy Spirit first impressed on my heart that He was bringing a Healing Revival to the region in which I live, I was thrilled! I have prayed for Revival for many years, expectantly, while about the Father's work, watching and fanning, and magnifying the sign of awakening.

So, I was happily surprised that day when Holy Spirit whispered, "Healing Revival", to me. I had never heard those words, *healing,* and *revival,* put together before like that. But my biggest surprise was what God impressed on my heart a week later: "Open a Healing School".

It was during a church service that I had an open vision from God. As I looked around the sanctuary, I saw many individuals dressed in doctor and nurse uniforms! Everywhere I looked, there were medical professionals who didn't even know this was their calling. The vision was so real that I was stunned and didn't know what to do. But I asked God, and that's when I heard the words, "Healing School!"

This book was birthed during the first three years in which Holy Spirit initiated Healing School was in session. From the very first class, we opened with 70 students who were willing to grow in wisdom, revelation, and boldness. Through Healing School, Healing Rooms were formed in our region. Out of this ministry we have seen countless miraculous healings. (Healing Rooms instruction is found in chapter three.) As He said He would, God has birthed a Healing Revival!

Many students have prodded me toward making the contents of this book available to all. I have been told that the material is life-changing (and many more cheering comments). With the prodding of the students, I present to you a book that can be as a Healing School for you, the reader.

In this book you will learn how to minister healing, the secret to increased miracles, how miracles are reproducible, and the way to sustain them! I believe that you will walk in personal divine health as you apply the revelations.

I also believe that you will find a fire ignited in your heart to help others come into the reality of God's personal love for them. You will heal many people, in Jesus' Name, and ignite many hearts with the fire of the love God's!

May you receive Holy Spirit revelation through this book, and may God ignite a Healing Revival in your own heart and region!

Expecting Miracles,

Linda Anderson

1

BECOMING A DOCTOR OF THE CROSS

The One who guaranteed His healing power is the One who resides in your hands and in your very being! Since the Almighty, all-powerful, all-knowing, all-life-giving God resides in you, how could you not affect the situations in your path?

Have you ever heard a doctor say, "I will heal ALL of your diseases?" Only God guarantees a freedom from disease that no one in the medical community has ever dared to promise! Yet, most people go to a medical doctor before they go to Almighty God.

Throughout biblical history, there was never a time when medicine alone was credited as a cure. Only God was known to heal and known as "Healer". Medicine and medical procedures may be aids in regaining health, but the supernatural healing power of God is the one essential component that cannot be left out.

I appreciate the time and price it requires to become a medical doctor. Not only does this type of degree require years of accredited education, but there are also the factors of getting over seeing the bared human anatomy, conquering any squeamishness about blood, and memorizing thousands of terms.

I wanted to go to medical school and become a doctor; but the aforementioned requirements were daunting to me. So, I took the cleaner route to become a psychology major in college. However, even now in my sixties, I still have a desire to go to medical school and become a certified medical doctor...if that would open more doors to help people become whole! Yet, whenever I pray about pursuing a medical degree, the Holy Spirit reminds me that He has qualified me to be a healer of people because He, The Healer, lives in me - and so I am a Doctor of the Cross!

As you know, we need a system in place in order to regulate medication (prescriptions) and to perform surgeries - we really don't want just anyone doing these kinds of things, as they require expertise. And we can appreciate the fact that we have access to doctors when needed. But seriously, we really don't need a medical doctor very often in our lives.

Certified doctoring is a relatively new concept in the world. In fact, for most of Jewish history, the priests were the physicians. It wasn't until the early 1800s in America, that any kind of regulations were established for practicing medicine. At that time, medical societies started setting up standards of practice, and began the certification of doctors.

The Johns Hopkins University School of Medicine opened in 1893 and is cited as being the first medical school in America of genuine university-type. It wasn't until after 1920, that physicians were freed from asking permission of the church before starting their practice or performing surgery (too bad!).

Like me, you may not have graduated from medical school, as most of the doctors in history did not, but you may be more qualified to bring healing to people than you think. There is a place for trained physicians and surgeons; but there is also a place for you.

Trained Medical Doctors Practice

According to recent polls, the number one concern of most people is good health. Consequently, doctors are sought after, paid a lot of money, and often idolized. Again, we appreciate so much when we are helped via a physician. But studies show that up to 20% of individuals are misdiagnosed, and even a higher percentage are prescribed medications that create more problems than remedies. To break down our illusions even further, consider the following history of medical science:

- **Bloodletting** - for thousands of years, medical practitioners clung to the belief that sickness was the result of 'bad blood.' With this in mind, patients with a fever or other ailment were often diagnosed with an overabundance of blood. To restore bodily harmony, their doctor would simply cut open a vein and drain some of their blood into a receptacle. In some cases, leeches were used to suck the blood directly from the skin. Bloodletting endured as a common medical practice well into the 19th century! Praise God we have moved away from this practice.

- **Microscopic Ignorance** - in the mid-19th century, one out of every six women died who gave birth in a hospital maternity ward. The obstetricians ascribed the deaths to constipation, delayed lactation, fear, and poisonous air. It was only when a young man, Ignaz Semmelweis, accidentally noticed that washing his hands after performing autopsies on the dead, and before going in to examine the living, changed the mortality rate! No one believed that there was actually something invisible on the doctors' hands (which of course we now know as bacteria), and Semmelweis was scorned and laughed out of the medical community. Eventually, the microscope was invented which could look into the microscopic realm where germs were observed. Only then did Doctors begin to perform the act which God taught Moses many centuries before, about cleansing the hands (Numbers 19)! Nowadays many people are phobic about germs and worry too much.
- **Animal Dung Ointments** - during the same time that Moses was receiving instruction from God about how to live healthy, the Egyptians (who held the most prominent place in the ancient medical world) published a famous medical book, the Papyrus Ebers. In this book, lizard blood, dead mice, mud, and moldy bread were all used as topical ointments and dressings, and women were sometimes dosed with horse saliva as a cure for their issues. Egyptian physicians used human and animal excrement as a cure-all remedy for diseases and injuries. According to 1500 B.C.'s Ebers Papyrus[1], donkey, dog, gazelle, and fly dung were all celebrated for their healing properties and their ability to ward off bad spirits.
- **Isolating the Sick** - in the fourteenth century, the Black Death took the lives of one out of every four persons. The plague was out of control, with no seeming way to stop it . . . until the church was consulted! God had already given the way of health as He

> had instructed His people about quarantine and isolating the sick (Leviticus 13). Historians credit the instructions in Scripture for halting the plague. The sickness stopped spreading when contact with the sick ceased. Millions of lives were saved through the wisdom of God's Word!

There are many more examples which could be cited which show the value of seeking God and His Word above the cultural norms. (What will the people living in the centuries beyond us laugh - and groan about, as they read about our primitive medical practices?)

What Type of Qualifications Does a Doctor of the Cross Have?

Jesus Christ appointed many ordinary people to bring real cures and freedom to masses of people! Your qualification to heal men and women, boys and girls is this: The One who lives inside of you, and what He said you can do.

All around us there are people in need of healing and deliverance. Who will help them? We are the ones who the Savior has invited to partner with Him in His compassion for people. Oh, that many of God's people would rise-up and believe that they can do what Jesus Christ said we can do - heal the sick and cast out demons.

God wants you to be empowered with the fact that you are full of the healing power of the Holy Spirit, simply by asking. Jesus Christ said, *"How much more will your Father give the Holy Spirit to those who ask Him"* (Luke 11:13)! And if this isn't enough for you, consider that Jesus Christ Himself, prayed for you to be given the Holy Spirit: *"I will pray the Father and He will give you another Helper . . ."* (John 14:16).

The One who guaranteed the flow of His healing power is the One who resides in you. Since the Almighty, all-powerful, all-knowing, and all-life-giving God resides in you, how could you not affect every situation in your path?

Your Medical School Manual

Instruction for receiving healing personally and for administering healing to others is given in the Bible. The Bible is our healing manual and it is full of perfect examples and wisdom. Our Heavenly Father is the only One who knows everything about the human body; He made it, He loves it, and He heals it. Therefore, we are not instructed to call the doctor; but we are instructed to call Someone - God!

"Is anyone among you suffering? Let him pray. Is anyone cheerful? Let him sing psalms. Is anyone among you sick? Let him call for the elders of the church, and let them pray over him, anointing him with oil in the name of the Lord. And the prayer of faith will save the sick, and the Lord will raise him up. And if he has committed sins, he will be forgiven. Confess your trespasses to one another, and pray for one another, that you may be healed. The effective, fervent prayer of a righteous man avails much" (James 5:13-16).

Extremes of Opinion

Later in this book, we will expose some ideas we may hold about healing that need to conform to God's truth. We all have opinions that have been formed through life experiences, other people's prejudices, and our own misconceptions. Praise God that we have the Spirit of Truth to help us and to change us (John 14:17).

One of my heroes, the great faith healer, John G. Lake, founder of Healing Rooms, wrote, *"When you become a Christian with a consecrated body, soul, and spirit, your privilege of running to the doctor was cut off forevermore."*[2]

One of the problems with this statement is the human lens in the person reading it. A person could take it and decide to make it a rule for his or her life, thereby refusing to see a medical doctor when that is what is needed. It could be that God may want a person to go to a doctor to serve His larger purposes. Seeking God FIRST for healing means listening to His plan and obeying His voice.

Trusting God

Healing is multidimensional as well as circumspect because sickness is often complex. But the first factor that brings about healing is simple: we always begin with God.

God loves to heal people, and He wants to be called on **before** the medical doctors. When a person puts God first and trusts in Him, that person is in a good position for the supernatural flow of healing to take place.

In Scripture, we learn about Israel's king, Asa, and the reason why he died - he sought doctors before the Lord.

"Asa became diseased in his feet, and his malady was severe; yet in his disease he did not seek the Lord, but the physicians. So, Asa died . . ." (2 Chronicles 16:11-13).

Asa wasted precious time seeking doctors before he called upon Almighty God and, consequently, he ended up dying of a disease. I wonder what would have happened if King Asa had sought God's remedy first (and then if led by God, the medical community after that).

Scripture tells us that God is a consuming fire! Take a moment and ponder what a consuming fire might look and feel like. The Most-High God is not to be trifled with.

"They provoked Him to jealousy with their sins . . ." (1 Kings 14:22).
"For you shall worship no other god, for the Lord, whose name is Jealous, is a jealous God" (Exodus 34:14).
"For the Lord your God is a consuming fire, a jealous God" (Deuteronomy 4:24, Hebrews 12:29).
"Do you think that the Scripture says in vain, 'The Spirit Who dwells in us yearns jealously' (James 4:5).

Remember what King Asa forgot - we always trust God before the doctors. God is a jealous King and He will be first!

No Condemnation

When Jesus Christ healed a woman, who had spent all that she had on many doctors and was still suffering, He did not condemn her for going to doctors.

> *"Now a certain woman had a flow of blood for twelve years and had suffered many things from many physicians. She had spent all that she had and was no better, but rather grew worse. When she heard about Jesus, she came. . .He said to her, "Daughter, your faith has made you well. Go in peace and be healed of your affliction""* (Mark 5:25-34).

Whereas King Asa died when he sought doctors first, the woman with the twelve-year problem was healed when she reached out to Jesus after many years of paying physicians.

Let us also remember that Luke, the one who penned the books of Luke and Acts, in the Bible, was called the "beloved physician" (Colossians 4:14). We see that there is room in God's house for many different types of doctors. But we must always seek God first and above all others. Without God there is no healer. Throughout biblical history, there was never a time when medicine alone was credited as a cure. Only God was known to heal and known as Healer.

Medicine and medical procedures may be aids in regaining health, but the supernatural healing of God is the one essential component that cannot be left out. Without God there is no Healer. "For I am the Lord who heals you" (Exodus 15:26).

Seek God First

When I minister in the nation of India, I often have the opportunity to pray for people who have come to the healing meeting as their **only hope**. One day a mother brought a young boy for prayer who had been hit by a car three days before the meetings began. As she stood in line, waiting to bring her son forward to be healed, I saw that her son's leg was very damaged. The little boy was in terrible pain and was crying. As I invited the woman to bring her son to the front of the healing line, I saw desperation in her face, but I also saw hope. I put my hands upon the boy's leg and as I did, I felt the immense compassion of Jesus! And then, through the woman's faith and the Lord's healing power, the boy's leg straightened out and he was completely healed! As that mother sat her son on his feet, rejoicing broke out throughout the building! Faith rose sky-high and many more miracles occurred.

In America, I often minister to people who have come to a healing meeting as their **last hope**. Because of the affluence of our American culture, people have many options. In India, most people do not have the option of calling paramedics or a doctor. Consequently, we see many miracles on the mission fields of the world where God is called upon first.

I believe that seeking God first is a key to healing, as it is a key to life. *"But seek first the kingdom of God and His righteousness, and all these things shall be added to you"* (Matthew 6:33).

Who Does God Appoint To Bring Healing?

The fact that God would use me to bring healing to people is astonishing to me. I never get over being amazed by His use of little me. I live mind-blown because of the reality of the miracles which I am privileged to participate in.

Jesus Christ appointed ordinary people who were willing to work. He then gave them the authority to do the work. Not just a badge to wear, but the kind of power that speaks light into being - Heaven's power!

Jesus is ready to appoint you. He promises to give you His power and authority - and then you are qualified! I don't know of any medical school in the world that gives out that kind of God-credential! Jesus Christ appoints willing people like us and then gives instruction, protection and power: *"The Lord appointed seventy others also [besides the twelve] and sent them two by two before His face into every city and place where He Himself was about to go . . . Behold, I give you the authority to trample on serpents and scorpions, and over all the power of the enemy, and nothing shall by any means hurt you.'"* (Luke 10:1-19).

Taking the Command to "Go" Seriously

What does it take to become a healer of people: A Doctor of the Cross? You take seriously Jesus' command to "go". Miraculous Holy Spirit power is available to the one who replies, "Yes, I will go!"

"Jesus saw the multitudes, He was moved with compassion for them . . . Then He said to His disciples, 'The harvest truly is plentiful, but the laborers are few. Therefore, pray the Lord of the harvest to send out laborers into His harvest.' He called His twelve disciples to Him, and gave them power over unclean spirits, to cast them out, and to heal all kinds of sickness and all kinds of disease'" (Matthew 9:35-10:1).

I almost always feel like I am over my head - except when I remember and focus on what Jesus said, "I give you power . . ." Forming a Healing School, holding large conferences that cost a lot of money, planting a church in the "divorce capital of the world"[3], traveling the world to carry the torch of God's love, healing a person in a local store . . . I am a little laborer in God's great harvest with His immense power.

As people who are willing to attempt great things for God and who trust Him, we are conduits of His love and mighty power. God will show each of us what to do because He loves to work with a human agent on earth. That human agent is me and that human agent is you.

Prayer

Father God, until now, I didn't realize how important it is that I talk to You first. Please forgive me for each time I have reached out to another person before talking with You. I am sorry for seeking medical advice from anyone before You. Please help me to believe that I can hear You, and to become a person who seeks first Your kingdom and Your righteousness. Thank you for making me new today and giving me revelation. Now use me to be a conduit of healing to others. In Jesus' name, amen.

Reflection

1. What qualifies you to be a Doctor of the Cross (Luke 11:13)?

2. Sickness may be complex, but what does healing begin with?

3. Who is God's human agent?

4. Jesus Christ said that we should pray that willing workers will go and heal the sick and bring His Kingdom benefits to people. Are you a willing worker who Jesus is appointing?

"Let all that I am praise the Lord; may I never forget the good things He does for me. He forgives all my sins and heals all my diseases" (Psalm 103:1-3 NLT).

2

HOW TO RECEIVE

The essential element for the kind of faith that brings healing is a deeply personal understanding of who Jesus Christ truly is

Victory was in the air! The worship had just blown the roof off and we were preparing a tunnel of prayer up front for anyone at the service who wanted to receive healing from God. The chairs were pushed back, and the line of hopeful people wrapped around to the back of the sanctuary!

Many people went through the prayer tunnel, expectant, and received a powerful touch from God! Others hurried through with heads down, not realizing that the goodness of God was available to him or her **personally**. The Lord desired to minister His extravagant love deeply into all! I could hear the whisper of Holy Spirit through the entire tunnel of prayer, "Just receive!"

How we receive will determine what we will have. Our Lord said it like this, *"As you have believed, so let it be done for you"* (Matthew 8:13). Our Father takes great pleasure when His children open their hands and hearts, lift their heads up, and believe Him for good!

For many years of my life, I had trouble receiving God's love for me. Believing that God's generous and extravagant love could be for me personally seemed too good to be true. After all, I knew myself and I couldn't imagine deserving that kind of love. So, I would try harder to please God and usually end up feeling like I just wasn't good enough.

It was through the baptism of the Holy Spirit that I was so overwhelmed by the love of God that I was changed forever! During this encounter with

God, I could feel hot liquid love pouring into me and then pouring out from my own mouth to God. There was no previous experience in my life to compare with what I felt. Every temporal thing seemed to melt away as I was saturated with God's presence and love. It was as if all of Heaven was opened to me and swallowed me up in joy! I was so filled and transformed by Holy Spirit that nothing else mattered. The weeks and months following this experience were filled with incomparable joy and wonder. I could hardly sleep - my heart was so full of fire, love, and joy!

This true experience didn't happen because I had done all the right things. It happened because I was so hungry to receive from God that I was wide open to His Spirit. God can't resist pouring His merciful kindness and love out on anyone so desiring to receive from Him!

Receiving from Our Good Father

It is not uncommon for people to walk into our Healing Rooms who are unwilling to receive from God. The very fact that they walk into a prayer clinic should indicate that there is a desire to receive something they need. But the desperation to feel better that brought them in may not mean that he or she is willing to make the necessary changes afterwards. A quick fix is often a person's hope, instead of a full-fledged transformation which requires the individual to believe differently.

When Jesus healed a man, who had been sick for 38 years, he gave him this strong warning: *"See, you have been made well. Sin no more, lest a worse thing come upon you"* (John 5:14). I wonder if we should put up signs in our Healing Rooms with these words of Jesus on them.

I desire to know the rest of the story. Did the healed man stop sinning and stay well? Did he continue to live as he had before he was healed and end up worse off?

I have also desired to know what happened to the women who was caught in adultery. Jesus told her, *"Go and sin no more"* (John 8:11). Did she change her ways and become a lover of Jesus, or go back to a life of sexual sin?

In the case of this woman, it would seem likely that she was most certainly transformed. Having come face to face with God's mercy and goodness, surely, she would "go and sin no more". No doubt, she needed strength and revelation to be able to stand when the people around her expected her to be the way she used to be.

We all have people around us (especially family members) who expect us to behave as we have always behaved and do what we always have done. Breaking out of a mold, changing habits, and thinking in a whole new way is challenging. Only a true encounter with God's love will *keep us receiving* His love.

The man who laid by the pool of Bethesda, crippled for 38 years, who Jesus told *"take up your bed and walk"*, probably did not know how to live differently (John 5:8). The healed man was immediately in trouble with the leaders for carrying his bed on the Sabbath. Obeying Jesus' words was a whole new world for him. What a radical upheaval that man must have felt after being incapacitated and immobile for so many years. Could he make the shift? Scripture tells us that the healed man did not know who Jesus was and eventually stirred up trouble for Jesus with the leaders (John 5:16). If only he had believed that it was God's love which touched him. Then he surely would have fallen in love with Jesus, started giving his testimony, and become a preacher of the gospel!

Sometimes I hear back from people who were healed at our ministry but relapsed back into their former troubles. There are some commonalities we see in those who relinquish their healing. There are also similarities in those people who are healed and sustain their healing. The outcome often depends on *how* a person receives from God, and not *what* a person receives from God. How we receive *will* determine what we will have.

Your Love Receiver

How a person receives love from God is very important. In order to make the deep connection Father God longs to have with you, He may need to heal and restore your ability to receive love.

When speaking at the first night of a conference, I sometimes share about a little-known part of the soul called 'The Love Receiver'. I explain that there are body parts that we don't think about very often - if at all. Like 'The Truster', 'The Recorder', and 'The Love Receiver'. These inside parts are frequently in need of repair or updates.

Next, I explain that every person has been given a 'Love Receiver' formed by God. But because of life's experiences, especially personal sin, most people have difficulty accepting the generous, lavish, extravagant, amount of love offered to them by Father God.

To help illustrate the way a 'Love Receiver' operates, I have the individuals make a funnel out of a sheet of paper. The opening on one end is wider than the other, and the participants tape the sides together to form a cone-shape. Then I have them put the funnel on their heads, widest side up. This is a symbol of a healthy Love Receiver; wide open to God's love and a channel into themselves.

As I walk people through the illustration, I ask if perhaps one (or more) of the following things have happened to their Love Receiver:

- An off/on switch has been installed: when you feel good about yourself you turn on your ability to receive good things. When you mess up or fall short, you switch it to off.
- The Love Receiver is under your chin instead of open to heaven: your intellect is in the way, telling you that God's extravagant love is just too good to be true and just not logical.
- The receiver is bent; therefore, the wrong frequency is being tuned in: people who you have trusted have failed you; and now, you are looking for love in all the wrong places.
- Pain has squeezed it shut: you have decided that getting close to anyone is too painful and staying surface is safer (God seems far, far away).
- The opening is clogged through being filled with earthly stuff: you've tried to satisfy your desire for God's love with food, outward appearance, possessions, alcohol, etc.
- The funnel is upside down on your head: you give to everyone else; but when it comes to receiving, you feel like hardly anyone gives back to you, let alone God.
- Unforgiveness has shriveled up the receiver: you are mad at yourself, other people, and God. Therefore, your potential for receiving no longer feels possible (or wanted).

After going through this list, I give the people an opportunity to repent. Having realized that it was they themselves who blocked their own ability to receive from God, revelation and conviction comes in. Then the listeners are invited to ask Father God to forgive them and to repair their ability to receive His extravagant love. After the listeners *willingly* ask Father God to repair their Love Receivers, He does - for all who are willing to receive.

If the repair is resisted or refused (or received only a little bit), that amount will be measured back. The Lord said it like this, *"Take heed what you hear. With the same measure you use, it will be measured to you; and to you who hear, more will be given"* (Mark 4:24).

Gaining revelation of the truth of receptivity is a key to actively living the supernatural life; a key we all need. Whatever action you take in obedience to God - there will be a response from Heaven!

For This Reason

Paul might have been writing about the Law of Receptivity when he addressed some of the problems that were happening in the church at Corinth. The people of Corinth were gathering at church, taking Communion, but, in Paul's words, "not for the better but for the worse" (1 Corinthians 11:17). He went on to say that the people were gathering to eat the Lord's Supper; but they were not gathering **for** the Lord's Supper (verse 20).

Paul explained that because the people had not judged the body and blood of Jesus for what it truly is, they would not receive the benefits of what it truly means. Many were just going through the religious motions without recognizing what they were actually eating and drinking. Paul was saying that Jesus' broken body and shed blood was both a powerful payment for their sins and health to their bodies. The Corinthians, not paying attention, were missing the depth of what was offered to them.

It is the same today . . . churches all over the world partake of Communion simply as a reminder of something that happened a long time ago, instead of a physical, touchable testimony of the present reality: *Jesus paid for my miracle*!

Paul wanted the people to have a conviction that burned in their souls about what Jesus died to give them. He wanted Communion to grip them (and us), not just with a nice remembrance, but with the living, physical, and personal testimony: my healing was already fought for, *and won*, by Jesus.

This passage tells us that, in Communion, there is something very special and miraculous. Sometimes we change what Jesus says to make ourselves more comfortable. For example, the Lord told us to heal the sick; but we change it to *pray for the sick,* because we think we can't heal anybody. We think our job is to pray our best prayer. But Jesus didn't say that, He said *"heal the sick"* (Matthew 10:8, Luke 10:9). Jesus didn't say this because we have the ability but because He put the ability within reach. He said that there is a gift, an anointing available, and that if we will contend for it, He will give it to us.

In 1 Corinthians 11:24, Paul quotes Jesus' words exactly: *"Take eat, this is My body . . ."* (also see Matthew 26:26, Mark 14:22). Jesus did *not* say, "here, take some bread, this *represents* My body." Have you ever been served Communion and been instructed with words like these, "Here, this is a hunk of the body of Jesus Christ and you need to eat it"? I have never heard those words from anyone besides Jesus who said, *"He who eats My flesh and drinks My blood abides in Me"* (John 6:56). During Communion we hold a piece of bread that is far more than just a piece of bread.

The people in Corinth were having problems with how they received. They were not discerning that the symbols they were ingesting were truly the body of Almighty God who had come in the flesh to save them. And in not receiving the symbols *as* the body of Christ, they were not receiving the healing He bought.

Consequently, some were sick, and others were dying. Paul explained to the people that to drink the blood and eat the broken body of Jesus Christ, *"without discerning the Lord's body"* (1 Corinthians 11:29), would make them sick. Why? I believe it was because the people were not viewing Jesus as God. They were gorging on bread and wine without receiving the reward of knowing God in all His immense healing power, authority, and identity.

Paul sent out a warning, *"Whoever eats this bread or drinks this cup of the Lord in an unworthy manner will be guilty of the body and blood of the Lord. But let a man examine himself, and so let him eat of the bread and drink of the cup. For he who eats and drinks in an unworthy manner eats and drinks judgment to himself, not discerning the Lord's body. For this reason many are weak and sick among you, and many sleep"* (1 Corinthians 11:27-30).

This means that if I have sin in my life that I am unwilling to deal with through confessing to the Lord, then I will not receive from Him. Paul is not saying that people should not take the Lord's Supper. I believe he was saying, *when you take the meal, repent of your unbelief.* The point is not to stay away from the Lord's meal, but to examine yourself and be healed.

Throughout Scripture, we find that there is a law of sowing and reaping. What we sow, we will reap. *"Do not be deceived, God is not mocked; for whatever a man sows, that he will also reap"* (Galatians 6:7).

Why were some of the believers in the church at Corinth sick and dying, when they were doing something which should have made them well?

Think about this principle in the context of Jesus' words about receiving a prophet: *"He who receives a prophet in the name of a prophet shall receive a prophet's reward. And he who receives a righteous man in the name of a righteous man shall receive a righteous man's reward"* (Matthew 10:41).

If a person who is a prophet is viewed as just a nice man or good woman, it is likely words spoken by him or her will be forgotten. Instead of listening intently to one who can foretell the future you may walk away thinking that what he or she said *was nice.* But if you believe that the person who spoke something about your future is a true prophet, you will begin to look for what was said to manifest and lean into the prophesy you were given. Once again, the important part is how you receive.

Jesus is the Everlasting Father

A true prophet, Isaiah of the Bible, looked into the future and saw the perfect likeness of Father God. Isaiah saw that the Child who would be born, looked so much like the Father that he called Him, "the Everlasting Father" (Isaiah 9:6).

"For unto us a Child is born, unto us a Son is given;
and the government will be upon His shoulder. And
His name will be called Wonderful, Counselor,
Mighty God, Everlasting Father, Prince of Peace" (Isaiah 9:6).

If you believe this prophet, Isaiah, who spoke the truth, you will receive the reward of seeing miracles. The miraculous has everything to do with an intimate relational understanding of the Father.

Jesus was asked by His disciple, Philip, "Lord, show us the Father". And Jesus replied, *"He who has seen Me has seen the Father"* (John 14:9).

Paul wrote to the church at Colossi, *"He [Jesus Christ] is the image of the invisible God..."* (Colossians 1:15).

Many people point to the Old Testament and conclude that Father God brings sickness, calamity, and punishment on His people. But all we have to do to understand what Father God truly does on earth, is to look at what He did when He walked here as the Son, Jesus Christ.

When Jesus freed the demon-possessed man who came running at Him in the Gadarenes, that was the Father (Luke 8:27); when Jesus had compassion on a mother and raised up her dead son, that was the Father (Luke7:13); when Jesus did not condemn the women caught in adultery, that was the Father (John 8:11). We know what our Father in Heaven is like when we look at Jesus and see what He did and why he did it.

Many people who come into Healing Rooms believe that their infirmity was given to them by God to perfect them. Sometimes a person will call a disease "mine": "my cancer", "my fibromyalgia", "my Parkinson's", etcetera. Therefore, when we gather and pray for an individual who believes his or her infirmity is his or her own, as that person believes, they continue to own the infirmity.

The great faith-healer, Smith Wigglesworth said this, "If I cannot make a person who is suffering from disease righteously indignant against that condition, I cannot help him. If I can make every sufferer know that suffering, disease, and all these things are the workings of the devil, I can help him."[1]

Every great faith healer throughout recorded times believed that all sickness is from the one who came to kill, steal, and destroy; sickness is from the devil. Almighty God did not come to bring harm, but He came to bring life! *"The thief does not come except to steal, and to kill, and to destroy. I have come that they may have life, and that they may have it more abundantly"* (John 10:10).

Can Almighty God bring good out of any situation, including sickness and suffering? Of course, He can. But does a person need to resist healing because he or she feels the need to suffer? Let us give our infirmities to the One who carried them for us and let Him do what He will! *"He Himself took our infirmities and bore our sicknesses"* (Matthew 8:17); *"Surely He has borne our griefs and carried our sorrows. . ."* (Isaiah 53:4).

What Father God has Put Within Our Reach

Sometimes there are infirmities which remain in a person's life in the area of torment or affliction simply because that person does not believe that God wants to heal him or her. The means which God has put within their reach is not employed due to a wrong concept of Him. Jesus told a parable about a man who was given talents to use but the man buried his talent instead of using them. Why? Because his concept of God was faulty. He said, *"Lord, I knew you to be a hard man"* (Matthew 25:24). Because he didn't see God as good, he didn't move into a realm of faith for the impossible.

The kind of faith that brings healing, deliverance, and abundant life, begins with knowing who Jesus is and knowing that He, God, is always good.

May we each receive Jesus' suffering personally: Jesus died for me so that I will not be afflicted any longer. He paid the payment completely; and, I get out of it as I receive it God's way. From Heaven's perspective, it is a settled issue, *"By His stripes we are healed"* (Isaiah 53:5, 1 Peter 2:24), *"He Himself took our infirmities and bore our sicknesses"* (Matthew 8:17).

May Holy Spirit open our eyes to who our Savior truly is. Let us thank Jesus for the adequacy of the payment He made for us on the Cross: completely enough and sufficient. Let us partake of Communion, knowing that Jesus Christ is God, and as God, is worthy of all our worship and our full attention. May we eat of His body and drink His blood and love Him with all our hearts!

As we fully believe and teach that Jesus Christ is God, and that God is good, we will see an ever-increasing number of people healed. May the Lord's Healing Revival continue and grow until Jesus Christ has everything He died to gain!

Prayer

Father in Heaven, thank You for sending Your exact representation, Your Son, Jesus Christ. Thank You for showing Your prophet, Isaiah, that Jesus is the "Everlasting Father"! Please forgive me for not taking in the fullness of this truth. I believe now and receive Your Son, Jesus Christ, as Almighty God! I believe that You are always good and now know that You will always be good to me. Thank you for healing my Love Receiver. Help me, Holy Spirit Helper, to be forever changed by the revelation which you have given me about who You are and about Your goodness!

Reflection

1. Why is it difficult for many people to receive the extravagant love of God personally?

2. How must one receive the word of a prophet in order to gain the full measure of blessing?

3. Who did Isaiah say that the Child to was to come would be (Isaiah 9:6)?

4. How can something supernatural happen when partaking of the Lord's Supper?

3

HEALING ROOMS – THE DREAM

"At the beginning, all we have is the vision. At that point God expects us to begin walking in obedience according to the dream He has given us." John C. Maxwell

When God begins to put something new into your heart, you know it is His idea because before that moment you had never had a thought about it before. And then the thought begins to grow.

Not having been raised in the charismatic movement, or a Pentecostal-type church, I knew little about the things that are *normal* to those who grew up in a culture that *flowed in Holy Spirit*. For example, I didn't know that anointing oil was still used these days and only knew that it was something I had read about in the Bible.

One day while reading the Scripture about Mary anointing Jesus with Spikenard oil (John 12:3), Holy Spirit spoke to me about making some of this oil for His use. I had no idea how to go about this, but the thought began to grow. It wasn't long until I began to research how to make the oil and the next thing I knew, I was ordering the components and purchasing little glass vials to put it in. I had no idea that other people made and sold Spikenard oil until sometime later. It was purely Holy Spirit initiated because, as I found out through the process, God really likes the smell of Spikenard and the devil hates it. hat a powerful tool God gave me to use and provide for other people to use.

I have had the same kind of experiences many times when God would instigate new things for me during prayer. I learned from God about the use of flags during worship. And so, it was with speaking in tongues, prophesy, soaking prayer, dancing in worship, and the concept of a Holy Spirit Car Wash (I found out later that others called this a *Prayer Tunnel* and that the activity had been around for a long time).

Holy Spirit also initiated the concept of opening Healing Rooms. I have never been to a Healing Room in my life! I only knew that Bethel Church in Redding, CA, offered this ministry to people; but I simply saw it as a piece of many parts that make up that great church.

One day, I was reading one of my books on healing (a book I had read through at least two other times) by John G. Lake. But this time as I read the testimonies from the author's healing ministry, I heard Holy Spirit say to me, "I desire to open Healing Rooms." I responded back to the Lord that I didn't know anything about establishing this kind of ministry. Immediately Holy Spirit responded, "I will teach you."

In order to stay accountable to what the Lord had spoken to me, I wrote the conversation He had with me about Healing Rooms in my journal; and promised that I would wait on Him for direction. I then wrote a letter to my husband, Tom, detailing my quest for direction and the idea of a Healing Rooms ministry in our church.

For the next several weeks, I reminded the Lord that He said He would give me the direction for His Healing Rooms. And I waited with patience, for I was in no hurry to run ahead without knowing what I was doing.

Then the floodgates opened, and Holy Spirit began to speak to me constantly about His desire for this ministry, even to the point of giving me dreams and visions about Healing Rooms all night long many nights! This continued for several months; and then in 2017, I sat with the Lord for a long time recording His instruction.

God's Big and Detailed Plan

The following plan was given to me that day and written in my journal. The instruction did not come from any source other than from Holy Spirit's leading.

1. I would choose Healing Rooms ministers in order to open Healing Rooms in less than three months. The people who served in Healing Rooms would receive training and would be called Doctors of the Cross.
2. To begin, we would provide the opportunity for people to come the first Saturday of each month, 9:00 - 11:00 am. (More days and times would be added as needed.)
3. The ministry would be held at the Horizon Ministry Center. People would enter the main room where there would be a sign-in sheet for them to write their name and the time he or she arrived. There would also be clip boards with information forms that the patients would pick up and complete. These forms would then be handed to the Doctors of the Cross as the individual arrived for their prayer time in a Healing Room.
4. The waiting room area would be a place of preparation; a place filled with the strong presence of Holy Spirit. The Lord specified the worship music He wanted played, expressed His desire that intercessors would be praying, chairs would be in strategic arrangements, candles would be lit and flaming, oil would be available, prayer cloths prayed over and ready, and blankets on hand.
5. To begin the ministry, we would open three Healing Rooms per hour: Pastor Tom's office, my office, and the counseling office.
6. The prayer appointments were not to be counseling sessions - each individual would be given 15 minutes in a Healing Room. (Cards for each of the counselors who we have on staff would be available to hand to any individual who needed counseling.)
7. In the beginning, we would need a minimum of eight Doctors of the Cross for the Healing Rooms (two Doctors of the Cross in each of the three rooms with an exchange of Doctors of the Cross for the second hour). We would also need an overseer, a person to greet the patients and give them a form, and workers to take each person to his or her appointment. Therefore, at least twelve workers would be needed for each of the Saturdays that we would host Healing Rooms. I would be the overseer each week to bring unity, anointing, and consistency to the plan.

8. Each Doctor of the Cross would wear a white doctor coat with a name badge to designate their role and authority. These coats would be provided and ready on each Healing Rooms day.
9. Each Healing Room would have a small table and a chair for the person receiving prayer. The table would have an open Bible, a stack of Healing Cards (the one from His Way with healing Scriptures), a box of tissue, a pen and paper, and a small jar with anointing oil in it. There would also be chairs for each Doctor of the Cross.
10. I would create a pamphlet to give to people with information about Healing Rooms. I was to design a logo, prepare a mission statement, and write about the Healing Rooms purpose.
11. I needed to design and order two banners to be used outside the Ministry Center whenever Healing Rooms were open (one by the street and one by the front door).
12. Communion (grape juice and water crackers) would be setup in the kitchen and available to all workers. There would be a journal to record the things God showed us; and, there would be a bulletin board to pin papers on of written miracle accounts.

Holy Spirit was very specific in all these instructions. I was to do all these things, as well as open a Healing School, the following year for anyone who wanted to attend.

Working the Plan

I made a long shopping list of all the items the Lord had specified. I began to design the Healing Rooms folder and the verbiage to go in it. I found doctor coats and ordered them in all sizes.

I shared God's plan with the Horizon Church staff, and I began to recruit workers. I wrote potential Doctors of the Cross, "We are embarking on a great quest with the King! I hope that you feel the excitement that He has for this ministry and that you are ready to jump in with Him! I see the Lord rubbing His hands together in anticipation - Christ Jesus loves to heal people!!"

Then I began counting down the days, hoping I could get everything ready in time for God's opening day of Healing Rooms in Reno/Sparks, NV!

A training session was held for everyone who would serve at Healing Rooms, and we role-played the setting and plan. During this 'role-playing,' the healing was already flowing as one of the workers was fully healed in her back!

The Big Day Arrived

I was up very early the morning of the opening of Healing Rooms and began pacing and praying! Would people actually come for healing? Would the workers come ready and be effective in prayer? Had we gotten everything done as directed; would it be pleasing to God?

At 8:55 am we welcomed our first patient! And that day, we facilitated healing prayer for 23 different people and families! Many individuals received healing in their bodies and souls! When the two glorious and Holy Spirit empowered hours were up, I felt as though I could fly! And several other Doctors of the Cross echoed my joy with words such as, "I was made for this purpose;" "I have found my calling;" "I love this ministry;" and "Can we do this every week?!"

Healing Rooms had launched; I was in awe of what the Lord had done - and it was only the beginning!

Many Miracles

The testimonies of what God has done for people through Healing Rooms abound! In just a few short months, we had facilitated many miracles through the love and healing virtue of Jesus Christ.

One woman who suffered for years with IBS (Irritable Bowel Syndrome) wrote this report: "I have gone back and forth all day, between meetings, after meetings, trying to find the words to describe today's Healing Rooms. I even thought to do a video to send to you, so you can see the emotion behind this message. Before I came into the Healing Rooms I prayed, not for a healing, but that I wouldn't be freaked out by any prayer or healing I might experience. While, yes, I was going for healing, it is a fairly new concept and way of life for me. I also prayed for me to be honest in what I asked for and to go in with no guard up, that I would be totally open to what I was walking into. Old hymns started playing in my mind and I was worshiping before I even walked in the door. I took a deep breath and in I went. What I experienced was to this moment, hours later, raw. Never in my life have I experienced what I felt today - I was overwhelmed and am still in tears as I write this message. I wanted to be skeptical because I'm a realist and it's hard for me sometimes to function off of a feeling. But I know the Lord touched me! And in a mighty way. I can't explain it; I can't put it into words completely. I walked out of the Healing Rooms, got in my car to race off to a meeting, only to be stopped as I just sat and cried. I wanted to share this testimony with you - not once today have I had one symptom of IBS - no cramping, no pain/discomfort, no running off to the bathroom. I've eaten TWO meals today, which hasn't happened in about 6 months, and have had no signs of it. I claimed that healing. Thank you so much for having the rooms. I'm so thankful! What I experienced today was real and that feeling I had, I'm in awe!"[1] (To date, several months later, she continues to be completely well! She recently wrote, "STILL walking in a complete healing!!! I pray that the doubts go away of those unsure if they should go . . . that people step out in faith knowing we have a good, good Father who wants to restore and heal us, even in this life!")

In the last month at Healing Rooms we received these reports: "Bones in my back clicked into place." "The lump dissolved!" "Healing waves of heat went through my knees and I stood without pain!"

One Doctor of the Cross wrote, "A man I prayed for immediately noticed a significant difference in his back and leg pain. He felt the tightness in the muscles lessen, and he had less pain in walking. Through this experience he and his wife have drawn closer to the Lord and deeper into understanding of how powerful the work of the Holy Spirit is."

The healing testimonies continue to flow in, and the Lord God is pleased with the plan He initiated, and we are obeying!

Developing Strategies for Victory

We are taking territory for God's Kingdom through Healing Rooms! Since terrain is being taken, there is an adversary on the other side who is having to give up land. That former squatter is, of course, not happy. The one who came to kill, steal, and destroy is seeing people come alive, become prosperous, and walk in health!

Recently, while reading the book of Joshua, I was struck by how the brilliant commander, Joshua, knew to call Father God, "the Lord of all the earth." Captain Joshua had a mandate from God to take the land and so, in the hearing of the people, he prayed and proclaimed that the earth belongs to God! He strategically knew to call Father God the *Lord of all the earth* when he instructed his army to take the ground (Joshua 3:11).

Like Joshua, we have a mandate to bring the Kingdom of God into our region and we are taking ground for the King - but not without warfare.

The defeated enemy has issued a battle cry and is enlisting willing people to do his dirty work. One month at our Healing Rooms, of those eight rooms, teams in three separate rooms encountered satanic strategy plans against them by people who came in as decoys and distracters.

In one of the Healing Rooms, a person came in who was not interested in being healed. That person confided a story of victimization, and then would not submit to prayer. One of the Doctors of the Cross on this team left the room and received prayer from me to counter this attack of intimidation and powerlessness.

In another Healing Room, one of the Doctors of the Cross experienced a sideswiping as demons left a patient. He had trouble sleeping that night and felt beat up from the battle.

The third incident happened to one of our counselors who serves as a Doctor of the Cross. She left Healing Rooms that day and felt that she could not get through to the Lord in prayer. She felt as though something was blocking her. Eventually she prayed through to victory (hours later). She wrote this to me, "There is so much warfare right now; the enemy is sending spies to spy out the great healing and miracles. We must be wise as serpents and harmless as doves."

In answer to these problems, we stepped up the prayer cover over the Healing Rooms Ministry. We cried out to God for greater wisdom, received more insight, and were better prepared for the enemy's schemes. *"For we are not ignorant of his devices"* (2 Corinthians 2:11). Consequently, at the next Healing Rooms day we had great victories and protection from the enemy. At this writing, we have not had any more incidents like those described above.

WISE AS SERPENTS

We are developing greater strategy for the victory as we go!

As Doctors of the Cross, we must remember to wash away the stuff the devil brings around us with the pure water of the Word of God. Satan is called the "prince of the air" (Ephesians 2:2), and what he deposits is not often visible to the eye - as air is not visible.

After a spiritual battle, I will bathe in Scripture by listening to the book of John (or any book of the Bible), reading Revelation 4 and 5, out loud, and calling out memorized Scripture with my voice. And I always ask Holy Spirit to wash me off and refresh me after Healing Rooms ministry.

Sometimes we underestimate the influence that people have to effect atmosphere - and us. To illustrate this is a simple way, here is an account of something that happened subtlety, almost imperceptibly, but real, in a restaurant. My husband, Tom, and I went to a restaurant that we hadn't been to in awhile and noticed that it felt *different*. When the food was ready, an employee called Tom's name instead of bringing us the food, as they usually did. When I went to pick up the food, I asked the employee why they didn't bring it to our table as customary. I was told that corporate had changed their policy and that they could no longer serve the food. This comment was made with an attitude of hostility. After lunch Tom and I both remarked that the food wasn't as good as it used to be. However, we both knew that it tasted as it always had. It was the atmosphere that had changed, and the atmosphere affected the food. We both recognized that people can alter atmosphere, and through their words, attitudes, and subtle actions, can create negativity that has a presence.

Bathing in the presence of God daily and after ministry is essential to well-being. The pure water of the Word of God cleans us and restores us.

Hydration is essential to survive a natural battle; it is also essential to survive a supernatural battle. Just as drinking clean water is urgent in hot, dry weather, we must drink in God's presence after ministering.

> *"You, God, are my God, earnestly I seek you. I thirst for you, my whole being longs for you, in a dry and parched land where there is no water"* (Psalm 63:1).

Survival experts warn us not to wait till we feel thirsty, but to drink as much as possible to keep the hydration level of our bodies high. Likewise, it is critical that we don't wait until we have a nightmare, or feel sick, before we do what it takes to be washed in God's Word and Spirit. Before leaving Healing Rooms Ministry, we gather with other Doctors of the Cross and pray for one another. Let us encourage one another with words of blessing and let us wash with the pure water of the Word of God (Hebrews 10:22, Revelation 22:1).

God's provision for our refreshment is His presence, and God's presence is found in Holy Spirit! Just as Holy Spirit is our comfort, shield, and help, He is also like water, the essence of life for our whole being. Jesus said, *"If anyone is thirsty, let him come to Me and drink. He who believes in Me, as the Scripture said, 'From his innermost being will flow rivers of living water'"* (John 7:37-38).

Recently, I met with a man who was having terrible nightmares. He'd had four consecutive nights with the same terrifying dream-encounter about people who were trying to kill him. As I listened to his dream and saw the anger that he was experiencing, I asked him, "What happened the day before the nightmares began?" He thought for a moment and then said, "I mediated an argument between two men who were very angry at one another."

The next question I asked him was about the atmosphere and what it felt like during the mediation. He answered that "It felt evil." I then asked him what he did to wash himself off from the environment he had been in. He answered, in surprise, that he had not thought of that.

I encouraged the man to ask for forgiveness (he had been reacting in anger toward those around him since the mediation). After he did so, I then encouraged him to renounce the anger he had walked into, and consequently had taken on. The change was full, and he was set free! His dreams have been sweet since this prayer time.

Wouldn't it be best to train ourselves to wash in the presence and the Lord, every time after we encounter the demonic?

In the Old Testament, anointing oil and blood were used to clean things, to purify them, and to consecrate them. There are many Scriptures that explain how to clean things off and make them holy (especially Leviticus 14-16).

In the New Testament, the Lord Jesus Christ told His disciples that they were made clean by His Word: *"You are already clean because of the word which I have spoken to you"* (John 15:3)! This is the same way we are washed - with God's Word!

The Word of God will fortify us from within, filling us with "streams in the desert" from the internal springs of the Spirit. This enables us to serve as Doctors of the Cross who are healthy, creative people, full of faith and spiritual vitality for others.

More Healing Room Instruction

The Healing Rooms team which encountered the *spirit of intimidation* needed to wash off and to remember how to battle negative thoughts (training is found further on into this book).

The Prayer Team Handbook[2] states, *"This hindering spirit will try to keep you from ministering to other people by causing you to feel that you have nothing to offer. It will get in your path and express a problem. When you try to deal with the exaggerated issue, you will begin to feel that you are powerless. Since the issue is not real but is a distraction, the only way to solve the problem is to either lead the person into repentance or, if he or she will not repent, move them on. Use 2 Timothy 1:7 as your sword and wash yourself off."*

The third area of attack, that was mentioned earlier, was against a Doctor of the Cross who was side swiped by a demon as it left a patient. He felt beat up and could not sleep the night after Healing Rooms. I spoke with him the following day, after the attack (a Sunday), and shared a secret with him (and his wife) that I have had the blessing of using for a long time. I encouraged him to ask God for a Holy Spirit massage! Many times, after a battle when my body hurts all over, I will ask Holy Spirit for a massage.

After asking, it is never very long until I notice that I feel better and better! Holy Spirit is our Helper, and very present! Sometimes the help we need from the Helper is a massage in our physical body.

We are Learning

The Healing Rooms ministry in Reno/Sparks, NV, is growing and prospering with many miracles because of all the workers who are willing to lay down their lives for others. We have a lot to learn and will depend on Holy Spirit to teach us. We are willing and ready to do what God has called us to do.

Last year, Tom and I were on vacation in Salt Lake City, Utah, where I picked up a magazine that had the words "Healing Ways" on the cover. Hoping to find out that Healing Rooms were making the cover of a secular magazine, I turned to the pages specified to read the article.

The piece highlighted four choices for healing in the Salt Lake City area: 1) Native American Medicine (the medicine being feathers, a sacred blanket, and going into the past), 2) Lifeline (included elements like chakras and shamanism), 3) Inca Shaman (past lives), and 4) Living Energy Center (vibration and light/sound therapies).[3]

All the things the article highlighted had at least one element of truth with a whole lot of mixture. And there was not a single mention of Christian healing or the Healer, Jesus Christ.

Why no mention of the true Healer? And why does the secular and the occult have such a big platform? As I prayed about this, Holy Spirit showed me that the church has not stepped up into its place. Groan!

Since we opened the Healing School, many people have come to me and told me that they grew up in Christian churches that did not teach on healing, or that they were taught that healing was just for Bible days and not for now. No wonder American churches are full of people who go to doctors just as often as those who don't believe in Jesus Christ.

After reading the magazine and being convicted by Holy Spirit about the state of God's church, I determined even more strongly to provide Healing Rooms, no matter the cost! We will give anyone who will come a chance to encounter the True Healer, Almighty God!

Inviting People to Come Back

Throughout the books that I have read by John G. Lake (the founder of Healing Rooms) and Cal Pierce[4] (Director of the Spokane, WA Healing Rooms), I have read many testimonies about individuals who went back to Healing Rooms several times until healing manifested. Needing quite a few sessions in Healing Rooms seemed to be the norm.

I am not saying that an individual cannot be healed on the spot during one Healing Rooms encounter. What I am saying is that we may need to encourage patients to come again and again. A person who will continue to come is desperate and is showing actualized faith for their healing!

The other thing that is evident is that we do not need to feel guilty, or powerless, when it appears that an individual we prayed for is not well later. It is up to that individual to pursue full healing, to hold onto what God did for them, and to give testimony of God's goodness.

On the other hand, let us believe God for miracles and fully expect healings to manifest! Let us do our part to prepare to serve at Healing Rooms through prayer, fasting, Communion, meditating on Scripture, and abiding in the pure love of God!

Our Purpose Statement

The purpose of Healing Rooms is to bring the reality of the personal love of God into the lives of as many people as possible, through the tangible experience of physical healing.

Healing is not one-dimensional. While a miracle may change a person's physical health, it also creates an opportunity for a heaven-on-earth place deep within the human heart - and a ministry of healing through his or her ensuing testimony!

Postscript

To say that God's big idea to open Healing Rooms has been successful would be an understatement! One and one-half years into this ministry, we have already seen over 500 patients walk into our free prayer clinic!

Sixty trained Doctors of the Cross serve at the Healing Rooms and more are being trained continually.

Prayer

Father God, I want to attempt great things for You. So, I tell You that I am willing again. I say "Yes" to anything that You want me to do. Please put ideas inside of me and then give me the strength and courage to do what You want! In Jesus' name, amen.

Reflection

1. Who enlisted the startup of Healing Rooms in Reno-Sparks, NV?

   How many specific instructions did God give for Healing Rooms?

2. What did the brilliant commander, Joshua, strategically pray in the hearing of the people?

3. What must the Doctors of the Cross do after ministering at Healing Rooms?

4. Who is responsible to bring the truth of healing, in the Name of Jesus Christ, to your region?

4

FRIENDSHIP WITH GOD

The Lord likes to be pursued. Those who pursue Him, find Him. This is probably because what we spend the most time on is really what we care the most about.

From the beginning of time, it was God's heart to build a dwelling place for Himself on the Earth, in and through people. Through us, He intends to live and reveal Himself. God **is** love.

The great Healer, Jesus Christ, is our example and pattern for how to receive personal healing, and how-to bring healing to others. The love of God is the key to doing what Jesus did.

A woman named Sarah, gave me an insightful testimony about her healing. Sarah had suffered greatly with pain in her hands, wrists, and forearms. The medical doctors called the malady, *arthritis.*

While in a church service, where healing prayer was offered, those in need were instructed to "find someone who loves you to pray for you". Sarah went to her husband, who loves her, and asked him to pray for her. Sarah said that her husband neither touched her nor prayed out loud, but that she felt his love for her.

As her husband prayed, suddenly Sarah began to feel a tingling in her hands. As she looked down at her arms, she saw strips of light, beginning in her hands and traveling up her arms! And then, the pain left her completely! Sarah was astonished and even now, sometime later, is still rejoicing in the love that healed her; God's love through a person.

Throughout the healing ministry of Jesus Christ, we read about the immense compassion He had for people. All through His earthly ministry, He demonstrated the love of the Father, and He showed it unfailingly, to the end. "*. . . Jesus knew He should depart from this world to the Father, having loved His own who were in the world, He loved them to the end*" (John 13:1). Jesus Christ was and will always be the lover of people!

It was the love of God which gave a blind man sight in Africa, as I prayed for him to be healed. The love which Father God poured into me for that stranger was without question, the supernatural love of God! (The full account of this healing is detailed later in this book.)

The Power of Love

The most important commodity which we possess, through the power of Holy Spirit, is love. This is that which catapults the healing virtue of Jesus forward into those we pray for. This is a factor which people do not usually find in a visit to the doctor. Love is the qualification for serving Jesus as a Doctor of the Cross.

Throughout Scripture, we find that God insists that love relationship is everything: "*'You shall love the Lord your God with all your heart, with all your soul, and with all your mind.' This is the first and great commandment. And the second is like it 'You shall love your neighbor as yourself.' On these two commandments hang all the Law and the Prophets*" (Matthew 22:37-40).

Because love relationship is primary to the heart of God, He wants to be pursued. As much as we sing songs about His pursuit of us, we may forget that the Scriptures speak a lot about us diligently seeking Him with all our hearts. "*You will seek Me and find Me, when you search for Me with all your heart*" (Jeremiah 29:13).

At this moment, Father God could demand trembling surrender from every human being on our planet. If He did this, there would not be a person standing, and rightfully so, since He is holy, holy, holy, Lord God Almighty! But rarely does He show up in the kind of power that zaps everyone in the room. Why doesn't He?

Love relationship is not satisfying unless it is chosen. God has chosen us, but He also desires to be chosen back. He desires the freely chosen love of people who He can call His friends.

Almighty God wants to have human friends. This amazing fact is seen throughout Scripture and points to the fact that God is a very personal-relating Father! If - since, God wants friends, do you want to be a true friend to Him?

Up On the Mountaintop

I have always loved the account in Scripture of when the Lord took His friends up on a mountain with Him and they witnessed His transfiguration (Matthew 17, Mark 9, and Luke 9). Up there, Peter, James, and John saw Jesus' face shine like the sun, and His clothes became as white as the light (Matthew 17:2).

Part of the reason why I love this story is because of the depiction of the radical highs, and then lows, that we also understand to be part of a disciple's life. In the evening, the disciples were seeing indescribable glory up on the mountain; but the next morning, they came down into the demon-possessed valley below. No doubt they felt like they could do anything while up on the mountaintop, but upon coming down they displayed powerlessness. They returned to the valley where there was a disputing crowd and a demon-possessed boy who they couldn't seem to help (Mark 9:18). This is an example for our lives too, as we navigate the high (great) places of faith along with the contrasting low times.

For most of us, life is a combination of setbacks and victories. Just when we think we are finally going to live in continual success and smooth-sailing, wham! Something comes up, testing and perfecting our trust in God. But if the trials and tests are walked through in obedient faith, they will eventually produce something far more satisfying than a smooth sail.

"Count it all joy when you fall into various trials, knowing that the testing of your faith produces patience. But let patience have its perfect work, that you may be perfect and complete, lacking nothing" (James 1:2-4).

Jesus was never flustered by the circumstances He encountered - whether people's opinions, mountaintop encounters or demon-possessed valleys. Jesus weathered anything that happened around Him without any loss of confidence or trust in His Father in Heaven. His friendship with Father God carried Him through all.

God's Design for Friendship

As with every good thing that exists, Jesus created the concept of friendship - friendship that includes people. Consider these words which Jesus Christ spoke, *"You are My friends if you do whatever I command you. No longer do I call you servants, for a servant does not know what his master is doing; but I have called you friends, for all things that I heard from My Father I have made known to you"* (John 15:14-15).

The Lord also said, *"Can the friends of the bridegroom fast while the bridegroom is with them?"* (Mark 2:19); *"I say to you, My friends, do not be afraid of those who kill the body, and after that have no more that they can do"* (Luke 12:4).

Before Jesus Christ laid down His life to save the world, He said, *"Greater love has no one than this, than to lay down one's life for his friends"* (John 15:13). And when the hour was at hand for Jesus to be arrested, He desired His friends to be with Him: *"Then He came and found them sleeping, and said to Peter, "Simon, are you sleeping? Could you not watch with Me one hour?"* (Matthew 26:40).

God's design for friendship is also shown in the Old Testament as we find that Abraham was called a *friend of God*: *"Abraham believed God, and it was accounted to him for righteousness. And he was called the friend of God"* (James 2:23). The prophets were friends of God: *"Surely the Lord God does nothing, Unless He reveals His secret to His [friends] the prophets"* (Amos 3:7).

This brings us to an aspect of the story of the Transfiguration that is important for us to see and be changed through. Remember that Peter, James, and John were not the only people up on the mountain with Jesus on the day of His Transfiguration: *"And behold, two men talked with Him, who were Moses and Elijah"* (Luke 9:30). These two friends of God showed up to have a conversation with Jesus about something very near and dear to the heart of God. They were not making small talk up on that mountain with Jesus.

Although the footnote in my Bible states that Moses and Elijah were on the mountain because they represented the Law and the prophets who were to come before Jesus, I believe there is another aspect that is much more personal and relational than that! Jesus wanted to talk with friends about what was going to happen to Him. Moses and Elijah knew about the Cross, and they understood that Jesus had to die. None of the disciples understood or agreed that Jesus must die. But God's friends, Moses, and Elijah, talked it through with Jesus.

Before we further address Jesus' mountaintop conversation with Moses and Elijah, let's see what Peter, James, and John might have been talking about with Jesus on their hike up the mountain. And let us understand why the Lord desired some real friends to converse with.

Fair-weather Friends

In this same chapter of Luke where the account of the Transfiguration is written (Luke 9), we find three discussions taking place among Jesus' closest companions. Peter, James, and John were: 1) Disputing with each other about who was the greatest, 2) Feeling exclusive and bothered that anyone else would do miracles who was not part of their group, 3) Desired to call down fire and kill people who didn't accept them. Wow.

In Luke 9:43 we read that *"everyone marveled at all the things which Jesus did."* But Jesus was not impressed with the people's marveling and told His disciples privately that He was about to be betrayed. *"But they [the disciples] did not understand what He said"* (verse 45). The very next verse - after the Lord's private conversation with His friends about His betrayal, states, *"A dispute arose among them as to which of them would be greatest"* (verse 46). Jesus was talking about being betrayed, and His closest friends were so caught up with themselves that they didn't even pay attention to His words.

Just three verses later, after Jesus had cleared up the *who is the greatest* dispute, John spoke and said, *"Master, we saw someone casting out demons in Your name, and we forbade him because he does not follow with us"* (Luke 9:49). The Lord again cleared up the problem, but just in time for James and John to come up with something else, *"Lord, do You want us to command fire to come down from heaven and consume [the village of Samaritans]?"* (Luke 9:54)!

Are you beginning to understand why Jesus wanted to talk with someone besides Peter, James, and John up on the mountain?! The closest companions of Jesus did not see Him or hear His heart. They saw what they themselves wanted, what they thought would give them the most power; plus, they had attitudes like terrorists who destroy lives in the name of religious ideas.

After the three areas of dialogue (competition, selfish ambition, and furthering one's own cause), right in a row, bam, bam, bam, the Lord turned to His disciples and rebuked them and said, *"You do not know what manner of spirit you are of. For the Son of Man did not come to destroy men's lives but to save them"* (Luke 9:55). Do you think He might have been frustrated and probably felt alone in His mission to save the world? I sure would have!

No wonder Jesus needed time to talk with real friends - those who understood His mission and knew about His soon coming betrayal and death. With Moses and Elijah, the Lord could talk about deep things, as the Scripture states, *"Behold, two men talked with Him, who were Moses and Elijah, who appeared in glory and spoke of His decease which He was about to accomplish at Jerusalem"* (Luke 9:31). Moses and Elijah talked with Jesus Christ about His coming death. Can you see that this would have brought the Lord companionship and comfort?

"O Lord, how great are Your works! Your thoughts are very deep" (Psalm 92:5).

Peter, James, and John couldn't seem to listen to the Lord's heart and so God's friends Moses and Elijah, showed up to talk with Him! God desired friends!

What Kind of Things Does God Like to Talk About With His Friends?

We are given a clue to the content of the dialogue Jesus had with Moses and Elijah. They talked with Jesus about His death, what it would accomplish, and where it would happen (Luke 9:31).

When you have extended time in prayer with God, do you ask Him what HE wants to talk about? Yes, there is a time to tell the Lord all your earthly needs; but there is also a time for true friends of God to converse with Him about what He desires. I have found that God likes to talk about Heaven, the coming end-of-the-age battle, the planets and stars, the treasuries of snow, wind, wild animals (see Job 39), and strategies for helping people. His thoughts are so much higher than mine (Isaiah 55:9).

God's friend, Moses said, *"Show me now Your way that I may know You"* (Exodus 33:13). The men and women of the Bible who desired to know God more than anything else were faithful to Him - not to a cause, not to their own selfish ambition, or a competition. They wanted to know God's heart and sought earnestly to listen to Him.

Hanging around the Lord, as even the elect who went up on the mountain with Him did, did not ensure a heart of love for Him. Those disciples walked in a mere shadow of His anointing, encumbered with their own self-centered ideas, they lacked power.

What About You?

Do you identify with the disciples' problems in their inability to hear God, due to their own ideas, ambitions, and cravings?

Most of us would protest that we do not want to be the greatest and that we put others first. But what if we apply putting others first to the places where we work, on the roads we drive, or when in line somewhere when someone else cuts in? Seriously, let us ask Holy Spirit to show us where we have a block in hearing God due to our own wants. Often it is the small, seemingly insignificant things or events that reveal our intentions, motives, and ultimately determine our destiny. Selfish ambition is a deadly sin, in that it comes between you and your friendship with God. James 3:16 states, *"Where envy and self-seeking exist, confusion and every evil thing are there."* Selfish ambition not only blocks your ability to hear God, but it also brings with it "every evil thing."

Ask yourself, and answer honestly: Am I listening to God to hear about Him and what He wants? Do I long to know God in the fellowship of His cross, His suffering, and His humility?

If you could not answer 'yes' to these questions, then probe deeper. What is the foremost desire of your heart? Do you want friendship with God, or the friendship of this world?

"Do you not know that friendship with the world is enmity with God? Whoever therefore wants to be a friend of the world makes himself an enemy of God." (James 4:4).

It may take a while for each of us to get the selfish ambition and love for this world out of our personal systems of operation. If we turn in our Bibles further in Luke, we will find that the disciples argued about *who was the greatest* again. More than ten chapters after the first recorded time in which they displayed their pride, they were at it again - and this time it was even worse. Their dispute arose immediately after Jesus spoke these words, *"Behold, the hand of My betrayer is with Me on the table"* (Luke 22:21).

How terrible for the Lord! To think that one of His closest companions would betray Him and hand Him over to the enemy; one of the men at the table, one who had lived and walked with Jesus all this time, who knew Jesus and was cared for by Jesus. Can you imagine the moment, and the pain, of this declaration?

It was as if the men at the table were not listening or could not listen. They could only hear: *What will happen to me*? Their love of self was revealed by their words and actions.

It is no wonder that the Lord understands our troubles and how alone we feel at times. He gathered His buddies for a last supper and was surrounded by them. He knew that He was about to be turned over to the chief priests and condemned to death; meanwhile, the disciples jockeyed for position.

You may think: If I had been there, I would have been a true friend to Jesus in His hour of need. This is exactly what Peter thought when he cried out *"Lord, why can I not follow You now? I will lay down my life for Your sake"* (John 13:37). To which the Lord replied, *"Will you lay down your life for My sake? Most assuredly, I say to you, the rooster shall not crow till you have denied Me three times"* (verse 38). Just as Jesus said, the fear in Peter's heart was soon to overcome his love for the Master.

After such denial (as all the disciples fled at Jesus' arrest), what eventually changed Peter and the other disciples into true friends of God?

Dying to Self-love

Before Peter's testing, Jesus had encouraged Peter, telling him that when he faced the trial again, he would come forth victorious (Luke 22:31). Peter would then be able to fulfill what he had previously spoken in pride when he boasted that he would die before denying Jesus. Up until that point, Peter had loved to the best of human ability, but that had failed him. The next time, Peter would be equipped with a love "not born out of man's desire for it but is shed abroad in our hearts by the Father" (Romans 5:5). God's love is not afraid to die for another. Peter came to the end of his own strength and cried out for God's help. In God's strength, we cannot fail because love never fails (1 Corinthians 13:8).

All the disciples (except one, Judas) eventually became men of depth who were selfless and true friends of God. But it took dying to self before they could become real friends of God. Isn't it interesting that watching a spectacular encounter happen on the Mount of Transfiguration did not fully change Peter, James, and John? As Peter himself later said, *"Though now for a little while, if need be, you have been grieved by various trials, that the genuineness of your faith, being much more precious than gold that perishes, though it is tested by fire, may be found to praise, honor, and glory at the revelation of Jesus Christ"* (1 Peter 1:6-7). They each needed a testing by fire, and a personal transformation by the power of Holy Spirit!

I long to see a company of Doctors of the Cross who listen to God because they can hear Him. They can hear Him because His interests have become their interests; His heart has become their heart.

In laying down their own lives, Peter, James, and John found freedom from the self-life. In the book of Acts, we find that Jesus' friends no longer sought to preserve their own lives but were happy to lay down their lives as they walked in the love of Holy Spirit: *"When they had called for the apostles and beaten them, they commanded that they should not speak in the name of Jesus, and let them go. So, they departed from the presence of the council, rejoicing that they were counted worthy to suffer shame for His name"* (Acts 5:40-41)!

What courage and what boldness! Love for God abounded in their hearts and caused them to obey no matter what. Jesus had told them earlier that if they loved Him, they would obey Him (John 14:15). Now God's love was finally fully evident in their lives; they were fueled by love for Jesus!

It is also clear from Peter that Holy Spirit is given to those who obey God. Peter said in Acts 5:29-32: *"We ought to obey God rather than men. The God of our fathers raised up Jesus whom you murdered by hanging on a tree. Him God has exalted to His right hand to be Prince and Savior, to give repentance to Israel and forgiveness of sins. And we are His witnesses to these things, and so also is the Holy Spirit whom God has given to those who obey Him."*

Too many Christians want grace without the obedience which is born out of love. Even if we go up on a mountaintop with Jesus, if we are not living in obedience to Him, our love will grow cold. With every disobedience, love can diminish.

We cannot obey God only when it is convenient for us, when we feel excited, or everything is going our way. We would call people who behave this way "fair-weather friends." The kind of friends that God desires are friends who walk in obedience to Him no matter the cost. Are you willing to be that kind of friend to God?

Prayer

Father God, there may be areas of disobedience in my life which You alone know about. Please shine a light on what needs to change in me. I will repent, and with Your Holy Spirit power, I will conform to Your way. I want to be a true friend of Yours! This is my heart's desire and commitment. In Jesus' name, amen.

Reflection

1. What does it mean to be a true friend of God? Use the following Scripture to contrast being a friend of God with being a friend of the world: James 4:4, John 15:19, 17:14.

2. Do you long to know God in the fellowship of His Cross, His suffering and humility?

3. What changed Peter, James, and John into people who gave up their lives to serve God?

4. What is the key to doing what Jesus did (John 5:19)?

5

THE LIVING SUBSTANCE

The healing virtue which flowed from Jesus into a woman who touched His clothes was a substance. Generally invisible to the human eye and often unrecognizable except by the evidence, nonetheless healing virtue is present and real. Just as faith is the substance of things hoped for, and the evidence of things not seen (Hebrews 11:1), healing virtue is a living manifest substance of faith.

It has often been my privilege to be asked by a parent to seek God's answers on behalf of a sick child. One of the families I have been working with needed healing for their youngest child. As I prayed and diligently sought the Lord for wisdom, one night He gave me dreams about the remedy. I dreamt that I was to put a 'mustard poultice' on the child.

When I got up in the morning, I asked God how to apply the poultice. In the back of my mind, I was thinking about the fig poultice, which Isaiah instructed people to put on Hezekiah (Isaiah 38:21). I knew that a poultice was a soft moist mass, often heated and medicated, that is spread on cloth over the skin. I wondered if I should pour mustard on a cloth, heat it up with my prayers of faith and take it to the child.

As I prayed, Holy Spirit instructed me to find the word 'mustard' in the Bible. I searched the Scripture and found that every mention of mustard was about the mustard seed of faith (Matthew 13:31, 17:20; Mark 4:30-31; Luke 13:18-19, 17:6). The Lord was showing me, through my dreams, that the remedy for the malady was FAITH! And just as the woman who touched the hem of Jesus' clothes felt His healing virtue flow into her, an actual piece of cloth, soaked in prayers of faith, would be used.

> *"If you have faith as a mustard seed, you will say to this mountain, 'Move from here to there,' and it will move; and nothing will be impossible for you"* (Matthew 17:20).

In thinking about the mustard seed analogy for faith I wondered, why didn't the Lord say faith <u>is</u> a mustard seed instead of faith <u>as</u> a mustard seed? Wouldn't it be easier for us if the Lord said, "If you have a mustard seed, you can move a mountain?" Then we could all go out and buy all the mustard seeds we need and use them for every problem (no doubt they would cost more than diamonds though!)

Most of us want to hold something tangible in our hands that we can feel, see, taste, or touch; a substance - like a seed that we know is *real,* tangible, and not imaginary. If we were to hold out our hands and say we have a living substance in them, but our hands appear empty, the people around us might ridicule and scoff at us.

Yet Jesus said that His Word <u>is</u> a seed (Luke 8:11). A word-seed cannot necessarily be seen but can be heard! The words which Jesus Christ spoke while He was here, in bodily form over 2,000 years ago, still have weight and are still available here on earth; and, anyone can come into agreement with them. Believing in Jesus and His words is actualized faith, faith that has substance and evidence.

Many people say that they wish they could see or touch Jesus physically, and then they would be willing to believe in Him. But even if Jesus appeared today, He would still speak words that must be believed in order to be saved and healed.

In Mark 4:1-9 we read, *"Jesus began to teach by the sea and a great multitude was gathered to Him, so that He got into a boat and sat in it on the sea; and the whole multitude was on the land facing the sea. Then He taught them many things . . . 'The sower sows the word . . . If anyone has ears to hear, let him hear.'"*

When Jesus got into that boat and sat down, they pushed Him out into the water, and away from the people. Jesus preached from the boat and the people sat on the shore. What was He demonstrating? He was out of reach; yet even though He was out of reach physically, the people could hear His voice from the boat. Words carry well across water, and the sound of Jesus' voice reached the multitudes! His words were there as the people listened to His voice across the water, just as He is here as we listen for His voice across time.

Many people say, "If only Jesus were still here in bodily form," or "if only I had lived back then when I could have been around Jesus." But it would still be the same as it was back in Bible days - those people had to decide to believe what God said - and so do we. Most people were healed by Jesus' Words. We have the unchanged thing that the people in the Bible had - God's words. And we also need to believe them. Jesus' words have substance!

Holy Spirit Teacher

In writing this chapter, I spent way too much time trying to simplify some of the physics in order to make it easier to understand. In struggling with the simplification, I asked the Pastors Prayer Shield ministers to pray for me. I received a word that set me free to leave this chapter as it is. A word can bring change and did for me. *"Don't simplify it, just state it as you know it! God will teach us and give insight, He will teach us as He has promised, but the raw information is the best!"* Therefore, as you read the somewhat complex concepts that follow, ask God to teach you!

Understanding Substance

Have you ever smelled fear? Have you tasted anger? Have you felt love in the air? Have you seen a shadow cross someone's face? Have you heard a song on the wind? Any of these can be perceived, but none of them are classified as a material substance.

The dictionary defines a substance as a physical material from which something is made and exists. But the definition of a substance also includes some unseen things such as gas, air, and microscopic particles.

If we think about the substance of gas, we can understand a little more about the possibility of a substance being unnoticeable through our human senses. For example, Natural Gas is colorless and odorless and is generally only detectable when an odor is added to it. Mercaptan is a chemical substance that smells like a rotten egg and is added to Natural Gas for safety. In the event of a gas leak, people would smell the Mercaptan before the gas built up enough to become explosive. Without the added Mercaptan, Natural Gas is without any human means to detect through smell, taste, touch, sound, or sight, but nonetheless is a real substance. The proof of its existence is in the evidence of what it does as it generates electrical power or burns as fuel.

Invisible ink is a substance that a person can use to write a message which is unobservable until the ink is revealed. Even human body fluids can be used as an invisible ink but will be undetectable until the right codebreaker is used. Most invisible inks are revealed through the means of heat.

In the Bible, food that fell to the ground out of heaven was called "manna" and was a substance which fed the children of Israel for forty years (Exodus 16:35). Manna was a "small round substance, as fine as frost on the ground" (Exodus 16:14). God spoke the word "manna" and it appeared from His words. The people could bake the manna or boil it; but if they didn't gather it, it melted. What an interesting substance, and obviously supernatural!

These examples of things that are invisible or supernatural are designated as substances, each having a unique composition. All have a real structure that qualifies them as a physical material by the evidence of what they do. Faith is also a substance that is verified by what it does.

When Jesus Christ felt healing virtue leave His body and go into the body of a woman who had faith to be healed, what kind of substance left His body and went into her body? Is faith released as a particle, a chemical, a wave (light or sound beam), heat, or something we cannot explain at all?

The word "real" (in physics) only makes sense in relation to a human observer. But we are people who believe in God, and not just what a human being can observe. "For since the creation of the world His invisible attributes are clearly seen, being understood by the things that are made, even His eternal power and Godhead" (Romans 1:20).

The Bible says that God sees a substance before it even forms, like He saw you before you were conceived. *"Your eyes saw my substance, being yet unformed. And in Your book they all were written, the days fashioned for me, when as yet there were none of them"* (Psalm 139:13-18).

I wonder if God sees the substance of faith that is about to form in you to enable you to speak His healing word into a person and bring a miracle!

"By faith Moses . . . endured as seeing Him who is invisible" (Hebrews 11:24-27).

Information Received Through Dreams

As I share some of the revelations which Holy Spirit has given me through dreams, and through prayers, about the substance of faith, I prepare you, the reader, through accounts of great people who have received insight in the same way.

There are hundreds of examples of famous scientists who made amazing discoveries that were fueled or materialized from dreams. There are also untold numbers of great writers, poets, musicians, philosophers, and entrepreneurs throughout history who were given inspiration and information during their dreams.

The father of neuroscience, Otto Loewiln, was awarded the Nobel Prize in Medicine for work that came to him in a dream. He thought that nerve signals were possibly transmitted using chemical instructions. He could not think of how he could prove his new idea. In 1920, Loewiln dreamt about the problem. He awoke excitedly during the night and scribbled notes about the dream. In the morning, he could not remember the dream; and he could not read his notes either! The following night, he dreamed about the problem again. The dream was about an experiment he could use to prove his idea, and this time he remembered it. He carried out research based on his dream and published the work in 1921, establishing that signaling across synapses was indeed chemical.

The Periodic Table of Elements, of which I spent a lot of time coaching my husband Tom to memorize in college (for his degree in Chemistry/Biology), was composed from a dream! "In a dream I saw a table where all the elements fell into place as required. Awakening, I immediately wrote it down on a piece of paper." Dmitri Mendeleev, 1834 - 1907, Chemist. [1]

Even the Sewing Machine was invented from information given in a dream. Elias Howe had the idea of a machine with a needle which would go through a piece of cloth; but he couldn't figure out exactly how it would work. He was shown in a dream how to make a needle with a hole for the thread to go through so that it could be caught after it went through cloth, thus making his machine operable.[2]

Golfer Jack Nicklaus found a new way to hold his golf club in a dream, which he credits to improving his golf game. In 1964, Nicklaus was having a bad slump and routinely shooting in the high seventies. After suddenly regaining top scores, he reported: "Wednesday night I had a dream and it was about my golf swing. I was hitting them pretty good in the dream and all at once I realized I wasn't holding the club the way I've actually been holding it lately. I've been having trouble collapsing my right arm taking the club head away from the ball, but I was doing it perfectly in my sleep. So, when I came to the course yesterday morning, I tried it the way I did in my dream and it worked. I shot a sixty-eight yesterday and a sixty-five today."[3]

The samples you have just read are only a few of those that have been recorded. There are hundreds of examples of discoveries that have come through dreaming. But before you take all this inspiration as an excuse to go and take a nap, let us ponder again the subject of the substance of faith.

Faith has Weight

For many years, the Lord has given me dreams in the night about healing ministry. Most recently the dreams have become more scientific, the instruction more detailed and technical. God has shown me the light and sound properties in the substance of faith, and how faith is an actual substance. (Now for those of you who have studied physics and know that a "substance" must be pure and cannot have mixture, I remind you that we are studying a supernatural substance here. Think again of the manna spoken of earlier in this chapter.)

In dreams I have seen that injecting the substance of faith into a gap between the waves or frequencies of a sick person's malady will upset the malady's power source, shut a destructive door, and will open a new door of healing.

The belief that all physical matter is made up of vibrating elements called "strings" is officially known to physicists as "superstring theory" (supersymmetric string theory). It differs from traditional physics, in which all matter is made up of ball-like particles, because the strings are just what the name implies, line-shapes rather than round. But the theory of these strings is improvable currently because they are too small to see with any present magnification. However, I have seen these superstrings in dreams, and they vibrate with frequencies of sound.

Why is the operation of these strings relevant to your healing ministry? Because your primary instrument for releasing the healing virtue of Jesus into a sick person is your vocal cords or your vocal strings!

The fundamental component of strings is that they vibrate at resonant frequencies. This can be understood if you picture the strings of a musical instrument. Such strings vibrate at a distinctive frequency, as well as any multiple of that frequency. Each of these modes of vibration can be energized by plucking or striking the string or energizing one with the substance of faith.

To simplify this understanding, think of a time when words (sonic frequencies) were spoken to you which created a physical reaction in your body. Personally, I will never forget how my knees turned to water when a doctor told me that I had cancer. A chemical substance was released in my body by hearing the doctor's words and I had to sit down. (The complete healing from that cancer is another miracle story!)

We can make another person's heart skip a beat with our words, give someone a headache because of something we say, or make a family member's mouth water with words about the delicious meal we are preparing for him or her. These words go into our bodies in the form of sound waves and have effect on us physically.

Words create substance - actual materials and chemicals are formed as we just explained. You, with your vocal cords, have the power to speak words of faith that can bring healing to yourself and other people, in the name of Jesus.

You may already know that sound waves and light waves are closely related. If I pluck a middle C on my piano, sound waves will touch you. But if I were able to go up 700 octaves and hit a middle C, light waves would touch you.

I remember a retreat at which I was the speaker. After the message, there was a time of ministry in which two different women came forward and asked for healing prayer for Multiple Sclerosis. I prayed for many people that day, but these two women stood out because each of them had faith that moved a mountain! As I laid hands on the first, it was as if an electrical current flowed from me and into that woman! She felt that current of healing virtue in her body and she was completely healed. The other woman piggybacked on the testimony (words) of the first and God completely healed her as well! I injected the substance of faith into their bodies with the Word of God through my vocal strings and it became light!

"Every time we are in the presence of God, at least some healing occurs." R.J. Davidson[4]

Instruction in the Night

As we have already seen, God gives insight and direction through dreams in the night. "For God may speak in one way, or in another, yet man does not perceive it. In a dream, in a vision of the night, when deep sleep falls upon men, while slumbering on their beds, then He opens the ears of men, and seals their instruction" (Job 33:14-16).

The following is a journal entry on the morning of October 8, 2017, after a night of dreams about the substance of faith.

In the night I was given understanding about healing. On my bed I could see clearly and was amazed. On waking I need help, Holy Spirit, to remember and write Your instruction.

I saw that all healing prayer heals. Whatever the malady, the prayer breaks into it every time. Sickness has waves that surge and the waves have minute gaps between them. Depending on the type of the sickness, the gaps are longer or shorter between waves. Healing prayer interrupts the waves - either momentarily (before they begin again) or actually separates them long enough to disrupt their pattern and calm the waves.

Faith has substance and when it is injected between the waves, it interrupts the sequence of the waves. Sickness and even pain, due to something like a broken bone, have a frequency. The pain may seem constant, but it actually ebbs and flows but the gaps are usually imperceptible. That ebb and flow can and does seem like constant pain - but it isn't. It has waves that have a space between each one.

In healing prayer, I come between a wave and the next wave with God's spoken word - the light and sound of faith. Sometimes this interruption breaks the pattern apart long enough for a person's own faith to kick in. Other times the interruption is so short that no one notices, and the change is not believed.

In the night I had understanding of the makeup of different kinds of diseases. The makeup of each one was important as I could see how each pattern worked and I knew when and where to inject the healing interruption, the substance called faith. I saw that faith came as light and sound waves (God said, "let there be light").

The length of the healing interruption which the spoken light of God's Word brought varied according to the gaps between the waves. The strength of faith must meet the strength of the malady and challenge it. This is why people often lose their healing before they know they have it. It all happens so fast. "But they did not know that I healed them" (Hosea 11:3).

How do we widen the gap for the patient, Lord?! How do we hold that next wave back in order to interrupt long enough to get faith in there?! Please teach me more, Lord! And thank You so much for showing me that healing prayer ALWAYS heals - even if it is only for a nanosecond!

I received more from the Lord the following night:

"You are the light of the world. A city that is set on a hill cannot be hidden. Nor do they light a lamp and put it under a basket, but on a lampstand, and it gives light to all who are in the house. Let your light so shine before men, that they may see your good works and glorify your Father in heaven" (Matthew 5:14-16).

God's Word brings light throughout the house (body)! Light has heat. Heat causes the atoms in any material (including a human body) to become more fluid and expand, which means there is a little more space between them. The space between the atoms (which are the fundamental particles which make up all matter, including human cells) is very small, but now the gap is wider because of light and heat and there is room for the injected healing virtue. "Standing in the gap" in prayer has a whole new meaning for me now! Faith is knowing that God has already provided for our healing ("By His stripes we were healed" 1 Peter 2:24). And faith is the substance that comes into the gap and blocks the way of the disease's power and opens the way of healing. Faith has substance and is full of light.

"I sought for a man among them who would make a wall and stand in the gap before Me on behalf of the land, that I should not destroy it; but I found no one" (Ezekiel 22:30).

God is the Father of lights (James 1:17). *We are "children of light"* (Ephesians 5:8).

Faith is a leap into the light and out of the darkness. The Word of God is like a laser light beam in its operation! "God has delivered us from the power of darkness and conveyed us into the kingdom of the Son of His love" (Colossians 1:13).

Divine Healing is Scientific

Hebrews 1:3 beautifully describes the truth of how Jesus Christ is EVERYHING! Jesus Christ *"is the brightness of [God's] glory, the express image of His person, and upholding all things by the word of His power, when He had by Himself purged our sins, sat down at the right hand of the Majesty on high."* Jesus is the center of everything, and the Cross is the moment around which all history, present and future, pivot!

There is a "glue" which holds all things together. Scientists have found a substance they have named, "The Higgs Boson" (after one of the six physicists who proposed its existence). Too small to see, it is theorized to exist and comparable to a pool of molasses that "sticks" to the otherwise massless particles in all things that exist and converts them (the formless) into particles with mass, creating the components of atoms. The Higgs Boson is often referred to as "the God particle" by the media. Even scientists know that there is something that holds all things together!

Everything is made up of atoms, which are frequencies of energy. I believe that these frequencies (sounds) of energy are the voice of Jesus causing all things to be and holding all things together! *"All things were created through Him and for Him. And He is before all things, and in Him all things consist"* (Colossians 1:16-17). Jesus Christ is EVERYTHING and apart from Him there is no healing, there is no anything.

This is not a New Age teaching, nor were my dreams humanly inspired. But how do these dreams of sonic waves, frequencies, and gaps relate to you?

Divine healing is scientific. Contact with the sick while using God's Word in prayer causes the Spirit of God to flow into the gaps between the waves of the malady. There is such substance in our Lord's words spoken through a believer that they can interrupt sickness and present a moment to receive healing!

The Apostle Paul, knowing this power, laid his hands upon handkerchiefs and aprons and no doubt spoke the words of God while doing so. The Bible says that when these cloths were laid upon the sick, they were healed, and the demons went out of those possessed. The Spirit of God emanating from Paul transformed the handkerchiefs into conductors of Holy Spirit power. When they were laid upon the sick, they caused a disruption in the sickness of the body, and healing was the result (see Acts 19:12). This demonstrates that the Spirit of God is a tangible substance, a heavenly material. It is capable of being stored in the substance of cloth, as demonstrated in the garments of Jesus (the woman who touched the hem of His garment) or the handkerchief of Paul.

"Immediately the fountain of her blood was dried up, and she felt in her body that she was healed of the affliction. And Jesus, immediately knowing in Himself that power had gone out of Him, turned around in the crowd and said, 'Who touched My clothes?'" (Mark 5:30).

YOUR FAITH HAS MADE YOU WELL

Let us now look at the words of Jesus Christ about faith with a new lens. To be able to read the words which God spoke without discounting them, attaching your own meaning, or reducing them to your own personal experience takes the help of the Holy Spirit. Therefore, please invite His help before you read the following words of Jesus about faith.

- "They brought to Him a paralytic lying on a bed. When Jesus saw their faith, He said to the paralytic, 'Son, be of good cheer; your sins are forgiven you'" (Matthew 9:2).
- "'Be of good cheer, daughter; your faith has made you well.' And the woman was made well from that hour" (Matthew 9:22).
- "He touched their eyes, saying, 'According to your faith let it be to you'" (Matthew 9:29).
- "Jesus answered and said to her, "O woman, great is your faith! Let it be to you as you desire." And her daughter was healed from that very hour" (Matthew 15:28).

- “When Jesus saw their faith, He said to the paralytic, ‘Son, your sins are forgiven you’” (Mark 2:5).
- “Daughter, your faith has made you well. Go in peace, and be healed of your affliction” (Mark 5:34).
- “‘Go your way; your faith has made you well.” And immediately he received his sight and followed Jesus on the road” (Mark 10:52).
- “When He saw their faith, He said to him, ‘Man, your sins are forgiven you’” (Luke 5:20).
- “Then He said to the woman, ‘Your faith has saved you. Go in peace’” (Luke 7:50).
- “Daughter, be of good cheer; your faith has made you well. Go in peace” (Luke 8:48).
- “Arise, go your way. Your faith has made you well” (Luke 17:19).
- “Receive your sight; your faith has made you well” (Luke 18:42).

Faith was something which Jesus could see in a person. Are you like Jesus; can you see faith? What does it look like? Why not ask God to show you what Jesus saw and what Paul also saw - the tangible substance of faith.

“A certain man without strength in his feet was sitting, a cripple from his mother’s womb, who had never walked. This man heard Paul speaking. Paul, observing him intently and seeing that he had faith to be healed, said with a loud voice, ‘Stand up straight on your feet!’ And he leaped and walked” (Acts 14:8-10).

In the Scripture (above) from the book of Acts, it states that Paul “seeing that [the man] had faith to be healed” told the man who was born crippled (had never walked) to “stand up straight on your feet.” Paul had observed the man intently first. What did he see? He saw faith to be healed. Again, what did the faith look like? Have you asked God to show you the substance of faith, so you can recognize it?

I often pray for people who do not have the faith to be healed. I can tell that they are thinking past the healing prayer and onto which doctor they will go to or the medication they will take. Often one of the first things a person will say to me after the prayer is, “Well, I will let you know what the doctor says I need to do . . .”

What if we really believed that the prayer of faith we prayed, with our sonic frequency vocal strings, went into the gap of the sickness and made the sick one well (James 5:15)? You cannot control whether or not a person will let the faith work in them; but if you see the faith go in, you can speak with greater influence and authority. Ask for this kind of insight today - and ask for vision to see who has this kind of faith!

Remember that you are called a person: per means to pass through, and son means sonic, which is sound. Part of your purpose as a person is to be used for sound to pass through and bring healing to people.

Father in Heaven, please grant me sight like Paul, that I may observe intently whether there is faith for healing. And, oh Lord, please let there be faith for healing! Thank You, Lord.

What Wars Against Faith?

What wars against faith? Lack of love. There is a place in our hearts for the deep love of God and this kind of love cannot coexist with a lack of love for other people.

The Test of Knowing Christ is how we love. We keep the commandments of God because we love Him (John 14:15); and, His command is that we love other people.

"Now by this we know that we know Him, if we keep His commandments. He who says, 'I know Him,' and does not keep His commandments, is a liar, and the truth is not in him. But whoever keeps His word, truly the love of God is perfected in Him. By this we know that we are in Him. He who says he abides in Him ought himself also to walk just as He walked . . . He who says he is in the light, and hates his brother, is in darkness until now. He who loves his brother abides in the light, and there is no cause for stumbling in him. But he who hates his brother is in darkness and walks in darkness, and does not know where he is going, because the darkness has blinded his eyes" (1 John 2:3-11).

Choosing Love Increases Faith

How can we increase in faith - the kind that has real substance and brings real healing? I believe that the reason that Paul could see the faith in the man we read about earlier (Acts 14:8-10) was because Paul loved him. The Scripture states that Paul looked intently at the man. Why else would he stare so closely and with such concentration?

Faith is one of those things that we don't necessarily grow in by trying to grow in faith. Faith is one of those things that you automatically grow in when you grow in your capacity and willingness to abide in God's love. God's Word says that faith works through love. Faith is activated and released by love. I can choose love; without love, I cannot choose faith.

> *"The only thing that counts is faith expressing itself through love;" "Faith working through love"* (Galatians 5:6, NIV).

The disciples of Jesus asked Him, "increase our faith" (Luke 17:5). The answer Jesus gave to that request was not for the disciples to receive a sudden super-download of faith. Jesus told His disciples that even a mustard-seed-size of faith could move a mountain. Then He told them that faith is an action and was their reasonable service to Him. Faith is in the obedience of loving service; faith expressing itself through love!

When we love our coworkers, our neighbors, our kids, and spouse, when we lay down our lives and serve others in love, we grow in faith! True love knows no limits, and nothing is impossible for it! Love believes all things (1 Corinthians 13:7).

Through love, life is transmitted, experienced, and multiplied and it enables faith. Without love, there are only dead works and that will inevitably bring a shrinking, withering, and suffocating of what should or might have been.

Love involves our emotions; it is not just a mental assent. Deep and sincere emotion can accentuate a real connection to God.

Jonathan Edwards was a revivalist who participated with God in many miracles and is still called the father of the first Great Awakening in America. He spoke of emotion being the gateway to knowing God and encouraged people to allow their emotions to be deeply affected by

God. Edwards insisted that he could see little or no evidence of spiritual transformation without emotions in the lives of individuals.[5] Mental assent, it seems, did not produce true belief.

Loving God and loving other people deeply from your heart will involve emotion. Are you willing to let yourself care so deeply that your entire life is full of the light, heat, passion, and the sound of God's love through you? If you are, I believe that your own faith is about to take a giant leap forward, and your healing ministry is about to soar! In Jesus' Name!

Prayer

O Lord! I want to know that what I release through my vocal cords actually brings light. You spoke, "Let there be light and there was light" (Genesis 1:3)! I am created in Your image and therefore, have been given the magnificent gift of speech. Please make me a trustworthy vessel who can speak healing into the sick and see them made whole. I give You my tongue, O God! Take my tongue and use it. From now on my speech is dedicated to You and Your purposes. In Jesus' name, amen.

Reflection

1. Have you had a God-given dream in which you were shown things that you could not have known before the dream? (Do you desire to have dreams from God? Ask Him to give you dreams.)

2. What did the people who were separated from Jesus (by water) need to believe to be saved and healed? Is the way of healing and salvation the same today as it was in Bible times?

3. What is the essential thing that you need (which Paul demonstrated in Acts 14:8-10) to bring healing to another person?

4. What is God's sequence for loving Him with your entire being (what is first in the list and what is second, according to Matthew 22:37)?

6

BASIC REASONS FOR SICKNESS

The resurrection power within Jesus Christ was and is greater than any disease or infirmity. Jesus Christ has all authority on planet Earth, including over sickness and disease. "All authority has been given to Me in heaven and on earth" (Matthew 28:18).

Randy helped lead worship the Sunday before he broke his leg playing basketball. It was a great day at church and Randy was playing the guitar, tapping his foot, and singing his heart out. Then on the following Wednesday, he was at the evening prayer meeting, explaining about how the accident happened and asking for prayer to ease the pain of his broken leg. But God had another idea!

We gathered around Randy to pray and I felt that God's power was present to heal him (Luke 5:17); so, I began to ask Father God to mend the broken leg. As we prayed, I sensed that God was bringing the healing. However, it wasn't until the next day, when Randy went back to the same doctor (the one who took the x-ray that showed the break) that we got the report that Randy's leg had no broken bone and he had no pain! The new x-ray showed that the bone was whole! The following Sunday at church, Randy was playing the guitar, tapping his foot, and singing his heart out - louder than ever! God had performed a doctor-documented, indisputable, miraculous healing! (Oh, and by the way, Randy became the worship pastor at that church!)

Shouldn't this kind of healing happen all the time?

Randy broke his leg because, as a human, he was susceptible to the conditions of planet Earth, including gravity, force (collision), and bones that are made of breakable material. In other words, his infirmity was a condition of living in an earthbound human body, on a spinning planet that has a gravitational pull. Some sicknesses and infirmities are the result of being a human who lives on earth.

One Reason For Sickness: Living On Earth

Consider what happens to the food that you leave in the back of your refrigerator for too long. Eventually it spoils, grows mold, and smells bad, simply because it is susceptible to the air that we breathe every day.

When Tom and I lived in England and attended a DTS with YWAM (Discipleship Training School with Youth With A Mission), we had a teacher named Lawrence Singlehurst. The main thing I remember about his teaching was, "everything swerves to rot!" He explained that: because we live in a fallen world, the whole planet, and everything on it, is deteriorating and will eventually swerve to rot. So encouraging.

One simple answer for why people sometimes get sick is because there are germs where we live. Germs are spread through touch and through the atmosphere and some of them get on us. Of course, there are factors which contribute to our susceptibility, but basically, being around germs is not something we can completely avoid.

Recently I was on an airplane where people all around me were sneezing. I really wanted that aircraft to land so I could breathe without taking in the flu-germs. I noticed that I was holding my breath a lot and of course, I couldn't hold it for the hours I was on the plane. To counter my irritation and the fear of getting sick, I began to pray for the people around me. Eventually the sneezing stopped, and the flight became more peaceful.

What a Committed Life to Jesus Christ Means

God's intention is that we become like His Beloved Son, Jesus Christ (Romans 8:29). Father God allows and uses many different circumstances to bring about that transformation. Sickness and the need for healing, whether gradual, partial, instantaneous, delayed, or through medical professionals, is part of that process. As we look at the basic reasons for sickness, let us endeavor to look deeper into the ways and purposes of God, without creating formulas to try to protect ourselves from life.

As I was typing these lofty (but true) words, a real-life situation popped into my phone messages. I read the prayer request, written for a coworker of a friend, who has been diagnosed with very serious cancer. Would I sit and ponder whether God wants to help that woman? Of course not! Immediately, I asked Father God to heal her, texted back, and asked that she be brought to me for healing. My job is not to figure it all out; my job is to put my hands on her and pray for healing, expecting a miracle!

Another Reason for Sickness is User Error

Medical science recognizes that our negative responses to life (such as fear, resentment, worry, hatred, envy, etc.) are responsible for 60-95 percent of our sicknesses. Emotional stress can cause ulcers, migraine headaches, high blood pressure, heart disease, arthritis, autoimmune illnesses, and countless other serious diseases.

Although we cannot avoid emotional stress completely, we can choose to keep ourselves in hope. Negative responses to life's issues can be managed through the power of our resident Holy Spirit Helper. (Dealing with disappointment and staying hopeful is outlined further in this book.)

We all know that what we choose to eat, and drink, can wreak havoc with many functions of our bodies.

As I was seeking the Lord in preparation for writing this chapter, Holy Spirit showed me that many of our health problems are *user error!* Is God willing to heal us when we are the ones who messed up our own temples? The answer is unequivocally, "YES"! Do not let yourself deny God's merciful kindness by thinking you deserve punishment and must pay. Jesus paid the full price for your healing and freedom! Father God is rich in mercy!

Simple User Error

Our Lord is also very rich in wisdom and He gives it liberally. In God's Word, He promises to give us wisdom (James 1:5) and to show us hidden things, which we do not know (Jeremiah 33:3). One convicting reason for sickness is simply: we don't take time to cultivate the act of waiting on God to show us the cure.

I have had many simple user-error problems for which God has given me the secret for the cure. For example, my right arm had become very painful, to the point where any task was miserable, including getting dressed. As I waited on God to heal me, listening for instruction, I heard "handbag." Suddenly, I realized that the new, large, in-style handbag that I was carrying was too heavy for me. When I repented of my vanity for carrying it and gave it away, my arm got better and better until there was no pain at all! And although my heavy handbag problem may have been obvious to those around me, no one told me. There is One who cares enough, is intimate enough, and knows everything about me who can help me!

Another case of simple user-error was a cleanser I was using on my face. It was expensive, did the job, and smelled nice. But for several years, I experienced recurring eye infections. One night, when I opened the bottle, I heard Holy Spirit warn me to close it. My common sense wanted to continue what I was doing; but I obeyed the prompting of the One who knows all and did not use the cleanser again. Since that time (it has been years), I have not had a single eye infection!

A friend of mine had been having a terrible time due to not feeling well at all. She went to the doctor and he could not find anything wrong with her. One evening, when she was about to take a medication that she had been taking for years, Holy Spirit stopped her and impressed on her thoughts that the medicine was not right. She closed the bottle and made an appointment to see her doctor again. When she saw the doctor, he discovered that the medication she had been taking was incorrectly dosed. She'd been taking way too much. Her malady cleared up completely when she listened to the Holy Spirit's prompting and acted on what God showed her.

Some people are ill because they do not take the time to go to God and wait for His answer.

What are the benefits of waiting for God's insight, and being led by His word? A sense of shalom (wholeness), the ability to rest and sleep well, even in a storm; a sense of confidence, hope, steadiness, clarity in processing thoughts, options, and information; the capacity to wait until God speaks and directs.

Easy!

Jesus Christ promised His followers that He would give them (us) an easy yoke. We see in this word 'easy,' the root word 'ease' and the opposite when 'dis' is added to 'ease': disease.

"For My yoke is easy and My burden is light" (Matthew 11:30).

Scripture gives us very good news about Who takes care of us! Jesus Christ, Himself, carried our sicknesses and diseases! *"Surely He has borne our griefs and carried our sorrows"* (Isaiah 53:4). In the original Hebrew, these words mean 'diseases' and 'pains.' Since Jesus Christ took my infirmities and my sicknesses, there is no reason for both of us to bear them!

How does Jesus Christ take sickness off me and carry it Himself? He often initiates my healing by convicting me of sin so I can repent and by so doing, close access to disease. He also shows me the things in my family line that I need to deal with so He can free me and the generations in my family line after me.

Most of us are quite capable of making simple things difficult. Yet, Jesus illustrated a simple lifestyle: one that was worry-free. How do we live like that?

Make sure your ease does not become dis-ed (disease); because according to internet insurance companies, there are more than 13,000 diseases. No wonder the word of God teaches us to forgive quickly (daily), guard our hearts, capture our thoughts, not to worry, and not to let the sun go down on our anger! God knows that a sick soul will contaminate the body!

A Sick Soul

"Anxiety in the heart of a [person] causes depression . . ." (Proverbs 12:25).
"Some patients I see are actually draining into their bodies the diseased thoughts of their minds." Dr. Zacharty Bercovitz[1]

Jesus Christ instructed, *"Do not worry"* on purpose (Matthew 6:25-34). There are physical and emotional symptoms which manifest when we continue in worry. Among those symptoms: the body is tense, we are reactionary and irritable, we have trouble relaxing and sleeping. What is the outcome of being worried? Exhaustion, fear, error, dissatisfaction, loss of physical health, loss of emotional peace, internal loneliness, and as the Proverb states, "anxiety in the heart causes depression."

Some people are sick because they 'are worried sick.' Fueling negative emotions by agreeing with them (as in worrying instead of choosing to trust God), can bring sickness into the physical body. When a person comes into agreement with worry (or other destructive emotions), and does not turn to God, place may be given to a demonic spirit.

Am I saying that demon can oppress a Christian? Because I have experienced deliverance from oppressive spirits so many times, I am not demon phobic. I much prefer to recognize what is going on and do what it takes to be freed.

Every day I put each piece of the Armor of Light on myself and many other people who I intercede for. Although the garment of praise is not included in the Ephesians 6:10-18, list of armor pieces, I always include it. Isaiah 61:3 instructs, *". . . Put on the garment of praise for the spirit of heaviness."* When I put on this covering of praise, I notice a tangible lifting of shadows and an increase in light. Does this mean that there was a foul spirit oppressing me? I believe it does.

Being a person who carries a torch for a healing revival, and one who brings Holy Spirit-filled speakers to minister at regional life-changing events, enemies often target me. Add to this the fact that my husband, Tom, and I planted a new church in the devil's territory, and you will understand that there is a lot of opposition. Sometimes that opposition attempts to lay upon me like a heaviness. But I can tell you that putting on the garment of praise and throwing off the spirit of heaviness brings an actual, noticeable, change in my physical body. For me to pretend that a demonic spirit of heaviness is not really real and ignore it would be foolish.

In the original purpose of God, humankind ruled over creation. When sin entered the world, creation was infected by disease, sickness, afflicting spirits, poverty, natural disasters, demonic influence, etc. Through the authority of Jesus Christ, we again have power to expose and undo the works of the devil.

Why do disease, addiction, and all the other tools of the enemy continue to torment humanity? If we knew more about spiritual warfare, we could thwart much of the devil's schemes and those things which hurt us personally.

Let us believe the warnings in the Bible and heed its wise instruction for our protection. Certain unchecked emotions can bring a person under demonic oppression. As Scripture warns, *"Do not let the sun go down on your anger"* (Ephesians 4:26). Why? The rest of the verse states that going to bed angry can give access to satan. If we truly believed that the one who comes to kill, steal, and destroy can touch us through our anger, we would get rid of that anger in a flash.

Scripture teaches that the Spirit of God gives life to our mortal bodies (Romans 8:11). Although the Holy Spirit wants to release life into each of our physical bodies, what happens when a person's soul is in opposition to the Spirit? Let's say that the Spirit of God speaks, "Peace be still" to you, but you believe you have a right to be angry and continue to seethe with anger. The mortal body will take on the nature of the soul's choice. A person can carry something with them that works against them which destroys their own health. (For an illustration of what this might mean, read my personal story in chapter 13.)

What is the remedy for a sick soul? Once again, the remedy is simple: we must be persistent and committed in conforming to the image of Christ. This always involves repentance (turning around and going God's direction), submission (yielding to God as Master), resisting the temptation to give into the devil's lies, and establishing God's Word as your meditation day and night!

"Repent therefore and be converted, that your sins may be blotted out, so that times of refreshing may come from the presence of the Lord" (Acts 3:19).

God's Healing School for me

In 2003, God put me into His extreme ten-month Healing School. Up until that time, I had many stories of successes when God brought healing to people through me. I saw and felt a large goiter disappear from a woman's neck as I prayed. Numerous individuals were healed of cancer when I prayed for them. Doctor documented cases of Multiple Sclerosis completely healed. The list could go on and on.

I personally experienced many types of healing in my own body. I had a heart condition that was healed after prayer. I was on a roll. Until 2003.

My husband and I had planted a new church in a city in California, in 2000. The church was growing quickly during those exciting days; and we invited some of our good friends John and Carol* to move to our city and help us build the church. After much prayer, they agreed to come. We were thrilled!

John became the church treasurer and Carol was part of my His Way Ministries Leadership Team. The church was growing; the fellowship of friends was sweet . . . Until 2002, when John was diagnosed with brain cancer.

Faith was high, and we fully expected John to be healed. In the months during John's illness, he had many visions of the healing that would flow through me into him and bring salvation to countless people. John recorded the visions, sharing them with anyone who would listen (including hospital staff). We were sure that healing was coming.

We had a trip planned to fly from California to New York in early 2003. The day before we left for the trip, I spent a couple hours with John and Carol, praying for John's healing. I knew that God had touched him during that prayer time and was confident that John would be fine while we were away.

The night before we left, I felt impressed by the Holy Spirit to watch one of our videos - the story of a man who was raised from the dead. I couldn't find it; but as I sat and waited for the Holy Spirit to show me where it was, He impressed on me to pull a certain binder from our library bookshelf. As I did, the video, which was tucked inside, fell into my hands. I wondered if Jesus was preparing me to raise the dead.

In New York, we visited a great church and the sermon (I will never forget), was about Jesus raising Lazarus from the dead. I pondered more about the miracle of John's healing. Maybe God would make it even bigger than we could imagine, by actually raising John from the dead. I felt excited.

We did not have any cell phone service on the flight home from New York. So, it wasn't until we arrived back in our city that I turned my phone on. That's when I received word that John had just died.

Without any delay, I headed for the hospital (Tom waited at the airport for our luggage). John had only been dead a short time and I was absolutely certain, without doubt, that he would raise from the dead!

For the next three hours, I commanded John to rise, in Jesus' name. I pulled him up from his bed by his arms and spoke life into him; I rebuked the enemy; I begged God to send him back; I commanded, and then begged, John to come back. I pulled him up repeatedly. I gathered others to agree with me in prayer for John's rising. I stayed until hospital officials insisted I leave so they could take John's body to the morgue. Still, I believed that he would come back to life.

I wrote these words in my journal that same night, *"This is about the will of sovereign God and what He said. Nothing else. His word stands forever. I give up my reputation. What does it matter? It will pass away. The word of the Lord stands forever. I will lay down my life and believe what God has said. John is not to die. Regardless of my life, I will believe God."*

But John did not come back to earthly life. This terrible disappointment and loss instigated an extreme pursuit of searching for God-answers. My time in God's Healing School consumed several hours every day, for ten months, as I asked Him questions and listened for His answers. I received answers that did not fit my paradigms - answers that jarred me out of my own ideas of healing.

Some of the Things I Found Out About God

During the months in God's Healing School, I learned some of the basic reasons for sickness and was instructed in the many combinations of factors that enlist illness. I also learned these characteristics about God:

- God doesn't get upset when someone dies; but He has compassion on those who are grieving (John 11:14).
- God doesn't need publicity *("I do not receive honor from men"* John 5:41; *"Tell no one"* Matthew 8:4, 12:16, 17:9, Mark 5:43, 7:36).
- Nobody dies without God's watchful eye of love.

"Not even a sparrow falls to the ground apart from your Father's will" (Matthew 10:29).

Consider the following statement made by a young woman in our church whose husband was suddenly taken to Heaven: "Satan's greatest weapon is to kill us, and our greatest weapon is to die. How good is our God that He designed it so that the last thing Satan can resort to is the single greatest gift God could ever give us - the unhindered fullness of Himself."[2]

God's perspective (absolutely right and true perspective) about a person's death is very different from ours.

Some observations about why God doesn't always seem to heal, despite our praying and proclaiming:

- God often deals with the root cause, not just symptoms (Hebrews 12:15).
- God will test our faith (James 1:3).
- Sometimes healing is progressive (Luke 17:12-19).
- We may not be willing to fulfill the criteria for healing (James 5:16).

We will further explore each of these aspects of God's healing ways, as well as the way to be free from demonic oppression, later in this book.

In God's Healing School (in which I am still enrolled), I learned to lay down the results of my healing prayers and trust God. I determined that if I prayed for 100 people and none of them was healed, I would pray for 100 more. (During the time following John's death, I had such a loss of confidence that I prayed for fewer people - which, of course, meant that fewer people were healed. When I regained my confidence, through the time of listening to God, I decided that I would pray for healing for anybody, every chance I got, including praying for the dead to raise.)

A few more of the many things Holy Spirit taught me during that time include: the part human freewill plays in health; the overuse of morphine in medical practice; how a spouse's choice can affect an outcome; how the devil attempts to set-up scenarios; and the very sensitive matter of respecting family members who don't appreciate an 'outsider' intervening with their loved one. I am wiser now!

One of the many gifts God gave me during that intense time of learning, was the gift of seeing percentages. I frequently see numbers over a person (especially in the hospital) who is critically ill. The numbers (as an example: 83%), do not mean that the person only has a 17% chance of being healed. The percentages relate to other factors which I will write about someday, as Holy Spirit gives me leave. Suffice it to say that Father God has given me a tool whereby the devil will not trick me again in the same way as before.

I also received a deep impartation about the sovereignty of God. The security which I now have due to this impartation is amazing to me.

Father God promised reward to any of us who diligently seek Him. His rewards are far beyond anything we could ask for!

Suffering that Brings God Glory

In the book of John, we find that God allowed a man to be born blind for the very purpose of bringing God glory many years later!

"As Jesus passed by, He saw a man who was blind from birth. And His disciples asked Him, saying, 'Rabbi, who sinned, this man or his parents, that he was born blind?' Jesus answered, 'Neither this man nor his parents sinned, but that the works of God should be revealed in him'" (John 9:1-3).

The blind man's healing brought glory to God (honor, respect, and tribute). The years of the blind man's suffering were not addressed in this Scripture at all. No sympathy or apology was given. God's purpose was accomplished as God was glorified.

Does this seem unfair to you? We know that God's ways are perfect (Psalm 18:30). I am personally looking forward to talking with the healed blind man in Heaven. I can't wait to hear about how God's grace was sufficient for him as he waited for his healing with a knowing that he was chosen for something great!

Some people have used the Scripture about the man born blind to insist that they must also suffer in order to bring God glory. We will address the problems with wanting to punish oneself later in this book. But for now, remember that in God's time, that blind man did receive his sight! We must also wait in faith for God's ultimate good plan.

One more: Lazarus' death was also allowed because it brought God glory. Can you imagine the rejoicing that happened when Lazarus came back from the dead? Such a great display of the glory of God!

"This sickness is not unto death, but for the glory of God, that the Son of God may be glorified through it" (John 11:4).

It can be challenging to know which way to approach a person who needs of healing. We need Holy Spirit guidance in order to know when sickness is to be rebuked - as the Lord demonstrated when He rebuked a fever and it left a woman (Luke 4:39); when to wait - as Jesus waited for two days, allowing Lazarus to die before going to raise him (John 11:6); or when a person needs to be freed from a demon (Luke 13:11).

We could find ninety-nine ways healing comes about (my New King James Bible lists the word 'healed' in ninety-nine verses) and memorize all of them. But the one way to bring healing to yourself and others is to start with Jesus. The Lord makes His way known as we step out in faith and serve others in love.

A long time ago the Holy Spirit told me that when I am afraid, I can't hear Him. Therefore, I always ask God for courage.

Armed with love and courage, we will not fail! The least that a person will experience from our healing ministry is love! And Love truly is the greatest gift of all.

In the next chapter we will go deeper into the ways of God in healing. You will need courage as you read, so go ahead and ask God now, for courage.

Prayer

Thank You, Lord, that You always know what You are doing, and everything You do is right. I join with You in Your great love for people! Give me courage, O God, and give me love! In Jesus' name, amen.

Reflection

1. Do you have a testimony from your own life of when you were suffering in pain from simple "user error" and the Holy Spirit showed you what to change?

2. According to Romans 8:11, what does the Spirit of God give to our mortal bodies?

3. Have you or someone you know, claimed that God was going to bring a spectacular healing so that lots of people would be saved? Ponder the concept that God doesn't need publicity.

- Can you find a Scripture to back up the idea that God heals people so that many people will turn to Him?

4. What does a committed life to Jesus Christ mean, regarding the viewpoint that God wants every person healed and whole?

7

HEALING IS CIRCUMSPECT

Healing is miraculous, but often humbling and can be messy. Sickness can turn us inside out, exposing our hidden faults and misconceptions, which Jesus wants to heal.

One day while seeking the Lord for deeper insight into how to bring healing to people, the Holy Spirit spoke very clearly to me, "Healing is circumspect." I had no idea what this meant or even the definition of the word, "circumspect." But it was obviously important; so, I went on a hunt to learn more.

According to the dictionary[1], the word circumspect means 'circum' (round) 'spect' (look, as through spectacles). Look around. Be careful to consider all circumstances and possible consequences.

Although healing is simple for God, it is still multifaceted and requires a listening heart to be able to see the whole circle. Healing is not a square that can fit in your brain box. We may need to get out of the tidy box we may have made and be ready to do things in a different way than we have done them in the past.

Recently, I was in the home of a very beautiful young woman who awoke one morning, out of the blue, with Bell's Palsy. One side of her face was not working, and her shining smile was limited to one side of her mouth. What a shock to be changed so suddenly in appearance in the very place where you face the world every day.

As I prayed for her, bringing her a word from God, it became clear that she was willing to suffer for the purposes of God and was ready to bring Him the most glory in her situation. Because of her love for God, I was stopped in my tracks from praying for instantaneous full healing. God wanted to use this infirmity for His glory! Here we come to one of the aspects of healing that is not popular in our culture: some infirmities are crafted to prove the devil wrong! This is a huge understanding. If we can gain wisdom from this truth, we will win far more battles against the fallen one and that which serves him!

Before we go further with our story, let us look at the Scripture for testimonies of when God used individuals to prove the devil wrong.

Consider the account of the man named Job: The devil was convinced and insisted that if God were to allow him to afflict Job, that Job would cave in. The devil told God that if He allowed Job to be sick in his body, then Job would curse God to His face (Job 2:5). But Job proved the devil wrong because he did not turn against God. Job said, *"Shall we indeed accept good from God, and shall we not accept adversity? In all this Job did not sin with his lips"* (verse 10)!

When human people walk through trials, troubles, and infirmity, without blaming God or turning against Him, a great spiritual battle is won in the unseen realm! The challenge comes in knowing which kind of situation we are actually in. Are we being tested to show God's glory? Or are we suffering because of our own choices? How do we go about fighting for our healing in the middle of a test?

The Lord showed me that sickness can turn us inside out, exposing the faults and sins He wants to heal.

Back to the case of the beautiful young woman who woke up one morning with Bell's Palsy. As I ministered to the woman, God spoke that He is jealous for her and will create opportunities for her to lock her gaze with Him and wean herself from the admiration of other people.

Later that day, after prayer, the courageous woman walked into her workplace and brought Jesus much glory! She wrote me, "It was so amazing! One of my coworkers broke down in tears after seeing me. I shared Jesus with her and all He's doing despite this affliction. I really felt Jesus all night right beside me! Thank you for all the prayers! I'm keeping my eyes on Him through all of this."

To further punctuate this woman's testimony, understand that she worked as a server at a busy restaurant. She served people who had to notice her lopsided smile and drooping eye. But she had the Lord's smile and His grace.

Wow - she proved satan wrong! Instead of blaming God, she brought God great glory as she gave testimony of God's goodness! She continued to walk through the affliction with faith and after Jesus received much glory through her, she was completely healed!

Some people believe that the devil was put on earth to torment us. I believe we were put on this planet to prove that the devil is wrong and show that God is always good! (Of course, we are here to glorify God and to be His friends.)

The Power of Testimony

A woman was baptized one Sunday at our church. She believed that she had a word from God, and that her obedience in being baptized would bring healing in her body. Afterward she gave this remarkable testimony:

> "It has been almost 2 weeks since my baptism and guess what? I've been pain free!!! God is so good when you are obedient to Him! I had one day in the last two weeks that I started to have doubt because I had a doctor's appointment and the doctor gave me an official diagnosis that was not good, an autoimmune disease with no cure. However, I prayed and remembered God's promise. So, I immediately sent that diagnosis to the Cross and the healing kept pouring out over me!! My thoughts have been what if this sickness and healing is part of a plan from God to be used as a testament of His goodness for the unbeliever? I felt compelled to share this with my husband, so I did. If my very literal husband can become open to the fact that God is real, and He does heal, who else do I need to share my testimony with? Isn't it funny how God works? He always knows what we need. We may fight it, and wonder 'Why me?' or 'This is so unfair.' But I've learned this is actually what I've been praying for. For years I've been praying for Jesus to soften my husband's

> heart to receive Him. I didn't know He would do it like this. I've also been praying for God to use me to be a light. I really believe He is using me through this whole process of sickness, praying, obedience, and healing!"

It was only a few months later that this woman's husband was radically saved because of her testimony. They have been a strong Christian family in our church for more than two years at this writing!

Instant Healing

While up front speaking at a meeting the Lord gave me a Word of Knowledge for someone who was experiencing pain in their hips. I expressed God's desire to heal; then I spoke the love and healing virtue of Jesus over those present. A man gave testimony that he felt warm liquid pouring into her body and all the pain left; he was healed instantly and completely!

Healing and Tenacious Love

A blind man in Africa, who received his sight, had a different road to healing. He was willing to be prayed for; however, I discerned resistance in him as I prayed. I was told that when a person receives healing in that area of Africa, the witchdoctor would take credit and demand payment. For the blind man to be willing to receive healing, he had to be willing to go against the witchdoctor, and that was a frightful prospect. As I understood the blind man's fear, the Holy Spirit gave me strategy - *minister the love of God that drives out all fear* (1 John 4:18). I began to minister the love of God, announcing that God loved this man with an everlasting love, and that Jesus shed His blood because of His great love for this man. I spoke God's passionate love and His desire for the man to know Him. For more than an hour, I continued to pour the love of God over the man who needed healing.

Then a change began to happen! Even though the man could not understand my language, the Holy Spirit was at work, making the love of God come through anyway (Romans 8:26). The man began to lift his head and face toward me, and I could see his eyes changing! But then fear would engulf him again and he would drop his head down again. This happened many times before the love of God finally overtook the man, and fear could not stop the healing love of God from pouring into the man's eyes! Pupils formed, and the man could suddenly see! There was an explosive, spontaneous praise and a dance party that ensued! The blind could now see, and everyone was jarred in the reality of a God who loves us and is with us to heal!

Although I am always thrilled when healing is instantaneous, experiencing the love of God pouring through me and into that man, for well over an hour, was incredible! God's love is like a multicolored waterfall in beauty and intensity!

Laying Down Half-Correct Ideas About Healing

We have just looked at four examples of how healing flows in different ways: 1) healing that proves the devil wrong 2) the power of testimony 3) instant healing 4) spiritual warfare breakthrough healing. Each different and orchestrated by God. Healing is circumspect!

I have many books on healing (eclipsed only by the multitude of books I have on prayer)! Sometimes different authors see healing from differing angels, basing their ideas on certain Scriptures, and not on all the verses in the Bible. (Please forgive me for when I have done this as well - and please remember that only the Bible is infallible!)

I have read or heard a speaker say, "Do not beg God for healing, you must command the healing to take place." Yet Moses begged God to heal Miriam:

> *"So Moses cried out to the Lord, saying, 'Please heal her, O God, I pray!'"* (Numbers 12:13).

Others say that Jesus did not tell us to pray for the sick, He told us to heal the sick, so heal them! (Read Numbers 12:13 again!)

Then there is the controversy over suffering. I just read a really good article by a writer who stated, *"For generations, religion has mistakenly assumed that God needs to send suffering to grow us into Christlikeness. According to 1 John 3:8, the Son of God was made manifest, not to afflict us with sickness and torment, but to destroy the works of the devil. It is theologically irresponsible for us to claim that God sends what Jesus destroyed in order to grow us spiritually."*[2]

While this is true in most aspects, we must not throw out the Old Testament and the many examples that show when God allowed troubles to come upon His people for a righteous purpose and/or for discipline.

King David stated, *"Before I was afflicted I went astray, But now I keep Your word"* (Psalm 119:67). God allowed affliction to *help* King David.

Many people do not want to look at the Old Testament with honesty and realize that God is the same yesterday, today, and forever (Hebrews 13:8) - He hasn't changed. The entire Bible is to be read, believed, and accepted. God is holy, holy, holy; He is to be loved first, but also to be feared and honored!

If you have been a person who was afraid of the violence of the Old Testament, there is a much deeper understanding coming for you! As we read God's Word with Him, in love relationship to Him, we can hear His passionate heart of love throughout all of Scripture.

The last book of the Old Testament gives instruction for the beginning of the New Testament (and God didn't divide the two halves - they are a whole). The last words in the last chapter of the last book before Matthew states, *"Remember the Law of Moses, My servant . . ."* In other words, don't throw out this part of the Word of God as you go forward into the time of Messiah!

> *"Remember the Law of Moses, My servant, which I commanded him in Horeb for all Israel, with the statutes and judgments. Behold, I will send you Elijah the prophet before the coming of the great and dreadful day of the Lord. And he will turn the hearts of the fathers to the children, and the hearts of the children to their fathers, lest I come and strike the earth with a curse"* (Malachi 4:4-6).

In the next book, the Lord Jesus said of John the Baptist, *"If you can receive it, [John] is Elijah who is to come"* (Matthew 11:14, 17:10).

The Untouchable Tool

Previously, I wrote about how Job proved the devil wrong. Here we come to an authority tool, which the adversary cannot touch. Remember, *healing is circumspect!*

The devil tried to steal the call of God on my life as a Doctor of the Cross, by disfiguring my left hand. How do I know that the accident, which happened to me when I was twelve, was an attack from the devil?

The left hand is a symbol of emotional strength, perspective, and sentimentality. The hand is an instrument of work, service, and spirituality: ministry activities that fulfill the Word and the will of God. *"I have spoken by the prophets, and have multiplied visions; I have given symbols through the hand (witness) of the prophets"* (Hosea 12:10). The Prophet's Dictionary states: *"Fingers - spiritual outreach and activity. Individual assistance or supports of the hand. The pointer finger refers to the prophet."*[3]

When I was twelve years old, I answered the call of God to become a missionary. I will never forget the night when I attended a service where the speaker was a missionary from Africa. At the close of the service, I went forward, dedicating my life to God!

A few weeks later, on a Sunday morning at church, I was walking down a hallway. On the wall was a switch box with a ring used to open it. The ring was extended and for some reason, I reached up to push the ring in. At that very moment, I felt that I was pushed forward (the boy who was walking with me said that he did not push or pull on me). Part of my pointer finger on my left hand was severed. I will spare you the details, except one - I picked it up off the floor and headed to the foyer to get help. Later at the hospital, the surgeon who worked on my finger did not believe it was possible to reattach it.

The next day was the first day of teen summer camp and I was not about to miss going. Even though there was pain in my hand and arm, my parents allowed me to leave for church camp.

The harmful things that happened at summer camp were unexplainable, and therefore, part of the reason why I know that the accident was an attack from the adversary. There is no other reason for the why the Christian leaders at the camp made fun of me and put me on display, as one who had lost her blessing. (FORTY years later, those same leaders sought me out and apologized to me! They also found my parents and made a trip to see them and to tell them how sorry they were for what they had done to their daughter. All these people stated that they did not understand why they treated me like they had, and that it was as though they had no control over their actions!)

Compounding the comments and condemnation I received from leaders, a lawsuit was filed on my behalf. During this time, I was required to have pictures taken of me with my hand and fingers on my face with the caption, "This pretty girl will never be perfect again."

Due to these, and other disturbing events following the accident, I became very self-conscious about anyone seeing my finger. I began to hide it, which entailed quitting piano lessons, getting out of my typing class at school, and making sure I never held hands with anyone. When I became engaged to my husband, Tom, I did not show off my engagement ring, but kept my hand in a fist. If I thought someone had seen my finger, I became sick to my stomach.

It is just like God to orchestrate our freedom from bondage and to renew His call and destiny for our lives! He had a plan for me. I needed to start new by going back to where the accident happened.

In 1988, 23-years after the accident, Tom and I received a phone call requesting that we interview for the pastorate of the very church where the accident occurred. We interviewed and accepted that call and were then pastoring some of the people who remembered the accident. Consequently, some of those people wanted to see my finger. I was mortified but felt that I had no choice other than to hold out my hand and show my finger. These occasions left me sick and wanting to hide.

The process of healing which Jesus brought to me, came through worship! I was in a season of hungering and thirsting for more of God; and had began to lift my open hands to Him in private prayer and worship. (Even opening my hand in front of God and letting Him see my finger was excruciating to me.)

But I was in a time of such desperation for more of God, that I told Him I would do anything to have more of Him. Little did I suspect that the next Sunday at church I would be tested about my "I will do anything." It was during the worship service that I thought I heard the still small voice of God say, "Lift your hands to Me - both of them." I could not! And I was miserable in my disobedience.

God is so gentle and kind - He continued to work gently on me every time I was in a worship service, encouraging me to open and lift my hands. And as you probably guessed, after many weeks of struggling, one Sunday I opened and lifted my hands!

I cannot tell you the grace and freedom that swept me up to Heaven with God at that moment! Instead of being sick to my stomach, suddenly I was freed and released from the bondage! I was amazed and astonished! I was healed when I publicly raised my hands to God in worship!

Up until that time, I had been stymied in my desire to move forward in healing ministry. I did not want to risk laying my hands on anyone and being seen as a maimed healer. But God had given me a strong desire to bring healing to people.

One day, Holy Spirit gave me a profound vision about the accident. In the vision, I saw clearly that demons had set it up to steal my potential. They had access to a book about me (the Scripture teaches us that there are books about each one of us in Heaven: Mal. 3:16, Heb. 10:7, Rev. 20:12). In the vision, I saw the day of the accident, that I was pushed, and that the demons of darkness laughed horribly about stopping a future faith healer. They thought they had won. (The laughter that I saw in the vision, as the demons laughed, was the same laughter I had seen and heard at camp when the leaders had laughed at me!)

In the vision, the Lord showed me that because I overcame, believed Him, and worshipped Him openly (displaying my finger), that my finger had become a sign to the demonic realm that they had failed! The display of my finger proclaimed, "FAILED!" to the devil. And, the Lord showed me that the displaying of my finger caused the demons to flee in terror! The vision was beyond amazing and changed me!! I could display a weapon, my lost finger, and prove the devil wrong because he had not been able to stop God's purposes through me.

In the years since my emotional healing, and the new power which I was given to scatter the demons while praying for the sick, I have had many people express opinions about my finger. I have had individuals come to me in church (after seeing my finger as I raised my hands to God in worship) and insist that I needed to be healed. I have had other individuals grab my finger and begin praying for it to come back (some becoming angry when the healing didn't manifest). The devil has sent many well-meaning people who imply that unless I am healed, I cannot be a Doctor of the Cross.

But I know something very important! I know that what is transpiring in the unseen realm is much more important than what the people around me think! I know that I am a healer with great power to lay hands on the sick and bring healing, because Jesus healed my soul completely! Healing is circumspect!

Isn't it crazy that there are individuals who want to steal my powerful weapon by insisting on *healing* my finger?

Jesus Only Did What He Saw the Father Doing

"Jesus answered and said to them, "Most assuredly, I say to you, the Son can do nothing of Himself, but what He sees the Father do; for whatever He does, the Son also does in like manner" (John 5:19).

In John 9, we find the account of a blind beggar who received his sight when Jesus touched him. As Doctors of the Cross, we must see like Jesus sees. He saw the entire circumference of the situation, person, and future.

In the case of this healing, many people were in an uproar in response to his healing, by the hand of Jesus:

- The Pharisees excommunicated the healed man (John 9:13).
- The healed man's family was persecuted and afraid (John 9:22).
- The healed man was reviled and accused by the leaders (John 9:28, 34).
- The healed man was cast out (John 9:35).

Sometimes the humility and the persecution that a healed person faces was more difficult than the infirmity itself. Jesus knows when and how to heal. Jesus is inside of you by the power of His Spirit! He will show you what He wants you to do.

Determine!

Determine right NOW to persist in your pursuit of God and His work through you. Your interaction, blessing, and peace in the Holy Spirit is not automatic. You will need to pursue encounters with God and will need to fight inertia (inactivity, apathy, lethargy, sluggishness)! As Heidi Baker said, *"I pray that God will continue to immerse you in His love until the only thing you understand anymore is His heart. I challenge you to make a lifelong commitment to go deeper still each and every day . . . Lord, come like a rushing river. I invite You to sweep me away to deeper places."*[4]

The invasion of God into impossible situations comes through a people who have said 'yes' to God, received Holy Spirit from on high, and are willing to step out in faith! Remember that other people need your help. You have something to give them - you have the King's domain inside of you, *"For indeed, the kingdom of God is within you"* (Luke 17:21).

Please take time to study the life of Hannah in the reflection questions below. As you see deeper into how God works, you will be able to join with Him in the depth of His love.

Prayer

Father God, please open my eyes to see the deeper ways in which You work. I need grace to accept Your perspective and see Your goodness. I request visions and dreams from You - of Your choosing. Do with me as You will, Father, I trust You. In Jesus' name, amen.

Reflection

1. Does God ever allow suffering in order to bring about His larger purpose?

   Let us look at the account of Hannah, the Prophet Samuel's mother. Read 1 Samuel 1:5.

   Why was Hannah barren?

- God will use the burden of your heart to bring about a surprisingly larger solution. Hannah's suffering over barrenness was also God's suffering over a barren nation! Hannah was key to the remedy for Israel as she cried out to God for a son and was given the savior for Israel!

2. What did Hannah do about her barrenness (1 Samuel 1:10)?

   Please understand that the Lord gave Hannah an assignment which was difficult because He knew that she could handle it with His power! The Lord was grieved over the barren state of His beloved nation, Israel, and wanted Hannah to join with Him in that barrenness so that she would cry out to Him. Please meditate on this concept until God gives you revelation! This is not the way most people think. (If we really thought, really knew, that God moves His hand on earth according to our prayers, we would pray! But we don't usually REALLY pray hard until it affects our own little world!)

3. It is important that we do not make lightweight or insincere vows to God. Hannah said, *"If You will only . . . I will give . . ."* (1 Samuel 1:11). What did Hannah tell God?

   Are there any promises that you have made to God and forgotten about? You can ask Holy Spirit (right now!) to bring any promise you have made to mind. Hannah's son, Samuel, became a savior for Israel (for one example, read 1 Samuel 7:3-4).

4. Does God also simply heal instantaneously? Do you have a testimony about this?

8

HOLD ONTO YOUR HEALING

Let your questions lead you to God instead of away from Him. "Trust in the Lord with all your heart, and lean not on your own understanding" (Proverbs 3:5).

Zacharias tarried in the temple longer than normal. He was expected to come out and pronounce a blessing on the people who stood outside praying and waiting for him. But when he finally came out, he could not speak at all! What had happened to this good priest on a beautiful sunny day in Jerusalem?

The Bible tells us that Zacharias was a good man, *"righteous before God, walking in all the commandments and ordinances of the Lord blameless"* (Luke 1:6). Yet, when he went into God's house and the Lord (the angel of the Lord) showed up, *"fear fell upon him"* (verse 12), and he asked a question that was not pleasing to God, for with his question came the evidence of a doubting heart.

Zacharias questioned God's word. Instead of believing the word of the angel, he trusted his own logic, which told him that he and his wife were too old to have a child. Zacharias was a good man; yet, he was still leaning on his own understanding.

The Bible calls a person who wobbles between faith and doubting, *double-minded*, and instructs us that questions must be asked with faith. *"Ask in faith, with no doubting, for he who doubts is like a wave of the sea driven and tossed by the wind. For let not that man suppose that he will receive anything from the Lord; he is a double-minded man, unstable in all his ways"* (James 1:6-7).

John G. Lake said, *"Make a consecration to God and stand by that and live by that and be willing to die by that. Then you will grow up into God, where your faith is active enough to get answers to prayer."* Healing, page 11[1]

It is prayer, that is accompanied by faith, that is answered; it is faith that stands on the Word of God that is strong!

> *"Indeed the gospel was preached to us as well as to them; but the word which they heard did not profit them, not being mixed with faith in those who heard it"* (Hebrews 4:2).

Where is Your Faith?

Jesus Christ asked His disciples the question, *"Where is your faith?"* (Luke 8:25). I had just prayed for a man to be healed from a hernia; and, I knew that the Lord was present to heal him. After prayer, the man thanked me kindly and then said that he would go to the doctor that week and schedule surgery. His faith was in the doctors and not in the Word of God, even though he, like Zacharias, was a good man.

Jesus Christ was serious when He instructed people to build their lives on the solid foundation of His Word. He taught very clearly that anyone who will listen to Him, and obey what He says, would have a secure place to live!

> *"Whoever comes to Me, and hears My sayings and does them, I will show you whom he is like: He is like a man building a house, who dug deep and laid the foundation on the rock. And when the flood arose, the stream beat vehemently against that house, and could not shake it, for it was founded on the rock. But he who heard and did nothing is like a man who built a house on the earth without a foundation, against which the stream beat vehemently; and immediately it fell. And the ruin of that house was great"* (Luke 6:47-49).

Here we find the crux of the matter - there is work to be done by each one of us to be ready for a storm. Each person must go after learning the Word of God for themselves to get out of the wobbly estate once and for all and into a solid place. Just as we know for sure that 2+2=4, may we be that certain that the Bible is true, concrete fact!

Recently, in a church service, my husband exhorted the congregation to read, study, and know what the Bible says. Tom asked if they believed what they read in the newspapers (and from the media or TV) and there was laughter, implying, "Of course not!" Then he asked the question, *"Do you believe what you read in the Bible?"* There was affirmation. Then he asked, *"Are you reading your Bible?"* Honestly, it got so quiet you could have heard a pin drop. Why? Because people are not reading their Bibles! His next question was, *"Why do we spend much more time reading what we don't believe than what we do believe, that which will give us wisdom and life?"* Great question!

New Christians, and those who are immature Christians, need to be encouraged to get a hold of the Word of God and to build their lives on it. Otherwise, when problems come, they will not be able to stand and hold onto what God has done.

I have had people say to me, "Pastor Linda, when you prayed for me, I felt the power of God go through me and I knew that God healed me. For days I felt great, but now the symptoms are back."

Maybe this very thing has happened to you or someone you know. The problem is usually that the individual did not have a foundation of the Word of God in them to help them keep a hold of their healing.

I have personally had so many experiences of healing in my own life that, no matter what symptoms present themselves, I am confident that I will triumph over them! For example, many years ago, I was diagnosed with an incurable autoimmune disease. I will never forget the look on the doctor's face, or his words, when he told me how sorry he was. After I got over the initial shock of the diagnosis, I began to diligently seek the Lord about the root of the illness (notice that I did not say, 'my illness,' since I know the truth about Jesus Christ carrying all my sickness and disease on Himself on the Cross).

As I sought the Lord for revelation of His healing path for me, He showed me a word-curse that I had put on myself as a child. I used to say to myself, "If something bad happens to me or I get really sick, then my (family member) will pay attention to me." I had invited sickness to come into my life and be my ally.

The process of finding the key to healing took me two years! But once found, I repented and closed the door, which I had opened as a child. I was IMMEDIATELY healed!

Since that healing took place, I have had times through the years when I experienced the same symptoms that I had with the actual sickness. But I refuse to give place to the ploy, standing firm on the healing power of Jesus Christ. I have found that if I will wait, not give place to fear or jump to conclusions, in about three days (or less), I am fine!

Psalm 107:20 tells us, *"He sent His Word, and healed them"*, and 1 Peter 2:24 assures us that the healing is done: *"[Jesus] bore our sins in His own body on the tree, that we, having died to sins, might live for righteousness-by whose stripes* ***you were healed.****"* We already have God's very Word, penned by the prophets in the Old Testament; and we have the Word made flesh in the New Testament, Jesus Christ. Therefore, in the economy of God, we are already healed; He has already sent His Word and healed us! And He has given us the written Word, so we will know what the Living Word did for us.

Getting to Know God Through His Word

When people are in a place where faith is strong, and the gifts of the Spirit are moving, it's comparatively easy for them to receive healing. However, when a person gets back home and is on their own, the devil comes and tries to put symptoms back on them. In that moment of temptation, the Scripture is clear: *"Submit to God, resist the devil and he will flee from you"* (James 4:7). If a person does not know the Word of God, they are likely to accept the symptoms as the sickness or disease itself, and the next thing they know, the sickness is back on them.

The One we must know is the Lord through His Word. We understand who God is by what the Word says about Him. He is everything the Word says He is, and we must get to know Him through His Word.

When we know and believe God's Word: *"by His stripes we are healed"* (Isaiah 53:5), and that *"He Himself took our infirmities and bore our sicknesses"* (Matthew 8:17), and that God wants to heal, *"I am willing"* (Luke 5:13), we will stand firm against the symptoms of sickness and hold onto our healing.

The Children's Bread

Jesus told a gentile woman that the healing she sought for her daughter was the bread of God's children (the "children's bread", Matthew 15:25 and Mark 7:27)! If you can get past the offence that might arise in feeling that the Lord acted differently than you think He should, and instead pay attention to the gold found in this Scripture, you will gain a healing promise to hold onto!

The following is a remarkable account, which shows us the fruit of persistent faith and humility, and which gives us license to persuade God(!) of what is rightly ours as His children. *"A woman of Canaan . . . cried out to Him, saying, 'Have mercy on me, O Lord, Son of David! My daughter is severely demon-possessed.' But He answered her not a word. And His disciples came and urged Him, saying, "Send her away, for she cries out after us." But He answered and said, 'I was not sent except to the lost sheep of the house of Israel.' Then she came and worshiped Him, saying, 'Lord, help me!' But He answered and said, 'It is not good to take the children's bread and throw it to the little dogs.' And she said, 'Yes, Lord, yet even the little dogs eat the crumbs which fall from their masters' table.' Then Jesus answered and said to her, 'O woman, great is your faith! Let it be to you as you desire.' And her daughter was healed from that very hour"* (Matthew 15:21-28).

You might be thinking, "but I am not a Jew and therefore not eligible for the *children's bread*." First, even a Gentile woman received "the children's bread" from God for her daughter when she persisted in asking; secondly, as a believer in Jesus Christ, you have been grafted into God's family and are now one of His children (please see Romans 11:17-24). We are now children of Abraham, part of God's holy nation, and part of His royal line and family!

When we know the power and authority of the Name of Jesus, and we believe that we truly do have a right, as children of God, to wholeness and healing, the devil will have no power against us! When the symptoms come, instead of being filled with fear, faith will reign out and we will have victory. This is winning the good fight of faith (1 Timothy 6:12).

There are countless passages in the Bible that show the healing power of God for us. It is essential that we study, memorize, meditate, and ingest the Word of God! This is how we build a healthy and strong house that cannot be blown down by the winds of life.

God is Good and ONLY Sows GOOD Seed

Sometimes a person will lose hold of their healing because they don't truly believe that God is good. I find that many people believe that they deserve to be sick because God wants them to learn a lesson, and they think that He wants to punish them, or that they just are not chosen for healing.

God is not random, haphazard, capricious, or arbitrary, in His promise to heal us. He does not choose to heal the person next to me and then say to Himself, "I will skip you." But He does give us "if . . . then" instructions so we can go after our healing.

Before we look into some of the Bible's most detailed words about the "if you will, I will . . ." stipulations, let us confirm that God is good and only sows good seed in His earth.

Jesus Christ illustrated what His Kingdom is like with the parable of a man who planted seed in his field. When the man went to bed and slept, an enemy came in and sowed tares (a problematic weed) in among the wheat. When the crop came up, it was full of wheat and weeds together. This caused the man's servants to ask the same question people ask about God today, "Sir, did you not sow good seed in your field?" Maybe you hear it phrased differently. "If God is good, then why doesn't He do something about the violence going on?" In other words, "Sir, are you responsible for evil?"

What was the reply of the Lord to the question? Jesus stated, *"An enemy has done this."*

Are you good, Lord? Yes! Then why am I sick? Because of an enemy.

The parable of the tares is one of the few parables that the disciples pursued asking about. We find the parable in Matthew 13:24-30, and then we find Jesus deciphering it several verses later. He explains, *"He who <u>sows the good seed is the Son of Man</u>. The field is the world, the good seeds are the sons of the kingdom, but the tares are the sons of the wicked one. The enemy who sowed them is the devil . . ."*

The enemy sows the wicked seed. There is no need to be confused about where sickness, death and destruction come from since Jesus told us clearly about it. And for sure, God only sows good seed. We are wise not to attribute to God anything of the disorder of our confused, diseased, and troubled planet.

If You Will, God Will

We stated previously in this book that there are reportedly hundreds of diseases to which humans are susceptible. In Deuteronomy 28, Moses lists some of the specific diseases for us that are consequences of coming under the law of sin and death, and then goes on to rope in all future diseases also, as coming under the curse of the law.

Before we list the specific diseases, let us state the good news first: No matter what the disease is, from of which a person is suffering, Christ has redeemed them from it; for we are told in Deuteronomy 28:60-61 that all diseases, without exception, are included in the curse. Therefore, ALL, without exception, are included in the Almighty's curse-breaking work on the Cross!

What is a curse and how can one affect you? Again, the pursuit of this understanding comes through learning God's Word. In the first four chapters of the Bible, there are no less than three major curses recorded (Genesis 3:14-15, 3:16-19, and 4:11-12). No biblical character ever treated a curse like a harmless prank, superstition, or an empty threat. Words have power; they can be used to bring blessing or a curse. The dictionary defines a curse as "an appeal to a supernatural power for evil to befall someone or something." When Jesus Christ took the curse of sin, all the evil that was directed toward you was put upon Him! This is the truth and should cause each one of us to live every day of our lives rejoicing in gratitude!

The listed diseases that are the curses of sin, as noted in Deuteronomy 28, include: Blindness, botch (although an unknown disease in these modern times, what does "botched" mean to you?), consumption (a wasting away of the body), hemorrhoids, extreme burning (acute inflammation, fever), swelling, itch (often a symptom of cancer or liver issues), madness (mental illness), pestilence (a contagious or infectious epidemic), scab, and tumors.

The curse of these diseases and all of the future diseases on our planet that can attack humanity were consequent upon failure to obey God's covenant and commands. In other words, disobedience to God's law puts men under a curse. A life of holiness is essential to a life of physical wholeness; both are ours through faith in the Lamb of God, who was made a curse for us and can be obtained in no other way.

Even if medical science could find the cure for every disease, as long as sin remains, it would inevitably be followed by sickness of some sort or other, for as James 1:15 states, *"Sin, when it is finished, brings forth death."* Disease is death begun. *"The wages of sin is death, but the gift of God is eternal life in Christ Jesus our Lord"* (Romans 6:23).

Is all the sickness that you experience tied to your own personal sin? No. Sometimes sickness is because of another's sin, generational sin, and as stated previously in this book, because you live in a fallen world. But is it possible to be healed of any and every disease? Absolutely, through the Blood that was shed on the Cross, by God Himself, for you. However, it may take your diligent going after God to get to the root and root it out.

Almighty God told the children of Israel that if they obeyed His voice and followed His commandments, they would be healthy and strong. If they would . . . He would. God's children sinned and could not fully obey the Law - just like us. So, God sent us a Savior and we have a choice of believing Him and His Word or staying in our sin.

Author, John Eldridge states, *"Our sins give the enemy a certain claim to our lives (Romans 6:16). As we renounce any sin, we also renounce any claim that we have given to Satan in our lives. This often comes in the form of 'agreements' - Satan has suggested something to us, and we have said, 'Yes'. He might have said, Don't ever trust anyone, or your heart is bad - never show it to anyone, or You are dirty . . . lustful . . . addicted and never will get free. Whatever we have agreed with, we renounce those agreements. We ask God to cleanse us by the blood of Christ; we command our enemy to flee (James 4:7)."*[2]

The Curse and the Cure

The Cure for our sin and sickness is offered to us by God - but is not automatic. Appropriating the redemption from the curse of sin, requires something of us, just as when the children of Israel needed to apply blood on their doorposts to be saved (Exodus 12:23). Jesus Christ became the curse that we might be cured: *"Christ has redeemed us from the curse of the law, having become a curse for us"* (Galatians 3:13). Our responsibility is to accept, believe, and appropriate the cure, the righteous blood of Jesus Christ, now through faith!

> "For as many as are of the works of the law are under the curse; for it is written, *'Cursed is everyone who does not continue in all things which are written in the book of the law, to do them'*. . . Christ has redeemed us from the curse of the law, having become a curse for us (for it is written, *'Cursed is everyone who hangs on a tree'*)" (Galatians 3:10,13).

It is clearly revealed in God's Word that Jesus Christ redeemed us from the curse of the law, including every sickness.

My friend, Vivian, would not give up on going after what God's Word promises. She absolutely believed that God had taken the curse of sickness for her and that by His stripes she was healed. For five years Vivian fought for her healing. As a child in South Africa, she was diagnosed with Sickle Cell Anemia. She was not expected to live past the age of 18 and was often hospitalized. One evening, she attended a great crusade where there was prayer for healing. Vivian knew that God healed her body that night; but she continued to be very sick. She didn't let go of believing that God had indeed healed her. For the next five years, Vivian continued to be in and out of hospitals. Sometimes she was very close to death. However, she continued to believe God and trust in the healing that she knew she had received at the crusade.

One morning, Vivian woke up feeling good. The battle was over; her healing was finally manifesting in her body. And her health continued the next day and the next. Today, Vivian is a vibrant, married woman in her forties.[3]

May we be like Vivian, tenacious in our faith and confident in God's Word and what He, who cannot lie, promised!

Father God looks for faith - it pleases Him! The next time someone tells you that he or she thought they were healed, but guess they were wrong, sock them in the nose. No, but really, encourage that person to get into a great Bible study and get strong in God's Word! The truth will set them free - if they will do what it takes to go after freedom.

I have been bought with a price. Therefore, I will live every moment so that the Great Purchaser of my soul will receive the full reward!

Prayer

O Lord, I need tenacious faith! I am sorry for the times I have complained at You for what I didn't do. Please help me to believe Your Word above all else. From this day forward, I commit myself to time in the Scripture of Truth. Holy Spirit of Truth, guide me into all truth, I pray. In Jesus' name, amen.

Reflection

1. What was the reply to the question in Matthew 13:27, *"Sir, did you not sow good seed?"*

   Do you believe that God is good and only does good?

2. According to Matthew 15:26, what is the *children's bread*?

3. Are you a child of God? What qualifies you to have all the benefits of being God's son or daughter (see John 1:12)?

4. What does it mean that Jesus Christ became a curse for you (Galatians 3:10-13)?

   Are you still under the curse of the law? Why or why not?

"Don't misunderstand why I have come. I did not come to abolish the law of Moses or the writings of the prophets. No, I came to fulfill them. I assure you, until heaven and earth disappear, even the smallest detail of God's law will remain until its purpose is achieved. So if you break the smallest commandment and teach others to do the same, you will be the least in the Kingdom of Heaven. But anyone who obeys God's laws and teaches them will be great in the Kingdom of Heaven."
(Matthew 5:17-19, NLT)

9

THE VAST IMPORTANCE OF THE ONLY BEGOTTEN

If I could somehow convey and establish the vast, sweeping, EVERYTHING of the Cross, this would be enough!

"Indeed I also count all things loss for the excellence of the knowledge of Christ Jesus my Lord, for whom I have suffered the loss of all things, and count them as rubbish, that I may gain Christ" (Philippians 3:8).

If you or someone you love has ever needed and received a blood transfusion, you have an idea of the immense value of blood. Likewise, if you are a person who receives dialysis treatments, or know someone who does, you understand that without this cleansing of the blood, there is no life. Scripture tells us, "the life is in the blood."

"For the life of the flesh is in the blood, and I have given it to you upon the altar to make atonement for your souls; for it is the blood that makes atonement for the soul" (Leviticus 17:11).

Blood is not duplicable. Although medical science has tried to formulate this priceless commodity, it has been impossible to inject the needed oxygen into the formula. There is no counterfeit - to obtain more blood, you must get it from another human being. Your blood is worth more than gold; it is no wonder that Jesus Christ had to take on a mortal body, with real blood, to redeem us! This is the extreme price that Jesus

Christ paid for our sins - shedding His own blood for our transfusion, on the Cross!

> *"Then Jesus said to them, "Most assuredly, I say to you, unless you eat the flesh of the Son of Man and drink His blood, you have no life in you"* (John 6:53).

When our daughter, Tamarah, was twelve years old, she had a 'routine' tonsillectomy. After the surgery, there were complications that resulted in her being rushed back into surgery to save her life. We had to make an important decision (during and after the second surgery) about whether or not to allow her to have blood transfusions. We decided not to give permission for this transfusion because of fear. (At that time, we did not understand that we could have cleansed the blood she would have been given through prayer.)

Because Tamarah had lost so much blood during the whole ordeal, it took over a year for her to fully recover her strength. For several months, she was very tired and pale. A person can have everything else - a nice home, a loving family, nutritious food, but without the life-giving substance - blood, there is no life.

Eventually, because of God's miraculous restorative repair (which He built into our human bodies), Tamarah's body was brought back into the full volume of blood needed for life and she regained her strength. The life is in the blood!

WHAT IS BLOOD?

Although I could, I won't write a long dissertation about the magnitude of the importance of your blood - the subject is inexhaustible! But in the way of a few comparisons to show the work of Jesus' blood, let us look at some facts. (Note - if you are squeamish about the subject of blood, please take time to ask God to deliver you from this. It is the devil who does not like the subject of his demise, and he is the one who tries to put an abhorrence for the subject of blood into people's minds!)

As blood flows from a wound, it looks like a uniformly red liquid; but turn the microscope on it, and you find a fluid with solid particles floating in it, some red, some white. These are the corpuscles. The bright scarlet color is due to hemoglobin, which carries and releases oxygen to the organs throughout the body.

What does your blood do for your body, in addition to supplying oxygen? Literally everything. Everything comes to the body through the agency of the blood. Your blood cleanses your body through the removal of waste and carbon dioxide, conveying the various excrement materials to the proper channels of elimination. The oxygen brought to the cells sets fire to the waste matter, and the blood carries off the ashes. Your blood cleans your body.

What a fitting illustration for the cleansing power of the righteous blood of Jesus Christ!

"The blood of Jesus Christ His Son, cleanses us from all sin" (1 John 1:7).

Human blood carries to each cell in the body (there are millions of them) the necessary food, making a complete circuit of the body in 45 to 50 seconds. Your blood defends your body by actually conquering deadly microbes when they get into the circulation. The soldiers of the blood, tiny white corpuscles, stand up and fight them to the death.

Likewise, Scripture reveals that the blood of the Lamb overcomes all power of sin, sickness, and death . . . if we will but believe and use it. We are made *"priests unto God"* (Revelation 1:6). As priests, it is our prerogative to use the blood. It will bring victory every time, if we apply it in faith, for faith will never let go till Satan is beaten down under our feet.

The blood also conveys emergency supplies (hormones - substances manufactured by certain organs for crises) from the place of manufacture to the organs that have to meet the emergency. For example, adrenalin made in the little cocked-hat shaped glands situated on top of the kidneys, is a most powerful stimulant, and is said to be the strongest restorative known. It is made by the pituitary, a hazelnut shaped gland on the floor of the skull under the brain and conveyed by the blood. Adrenalin seems to be able to conquer death itself!

Of the blood of the Lord Jesus Christ we read, *"through His death on the Cross He might destroy him who had the power of death, that is, the devil"* (Hebrews 2:14), so that we can now *"overcome Satan by the blood of the*

Lamb" (Revelation 12:11). Scripture tells us that the blood of Jesus Christ gives us access to His presence (Hebrews 10:19)!

By its marvelous power of coagulation, the blood stops bleeding, seals up wounds, and starts repair work at the point of any injury. So, the blood of Jesus heals our wounds, makes us "whole, and strong and sound" with "perfect soundness" (Acts 3:16).

As we study human blood, we realize that the things that our human blood does for us are reflections, shadowy representations of what the blood of the God-man, Jesus Christ, does for those who have believe on Him and have life through His Name.

It is imperative that we believe in the flesh and blood coming of Jesus Christ in order to access His blood for our cleansing, healing, and protection.

There is Only One

"The Word became flesh and dwelt among us, and we beheld His glory, the glory as of the only begotten of the Father, full of grace and truth" (John 1:14).

If you have ever glimpsed Heaven's view of the only begotten Son of God, the Savior of the world, bleeding on the Cross, you have been radically changed. I am one who has been radically changed.

For me, I was not satisfied with traditional answers to the difficult questions that beleaguered me. I wanted to understand why Jesus had to die such a brutal death, exactly how His Blood washed me, and why evil is on planet Earth. For answers, I decided to listen to the book of Revelation day and night until I had answers (and to receive the promised blessing for all who listen to this book, according to Revelation 1:3).

The content of the visions that the one whom Jesus loved, the Apostle John, records for us in Revelation, is nothing less than the revelation of the Absolute Sovereign and Omnipotent King: Jesus Christ. He is the central figure of Revelation; just as He is the central figure of all history.

God wants us to seek Him - which is actually a vast understatement! He truly wants us to diligently search for Him and find Him, to love Him with ALL of our heart, soul, mind, and strength. Our God is a God of self-disclosure - He throws wide the door and invites us to know Him!

Along with the book of Revelation, I also witnessed the unequalled, unparalleled, everything-points-to-the-Cross and shed blood of Jesus Christ, through Heaven's mandates found throughout the Old Testament. One of those revelatory books is Leviticus. Almighty God reveals Himself in Leviticus as a very interested, detailed, micro-managing Father. The One who knows how many hairs are on your head and who doesn't even let a sparrow fall to the ground unless He wants it to; He is very specific, precise, and not very concerned about your privacy.

Some of the things, which I am about to write, are born out of decades of asking questions of the Holy Spirit and are personal. However, if these revelations will help just one person to know Christ and Him crucified, I am willing to throw open the door.

Something I wanted to know was why God had created woman with a monthly cycle and then pronounced her "unclean" when it was His own invention. My question was sincere, and my diligent pursuit of the answer was a pursuit to know God and His ways.

I was rewarded with a revelation of the magnitude of the Cross and how everything, even a woman's most personal monthly appointment, hinged on that. I am not asking you to agree with my findings or even embrace them. But I am asking you to earnestly pursue knowing God for yourself in the power of His death and resurrection! (The side benefit of your deep relationship with Almighty God is that signs, wonders, miracles, and joy will be your companions too!)

> *"For I determined not to know anything among you except Jesus Christ and Him crucified"* (1 Corinthians 2:2).

Every single law, ritual, sacrifice, and battle in the Old Testament was pointing to the coming birth, resurrection, and redemption of Jesus Christ. Every moment of waiting for the Only Begotten to be conceived, from Eve to Mary, was focused on that moment in time.

Every son who was born, but who was not Messiah, was mourned 33 days. A female child was mourned twice that (66 days), as the coming Child who would save the world, would be a Son, and not a daughter. Heaven's grief doubled, waiting for One Son (Leviticus 12).

Every time a woman had her "customary impurity" (Leviticus 12:2), she was unclean because she was not pregnant with Messiah. What a grief to Heaven and the whole earth - no Savior yet. Unclean meant unaccomplished, unclean meant unsaved and in bondage to the curse of the serpent. Unclean meant that the Cleaner was not yet here!

Every woman prepared for Messiah every month. How many millions of collective moments went by as Heaven waited and Earth groaned? I wonder how many Hebrew women held their breath monthly, in hope, that this child would be that Child! Hundreds of years, countless cycles, everything waiting, EVERYTHING hinging on One Child, One Cross, and One Savior of the world.

Noting the "customary impurity" truly pointed to the great big love of Father God, who cared about every single period that every single woman ever had, noticing, acknowledging, and waiting.

Every detail was known and documented by Almighty God! His eye was on the most personal part of every woman He made caring and anticipating the moment - THE MOMENT - in time that would change EVERYTHING: The Only Begotten, who was conceived of a woman, and born to die on the Cross!

No wonder the mothers had to sacrifice a lamb with every birth (Leviticus 12:6-8). The Lamb of God was foreshadowed with this act.

Satan knew the prophesies - he knew the plan that Father God had made to sire His Son who would take back the authority on earth, which the enemy had stolen through deception. Satan knew that Messiah would be born to a human woman, and he set out to sire a counterfeit through women. But Satan is not Almighty God - he is not able to spawn "God with us." There has never been a begotten of Almighty God until He begot Jesus Christ in Mary, "the Only Begotten Son" (John 3:16)!

"For to which of the angels did He ever say: 'You are My Son, Today I have begotten You'? I will be to Him a Father, and He shall be to Me a Son."
(Hebrews 1:5, Psalm 2:7)

Satan knew that Messiah would come in the flesh, as a human, but also God. Every battle he instigated against God's people on Earth had at its core the goal to stop the Only Begotten of Father God, the One who would crush his head (Genesis 3:15, Romans 16:20).

There are two phrases that especially enrage and disempower demonic forces - when we proclaim that Jesus Christ came in the flesh (this is part of why the proclamation of the Lord's Supper is so powerful), and when we proclaim Jesus Christ as the Only Begotten Son of God.

Jesus Christ, the Only Begotten Son, disarmed the fallen angels and made a public open display of their powerlessness at the Cross (Colossians 2:15)! When Jesus Christ died, everything changed; when Jesus Christ rose again, after being dead, those changes were enacted. The adversary, who had been the administrator of the curse on this planet, a role he held since the Fall, lost his grip. Death was swallowed up in victory at long last!

Consider the following testimony I received from a woman in our church: "Last year in June, I had a scan for medical concerns, and a nodule on my right lung was discovered. The doctor said they would need to follow-up in one year. I just had the follow-up scan and it showed no sign of the nodule. I asked the doctor how it could be gone, and she said she didn't know. So, I replied that I knew, because I am covered by the blood of Jesus, for complete healing in my lung. Completely healed and feeling so blessed." This woman applied the blood of Jesus Christ to her lung by faith and she was completely healed!

The Blood Jesus Shed on the Cross Was Real Blood

Without the shedding of real blood, there is no remission of real sin (Hebrews 9:22). A person can only shed real blood if he has a body. Jesus Christ came in the flesh, God with us, to save us, with His atoning blood.

It is to the blood then, the blood of the only begotten Son of God, which we are indebted to for our healing and deliverance. Remember what God said to the children of Israel, *"When I see the blood . . . the plague shall not be on you . . . the Lord will pass over the door and not allow the destroyer to come into your houses to strike you"* (Exodus 12:13, 23).

Father God said, *"When I see the blood . . ."*! When God looks at you, and He sees that you have received His Only Begotten Son, Jesus Christ, as your Savior, He delivers you from the curse of sin and death! Just as He did with the children of Israel when they applied the blood of the lamb to their doorposts.

Carefully note these indispensable points regarding the blood - It had to be shed; the lamb had to be slain: *"Without shedding of blood there is no remission"* (Hebrews 9:22). The blood had to be applied: *"Through faith in His blood"* (Romans 3:25). The blood had to be applied openly: "Lintel and door post" (a public confession of Christ crucified). The blood had to be continually upon them: *"You shall strike the lintel and the two side posts with the blood"* (Exodus 12:22). This action was called the Passover - when the lamb was slain, and the death angel passed by and the people of God were protected from harm.

How Do We Apply the Blood?

The children of Israel owned live sheep, which they had to actually kill, and then take its physical blood, put it on a dried plant, and spread it on their real houses. How do we take this story and translate it into what we do with Jesus' blood?

A couple of weeks ago I stepped into my place of prayer, an upper room in our home, where Scripture is always being played. As I stepped in, I heard the Lord say (from my iPod), *"With fervent desire, I have desired . . ."* (Luke 22:15). Immediately, I was arrested and wanted to know what Almighty God fervently desired!

Jesus told His disciples (and us), what He fervently desired to do before He headed to His death on the Cross, *"I have fervently desired to eat this <u>Passover</u> with you . . ."* Jesus wanted to eat the Passover meal with His friends!

I thought about who I would want to be with, if I knew I was going to die tomorrow and what I would want to do. Would I want to celebrate the Passover?

Jesus Christ loved His friends so much! Even though they were self-centered, didn't meet His needs, and didn't understand His words, He loved them. Always loving, never seeking His own way, hoping for them (and us), and consistently giving grace - this is God!

Then the Lord told His friends that Passover would now be fulfilled in the Kingdom of God; His very blood would be over the door, opening the way for them to join Him in Heaven! The Kingdom of God would rush into people who applied His blood through faith!

"With fervent desire I have desired to eat this Passover with you before I suffer; for I say to you, I will no longer eat of it until it is fulfilled in the kingdom of God . . . This cup is the new covenant in My blood, which is shed for you" (Luke 22:14-20).

We see here that Jesus gave us a tangible and actionable thing to do. Not a law, but a privilege, to access the redemption He paid for on the Cross, to apply His blood which was shed and His love which He poured out for us.

"Whoever eats My flesh and drinks My blood has eternal life, and I will raise him up at the last day. For My flesh is food indeed, and My blood is drink indeed. He who eats My flesh and drinks My blood abides in Me, and I in him" (John 6:54-56).

We remember Jesus' shed blood, as He instructed, not out of ritual or duty, but because of the proclamation of love this act proclaims over us, our families, ministry, work, and the heavenlies!

"As often as you eat this bread and drink this cup, you proclaim the Lord's death till He comes" (1 Corinthians 11:26).

The Blood of Jesus Christ, the Lamb, causes the people of God to prevail because it answers all of the enemy's accusations. Satan controls and defeats humankind through guilt and accusations. But we know that the blood has satisfied all the charges against us, joined us to God, and provided us with every provision to defeat the adversary.

Put the blood of Jesus over the doorposts of your life, daily, as you take Communion with the Lord Jesus Christ!

As CS Lewis stated, "All things are by Him and for Him. He utters Himself also for His own delight and sees that He is good. He is His own begotten and what proceeds from Him is Himself. Blessed be He!"[1]

Give Jesus What He Died to Gain

If someone sacrificed to buy a ticket so you could go to Disneyland, or to the Super Bowl, or to Florida (choose a place that you would love to go), you would definitely go! You wouldn't save the ticket as a keepsake and just look at it!

Jesus Christ bought your healing; and, He paid for your ticket. We owe it to Jesus Christ to go after and believe for our healing! He bought it; let us not refuse it.

I recommend that you buy some grape juice and crackers and that you partake of the Communion of our Lord daily. I could write countless testimonies which individuals have told me about their healing through doing what Jesus instructed. You will have a testimony too! The more you learn to meditate on, to honor and to appropriate the Blood of Jesus in your life, the fuller and more abundant your life will be.

Prayer

Father, I, by faith, put the blood of the Righteous Lamb of God upon the doorposts of my life. O Jesus, true Passover Lamb, cover me with Your salvation, healing, and deliverance! Thank you that You have, and You will!

Reflection

1. What are the parallels that you see between the blood of Jesus Christ (as noted in the Scriptures used in this chapter) and your own blood system?

2. How might the laws given in the book of Leviticus show the importance of the coming birth of Jesus Christ?

3. Why is it so significant that Jesus Christ came to earth in a real human body?

4. Often, a person's last words are some of the most valuable words we can hear. What was on the Lord's mind before He went to the Cross, and why that specific event

10

SEEKING MEDICAL ATTENTION

Many people go to doctors at the wrong time and become immersed into a system that pushes them onward into tests and drugs that were never needed in the first place.

What a marvelous age we are privileged to live in. Advertisements in all forms of media declare that there is a *remedy* for everything: all you have to do is swallow a pill. There are pills to make you sleep, keep you from sleeping, help you lose weight, help you gain weight, make you feel 'happier,' conquer pain, and all kinds of concoctions which claim to fix wrinkles, get rid of fat, clear up pimples, and conquer mood swings. Wow!

We certainly live in a time when there is an extreme preoccupation with the physical body. Fitness centers are popping up everywhere; Healthcare Reform is in the news every day; cosmetics sales are in the billions. Yet, in this age, the timeless Word of God remains completely counterculture with these words about Abraham: *"Abraham considered not his own body"* (Romans 4:19-23).

In her excellent book, His Healing Power, Dr. Lilian B. Yeomans states, *"Having divine light upon conditions, why give a moment's thought to deceptive appearances? Under such circumstances, they are to be ignored utterly. This is the only course a believer can consistently and safely pursue . . . for whatsoever is not of faith is sin (Romans 14:23). When satan comes along with some bodily appearances or sensation that contradicts the covenant God has made with you covering healing and immunity from disease, what are you to do? Consider not your body. Consider the covenant . . . Do not accord to physical symptoms a passing thought: ignore them. Refuse to take them into your calculations . . . the blessedness of the relief from distressing symptoms of all kinds that invariably attends this Abraham method of meeting contradictions."*[1]

What a radical statement: Ignore one's own body! Picture a reporter on your favorite news medium saying such a thing - instructing listeners to pay no attention to their bodies! In an age when we are told to carefully monitor everything about our bodies, this would be scorned as heresy.

We Need Discernment

When is the right time to pay attention to symptoms in your body and make an appointment to see a medical doctor? We have probably all heard stories about parents who refused medical attention for their child based on religious convictions. The stories that make the news are usually the extreme cases - the loss of a life when a medical procedure or medicine could have been an effective treatment. (Statistics state that one child a month in the U.S. is known to die as a result of a disease or disorder which was curable with medical attention.)

How do we, as believers in Christ Jesus, the Healer, know when to seek medical attention and when to rely solely on prayers of faith? And how do we, as Doctors of the Cross, advise other people?

Take the disease of cancer as a case in point. Most in the medical community agree that everyone has cancer cells in their body (a scary thought). But we also know that our bodies are equipped with a God-created immune system that can recognize and dispose of cancerous cells. Therefore, of the trillions of cells in the human body, the abnormal or atypical cells that possess some of the characteristics of cancer cells, most will resolve themselves and never result in cancer. No wonder the Bible states that we are fearfully and wonderfully made!

"I will praise You, for I am fearfully and wonderfully
made; marvelous are Your works,
and that my soul knows very well" (Psalm 139:14).

Since God programmed our bodies to heal, what if a person goes for a medical test at the wrong time? What if a doctor diagnoses a cancer, which your body is currently in the process of eliminating? We can know what to do because we have Holy Spirit to help us.

In chapter one, I expressed that there are extremes of opinion in the body of Christ, noting John G. Lake's comment about forfeiting forever the right to go to a doctor if a person is a believer in Christ Jesus. In that same excellent (but controversial) book, Lake wrote, *"You cannot tell me anything about medicine. There never was a bigger humbug practiced on mankind than the practice of medicine. The biggest men in the medical world have declared it over and over again, but the mob does not pay any attention to it." The book continues with statements by respected individuals who agree with medicine being 'humbug', such as Dr. Magendie of Paris who stated, "We take up the attention of the patient with our medicine while nature cuts in and makes a cure."*[2]

Yet, it seems evident that there are times when medicine and medical attention have a part in saving lives. A John Hopkins spokesperson states, *"Traditional therapies, such as surgery, chemotherapy, and radiation therapy, work. The evidence is the millions of cancer survivors in the United States today who are alive because of these therapies."*[3]

It isn't just cancer that has had evident results through medical treatment. Numbers of children may have been saved if only their parents had not withheld medical treatment and medicine. (Most of the cases, which made the news, were either a ruptured appendix, diabetes, or meningitis. All treatable had the parents combined faith with medical treatment.)

Throughout Scripture, there is never a time when medicine alone is credited as a cure, nor is there a time when individuals called themselves a 'healer.' Throughout Scripture, only Almighty God was known to heal and known as "Healer."

According to author Fred Rosner, one of the sects which served the ancient people in history, as physicians, would *"gather herbs and roots, which they would employ in the treatment of the sick. However, they considered these physical remedies as aids in their efforts to bring about cures by supernatural means. Their main remedies consisted of prayer . . . they were convinced that faith could cure."*[4]

There may be a combination of aids, which work hand-in-hand; but, the supernatural healing of God is the one essential component that cannot be left out. Without God, there is no Healer.

Too Many Meds

It is time to become wiser as believers in Jesus Christ and come into a much-needed understanding of how to live healthy, fruitful lives - and help other people reach the abundance which Jesus Christ promised them (John 10:10).

Currently, there is a huge rise in our nation of prescription medicines being dispensed. Consumer Reports Magazine issued the following concern, "55% of Americans regularly take a prescription medication - four medications on average . . . far more than people in any other nation. Of those people, 75% of them also take at least one over-the-counter drug regularly. The percentage of Americans taking more than five prescription drugs has nearly tripled in the past 20 years."[5]

In 1997, there were 2,416,064,220 prescriptions filled by all Americans, including adults and children. In 2016, there were 4,468,929,929 prescriptions filled. This is an 85% increase! (Let's spell this out. There were four billion, four hundred sixty-eight million, nine hundred twenty-nine thousand, nine hundred twenty-nine prescriptions written in 2016, in a U.S. population of three hundred twenty-six million people.)

Have you noticed the increase in commercials and ads for drugs? Drug companies know that there is huge profit in selling their pharmaceuticals. And the majority of Americans are buying into this for-profit-marketing, to their own risk and possible harm! (Many prescription drugs in the U.S. cost up to 200 times what they cost in other nations.)

Here are a couple of pertinent questions: Do you ask Holy Spirit if you should fill a drug prescription that a doctor has given you? Do you ask Holy Spirit if you need to put a pill in your mouth before you swallow it? We need supernatural wisdom! Otherwise, we could be damaging our bodies and shortening our lives. We just do not want to take a pill instead of spending time with God, listening, repenting, and finding freedom. It may take time to get to the root of our problems; but God is faithful and will speak to those who take the time to listen to Him!

It is frightening to see and understand that the word *sorcery* in the Bible is the word "pharmakeia". According to Strong's Concordance, "Sorceries, pharmakeia, compare 'pharmacy' and 'pharmacist'; generally described the use of medicine, drugs, or spells."[6]

In Revelation 9:21 and 18:23, we read of the sorcery (pharmacy) that will be prevalent in the last days. We know that some drugs are most certainly not of God, but how do we know for sure about others?

Did God Formulate Penicillin?

The brilliant scientist Sir Isaac Newton said, *"All my discoveries have been made in answer to prayer."* He also stated that he could take his telescope and look millions and millions of miles into space. Then he added, *"But when I lay it aside, go into my room, shut the door, and get down on my knees in earnest prayer, I see more of Heaven and feel closer to the Lord than if I were assisted by all the telescopes on earth."*[7]

What new discoveries and remedies does God have for us, just waiting to be found through supernatural information from Him?! Think about the astonishing power of the antibiotic, penicillin, and the way it was discovered by humans. Many of us are alive today because of an antibiotic which aided our healing.

Penicillin is one of the most widely used antibiotic agents and is derived from mold. This powerful medicine was discovered *accidently* when a blue-green mold had contaminated a plate culture of Staphylococcus. It was observed that the colonies of bacteria adjacent to the mold were being dissolved. Eventually, through experimentation, it was found that the mold (in a pure culture) produced a substance that killed a number of disease-causing bacteria.

In the U.S., penicillin was made available to the general public in 1945. But before that, and during the great war, it was so scarce and such a precious commodity that none was wasted. Since penicillin is actively excreted, and about 80% of a penicillin dose is cleared from the body within three to four hours of administration, it became common to collect the urine from patients being treated, so that the penicillin in the urine could be isolated and reused.

And one more fact that is interesting: It was a strain of penicillin - from a moldy cantaloupe in a market - that was found and improved, which produced the largest amount of penicillin. Who figured that out? Certainly, it was God who gave the wisdom to unwrap the mystery and produce such a powerful medicine!

You may have a story of your own about being helped through a God-given medicine. When I was a child, I was so sick with infected tonsils that the doctors were concerned for my life. My mom and dad prayed for me and gave me an antibiotic that helped me. Both were tools of faith.

When Should Medicine be Taken?

As I was writing this chapter, I had intense pain in my back and shoulder, and I wondered if I was about to be given an illustration to help give some answers. I stopped typing and went to seek the Lord in prayer.

First, I asked God to heal me, and I thanked Him that He always does. I read His promises for me in the Bible about healing and thanked Him again. Then I waited to hear from Him. Holy Spirit gave me an inkling that I was to go and take some aspirin (which totally surprised me as I rarely take any medicine). I went and looked in the medicine cabinet, found a bottle of aspirin, took out two tablets and held them in the palm of my hand. I then asked the Lord again what He wanted me to do, waited, and felt impressed to take them. So, I thanked God for the medicine, asked Him to bless it, and swallowed the two tablets. Then I walked back into my office and continued writing.

Two hours later, there was absolutely no change in the pain level. Then I knew that I was being given an illustration. I was to use my situation to help explain how to know when a malady is spiritual warfare, and when it has an actual organic cause, that medicine might help.

For me, when pain medicine has no effect at all, I can be certain that I am being *bothered* by *something else*. That *something else* is often a foul spirit.

Consider the woman who Jesus healed and delivered from a spirit of infirmity. The Lord said of this woman, *"So ought not this woman, being a daughter of Abraham, whom Satan has bound - think of it - for eighteen years, be loosed from this bond . . ."* (Luke 13:16).

We see then, that satan can bind up individuals and cause infirmity (illness and sickness). Of course, we don't want to believe that this can happen to us or to the people we care about. But it is shown to be true by the examples in the Bible.

Since the aspirin that I took didn't help me at all (by the way, aspirin was also a miracle discovery and is derived from the bark of the willow tree), and the pain was very real, I brought it before the Lord again, asking Him to deliver me from an oppressive spirit. Then I went, found my husband Tom, and asked him to pray for me to be freed. After Tom prayed, the pain was completely gone, and I am now back writing this chapter in comfort.

How did the oppressive spirit gain access to me; and why did I need someone else to pray for me to be freed? I believe the deduction is simple about how the attack came - I am writing a chapter in a healing book and exposing the sorcery in the drug industry. The powers of darkness and greed do not want this out in the open.

The attack had no place in me, and so was not too difficult to combat. But it did take two or more *"gathered in His Name . . ."* (Matthew 18:16) to contest it. It usually takes humility to ask another person for prayer. It is humility to which God is drawn, and by which the enemy is repelled. (I recommend a diligent study on the benefits of humility!)

"You will save the humble people but will bring down haughty looks" (Psalm 18:27).

"For thus says the High and Lofty One Who inhabits eternity, whose name is Holy: 'I dwell in the high and holy place, with him who has a contrite and humble spirit, to revive the spirit of the humble, and to revive the heart of the contrite ones'" (Isaiah 57:15).

"All of you be submissive to one another, and be clothed with humility, for God resists the proud, but gives grace to the humble. Therefore humble ourselves under the mighty hand of God, that He may exalt you in due time, casting all your care upon Him, for He cares for you. Be sober; be vigilant; because your adversary the devil walks about like a roaring lion, seeking whom he may devour. Resist him, steadfast in the faith, knowing that the same sufferings are experienced by your brotherhood in the world" (1 Peter 5).

You may be thinking that the aspirin I swallowed took more than two hours to kick in, or someone might think that, of course I was healed because I have access to a man of God (my pastor-husband) who prayed for me. But the fact is: God led me as I asked Him what to do. He wanted me healed; and as I listened and followed His instruction, God brought the remedy. Our job is to listen; God will show the way for each of us, no matter who we are.

After I finished writing this chapter, a person who proofed it for me asked me this question, "Why would God lead you astray by having you take aspirin that would not help?"

God did not lead me astray, but rather confirmed something you may need to know. If we take medicine for a spiritual issue, it most likely won't help with the physical symptom (or will only help a little). Earthly medicine helps with physical issues. The Lord had me take the aspirin to prove that it was a spiritual problem and to illustrate, for the reader, that insight from God.

Through this valuable message, you were also given the way in which to swallow a pill: pause, hold it, ask God, wait, do what He says. Yes, you can hear Him as you ask and wait.

The Epidemic of Depression

The term 'depression' used to refer to a time in history, "The Great Depression," when an economic crash took place - and the ensuing decade of hardship. Today, this word is used to describe symptoms which everyone experiences from time to time but are now labeled as abnormal and dangerous.

Oswald Chambers wrote, *"If we were never depressed, we would not be alive - only material things don't suffer depression. If human beings were not capable of depression, we would have no capacity for happiness and exaltation. There are things in life that are designed to depress us; for example, things that are associated with death. Whenever you examine yourself, always take into account your capacity for depression."*[8]

Pick up any magazine at a newsstand and you will likely find a list of the warning signs of depression, with a checkbox next to each one to determine how many you have. All the symptoms are common emotions that everyone experiences. It is adding them up and coming up with a high enough count to warrant medication that is part of the cash cow of the pharmaceutical companies.

In one decade, in each of these two nations, the United States and England, antidepressant prescriptions doubled. The number of new antidepressant drug prescriptions written in one year, in the United States, was 254 million. More than one in ten people (12 and older) are currently taking an antidepressant medicine in the United States.[9]

If these drugs were truly effective, then why is the suicide rate in America rising steadily? In one decade, from 1999 - 2010, the suicide rate in America rose 30%.

Something is obviously very wrong, and that something will not be fixed by just taking another pill. You, a true follower of Christ Jesus, have the one and only answer - the Life-giver, Jesus Christ! People need a real encounter with the Savior, Jesus Christ.

Please understand that I am not implying that there is never an occasion to seek medical help for the symptoms of depression. Many people have sought my counsel as to whether to take an antidepressant drug or not. There have been cases when the serotonin levels in a certain individual's brain needed a boost - for a season. But an antidepressant drug will not bring a cure - the underlying cause of the depression still needs to be healed by God.

10,000 Times

The founder of the largest church in the world, South Korean, Paul Yonggi Cho, once told my husband, Tom, and me, a story about a woman who needed healing. The woman had come to Dr. Cho for healing prayer because she was very sick; in fact, she had been given a death sentence from doctors. Dr. Cho prayed for her to be healed, but in two weeks' time, the woman was back, complaining that she was sicker than ever. Dr. Cho prayed for her again and the same thing happened - soon she was back, asking for more prayer. Finally, Dr. Cho instructed the woman to go up to Prayer Mountain and write the Scripture "By His stripes I am healed", 10,000 times. (There are mountains in South Korea, where people go into little dugouts in the mountain, and then pray and fast for extended periods of time. Tom and I have had the privilege of visiting these Prayer Mountains.) The desperate woman did what the pastor instructed, and, in a few weeks, she was back again - but this time she came in praising

God because she was completely well and whole! She had done the work that was needed, and by faith, she had written about what Jesus had accomplished for her, at the Cross, 10,000 times.

Realize that this task was very time-consuming and was work - but it demonstrated faith in action and was obviously worth the time and sacrifice.

QUESTIONS WILL CONTINUE

The questions that you will have as to when to seek medical help or when to write, "By His stripes I am healed" 10,000 times (or any other instruction from Holy Spirit), will continue as long as you are alive. However, the Answer will always be the same: we must be able and willing to seek God and hear His voice for direction. He promised to direct your path; He **will** answer you (Proverbs 3:6).

If you have not been in the habit of asking God before you take medicine, begin by asking God for much grace. Start with asking Him to remind you to ask Him! Holy Spirit is faithful; part of His job description is to bring Jesus' ways to your remembrance.

> *"But the Helper, the Holy Spirit, whom the Father will send in My name, He will teach you all things, and bring to your remembrance all things that I said to you"* (John 14:26).

If you don't know if you should submit to a certain medical test or if you should see a specialist; again, ask God. We are not Christians who live as practical atheists - we are people of faith! We have a God in Heaven who promised to answer us if we would but ask Him. (And you may get help from godly counsel if you need it.)

Father God is raising up men and women who know their God and are strong. He is raising up Doctors of the Cross who will carry His healing to many people and do great exploits for His Kingdom's sake. You can be one of these; because, you are willing to seek God and receive HIS answers.

Prayer

Father God, please forgive me for swallowing medications without consulting You. I believe that You care about my health and that You direct my life. Please increase my wisdom and show me what to do in every circumstance. I dedicate my life to You, and I trust You to teach me how to walk in Your ways. In Jesus' name, amen.

Reflection

1. Why did Abraham not give credence to his own body (Romans 4:19)?

2. What do you think is the driving force behind the epidemic of so many people relying on drugs for their *health*?

3. Did you know the story of how Penicillin was discovered?
   Do you feel that this finding was a gift from God? Why or why not?

4. What drugs might be of the world system and not of God's good plan for Earth?

   (It is interesting to note that part of the curse of the Fall of man (Genesis 3:18) was that weeds would grow in the ground along with thorns and thistles. Is marijuana called 'weed?')

11

STANDING ON YOUR FEET!

"Take everything the Master has set out for you, well-made weapons of the best materials. And put them to use so you will be able to stand up to everything the Devil throws your way." Ephesians 6:10-12 (The Message)

As I closed the email I had just received, I could almost hear the swish of the flaming arrow as the string of the bow was pulled back and the arrow came flying. Then I felt the sting as it hit me with "dread." The sting spread, and I felt powerless to resist the trouble it forecast. "People will scatter, and the ministry will fail," it said.

My arm felt so heavy as I reached to pick up my sword; the fight felt hopeless; my arm looked small; the feelings felt real. I cried out to God to strengthen me and I grabbed my sword: *"It is written: I am simply to 'scatter the seed but the Lord will bring the increase'"* (1 Corinthians 3:6-7).

The flaming arrow fell to the ground and went up in smoke. The feelings began to dissipate immediately.

"Zing," another arrow came whizzing in. This one yelled, "Unfair!" And I felt, "I cannot fight all of these arrows, there are too many."

"But I must," I resolved as I picked up the shield of faith. "It is written, 'I can do all things through Christ who strengthens me!'"

I pulled the arrow out and broke it in half. My skin instantly healed and was smooth again. I reached over and cinched up the belt of truth, which was girding my waist. I had some wins under my belt and was feeling strength come in. I prepared for the next arrow.

Power Weapons to Use

When Christ Jesus summoned His disciples, the first thing He did was give them authority over unclean spirits (Matthew 10:1). First things first. The Lord got them ready to win against the devil! You also have power over these spirits and have authority to quench their flaming arrows!

As believers in a battle for our inheritances, we face warfare all the time. Some days it could be fighting a lying spirit who is telling you to give up and quit. Other days it might be self-pity, as the enemy's arrows fly in with feelings of being alone and friendless. Or it could be fear - fear of the future, fear of an illness, fear of violence, worry over finances, or anxiety about a family member.

When was the last time you said, "Devil, it is written!" and "It is written again!"? You have power weapons and your very best counterattack, is the one Jesus Christ himself modeled for us:

"Jesus was led up by the Spirit into the wilderness to be tempted by the devil . . . the tempter came to Him and said, 'If You are the Son of God, command that these stones become bread. 'But He answered and said, ***'It is written,*** *Man shall not live by bread alone, but by every word that proceeds from the mouth of God.' Then the devil . . . said to Him, 'If You are the Son of God, throw Yourself down'. . . Jesus said to him,* ***'It is written again****, You shall not tempt the Lord your God'"* (Matthew 4:1-11).

The Sure Foundation of God's Word

The year was 1988 and it was the first time that Tom and I would serve as the senior pastors at a church. We had just moved from Oklahoma (where we were youth pastors) to Northern California, where we would lead a body of believers. We were excited! And little wet behind the ears. We had never had the responsibility of being at the helm of a church before, nor the experience for the spiritual warfare that comes along with that.

Starting a new profession, and the learning curve that often ensues, is a challenge. There are usually times for any of us, in a new job situation, when we feel unqualified, undertrained, or like we *will just never get it.*

Tom and I had been pastoring the church for about two months when we felt like we were in way over our heads. To understand a little of our history, my husband, Tom, had come out of the corporate world, where he had managed company branches in various cities with great success. He was being groomed for the presidency of a corporation when we answered the call of God to go into full-time ministry. Tom and I knew what pressure felt like - but the oppression we were experiencing as the pastors of a church was not *pressure*; it was demonic opposition.

We wanted to quit. Our sleep was being interrupted constantly with strange things happening in our house; I was diagnosed with Epstein Barr Virus; and, our teenaged kids were having a difficult transition at their schools. But the difficulties were not just at school - there were people at church who were mistreating our kids. One Sunday, a big man grabbed our son by the collar and told him that he was "a disgrace to his father," simply because he was talking to his friends during church! We felt like *something* did not want us to be pastors of a church.

One day, Tom and I were sitting on the floor in our bedroom crying out to God. The oppression we felt was tangible. I took my Bible and asked Holy Spirit to give us a word that would rescue us, and my Bible fell open to 2 Corinthians 4: *"Therefore, since we have this ministry, as we have received mercy, we do not lose heart."* As we read the words out loud and continued to read the chapter, we were amazed by what God was saying to us through those words.

> *"Therefore, since we have this ministry, as we have received mercy, we do not lose heart . . .For we do not preach ourselves, but Christ Jesus the Lord, and ourselves your bondservants for Jesus' sake . . . But we have this treasure in earthen vessels that the excellence of the power may be of God and not of us. <u>We are hard-pressed on every side, yet not crushed; we are perplexed, but not in despair; persecuted, but not forsaken; struck down, but not destroyed</u> - always carrying about in the body the dying of the Lord Jesus, that the life of Jesus also may be manifested in our body. For we who live are always delivered to death for Jesus' sake, that the life of Jesus also may be manifested in our mortal flesh. So*

> *then death is working in us, but life in you . . . knowing that He who raised up the Lord Jesus will also raise us up with Jesus and will present us with you. For all things are for your sakes, that grace, having spread through the many, may cause thanksgiving to abound to the glory of God. Therefore, we do not lose heart. Even though our outward man is perishing, yet the inward man is being renewed day by day. For our light affliction, which is but for a moment, is working for us a far more exceeding and eternal weight of glory, while we do not look at the things which are seen, but at the things which are not seen. For the things which are seen are temporary, but the things which are not seen are eternal."*

That powerful and gripping word from God fit our situation to a 'T'. After reading the Scripture Tom and I both felt the Holy Spirit strengthening us, because we knew that God had spoken directly to us, through His Word. We made a pact that day to read 2 Corinthians 4, out loud to each other, three times a day for the next month.

I will never forget the phenomenon that happened to me (us) next. As we strengthened ourselves three times a day through God's Word, I began to feel different. I felt stronger, surer, more able, and confident to handle the situations that arose. It is impossible to describe the change - but the change was palpable and truly astonishing to me! That strength has continued to grow as I continue to use my spiritual muscles.

We built our house, and the church, on the strong foundation of 2 Corinthians 4, and eventually adjusted to living in a constant state of spiritual attack. The battle did not decrease, but our strength increased greatly for the battle. The church grew, the mortgage was paid off, many people were saved, and the Kingdom went forward in power!

Where is Your Battlefield?

None of us wants to fight with invisible, opposing spirits, and, consequently, many people pretend that the battle is not real. But there are signs all around us that the battle is indeed raging. We must not take refuge in our illusions! We are to be actively engaged in winning a war for the King and the world He loves.

I don't need to list for you the issues facing our nation, our friends, and our own families. Each one of us has a battle to fight for our own victory, and for the call of God to help others.

The redemption of God comes into impossible situations through people who believe God's Word, have received power from Holy Spirit, and have stepped out in faith to release that power into the circumstances of life.

The question is, "How is your wrestling match going? Are you winning?"

"For we do not wrestle against flesh and blood, but against principalities, against powers, against the rulers of the darkness of this age, against spiritual hosts of wickedness in the heavenly places" (Ephesians 6:12).

You may have been taught that, as a Christian, you have to wrestle with your old nature. But how are you going to win if your enemy is you? You are in a wrestling match, but that match is usually not against yourself. You do not wrestle against flesh and blood, but against evil spirits.

Before we were born again, every one of us had an old nature that was contrary to God. However, when you were born again (pause and really think about these two words, which Jesus Christ said, which must happen in order to live), you were born from above. God did not fix your old nature - He made you a new creation with a new nature. God did not repair you; He remade you. Just read chapters 5, 6 and 7 of Romans - you will find that your old nature is said to be dead, over and over again!

"For if we have been united together in the likeness of His death, certainly we also shall be in the likeness of His resurrection, knowing this, that our old man was crucified with Him, that the body of sin might be done away with, that we should no longer be slaves of sin. For he who has died has been freed from sin. Now if we died with Christ, we believe that we shall also live with Him, knowing that Christ, having been raised from the dead, dies no more. Death no longer has dominion over Him. For the death that He died, He died to sin once for all; but the life that He lives,

He lives to God. Likewise you also, reckon yourselves to be dead indeed to sin, but alive to God in Christ Jesus our Lord." (Romans 6:5-11)

The fight is often outside of you, even when it feels like it is on the inside. The evil thoughts that you are tempted with will look real, but they won't be true. All things have become new. But you say that you are wrestling with your flesh. No, you are wrestling with something that wants you to think it is you, so that you will give it power. But the spirit you are wrestling with does not have any power unless you give it to him.

CS Lewis wrote the following about a man who was pestered by a demonic spirit: "The evil thoughts which had proceeded from the appearance of the enemy had been poured into his own mind by the enemy's will. The knowledge that his thoughts could be thus managed from without did not awaken horror but rage."[1]

We must not fear the enemy nor turn and blame ourselves for the enemy's interjected thoughts. We can battle the temptations and win.

Before you throw out this chapter and decide that you don't agree, pause, and ask Holy Spirit to give you wisdom and revelation. Perceptions about what you just read may not be pure nor accurate. Lean into God and let Him tell you the truth about what you are battling.

Wrestling is Not a Game

Wrestling against the principalities, powers, rulers of darkness, and spiritual hosts of wickedness (Ephesians 6:12), is hand-to-hand combat. It is engagement, touching, personal involvement. Wrestling is different from standing far off (as with a gun), where you never touch the opponent. Wrestling is a struggle that you are actively involved in with another being. Who is that other being? The Message Bible puts it this way: *"This is no afternoon athletic contest that we'll walk away from and forget about in a couple of hours. This is for keeps, a life-or-death fight to the finish against the Devil and all his angels"* (Ephesians 6:12).

Yikes! We are in a wrestling match with the devil and his fallen angels.

Some readers will be tempted to stop here and not go any further into this book. The thought that there are spiritual forces **actively** opposing - wrestling with us - is too much information for them. But the church is in desperate need of revelation to do the work which Jesus Christ gave us to do!

We are spiritual people; and yet, we seem to have little understanding of the spiritual world. Christians are people who were born into the Spirit (born again, as the Lord said, of the Spirit); and yet, many don't recognize that their temptations (poverty, addictions, anger, etc.) are a spiritual battleground. People relegate spiritual warfare to something to analyze with their minds instead of accepting that there is something they need to battle and destroy. This is our mission: destroy the works of the devil (1 John 3:8).

Notice that Jesus' words in the following Scripture are for any believer: *"These signs will follow those who believe: In My name they will cast out demons; they will speak with new tongues; they will take up serpents; and if they drink anything deadly, it will by no means hurt them; they will lay hands on the sick, and they will recover"* (Mark 16:17-18).

To do any of these things, you must engage in a very real spiritual battle. Be encouraged: The weapons of YOUR warfare are mighty!

A Conversation With a Spiritual Leader

The Lord had a very profound conversation with a man who was supposed to be spiritual. Nicodemus was obviously interested in spiritual things, since he sought Jesus out to talk with Him. But when Jesus began to share about the Spirit, Nicodemus was completely befuddled.

At one point the Lord stopped and said, *"Are you the teacher of Israel and yet you do not know these things?"* (John 3:10)

I cringe to think what the Lord might say to the corporate church body in America.

Jesus talked with Nicodemus about being "born again" and said to him, "If I have told you earthly things and you do not believe, how will you believe if I tell you heavenly things?" Do you think that Jesus expected Nicodemus to know about the spiritual realm? Does the Lord also expect you to know, and believe, in the realm of the unseen?

Pause and ask God to open your eyes even more to the things of His Spirit. If you ask this, you will need to do something though! You must be willing to obey the Spirit. God does not give His power to someone and then say, "You can do what you want to do and obey Me when you want to." If you want to be filled with God's Spirit, you must be willing to obey God's Spirit!

> *"Jesus said to [Nicodemus], 'Most assuredly, I say to you, unless one is born of water and the Spirit, he cannot enter the kingdom of God'"* (John 3:5).

THIS IS OUR MISSION

It is important to realize that there are evil spirits who are opposing your life in the Spirit and your work for Jesus. Most often, these evil spirits attack by giving you thoughts, called "flaming arrows", that can seem difficult to resist (Ephesians 6:16). Evil spirits attempt to make you feel that you want to do something that is contrary to your born-again life.

In the Bible, we find that there is no hesitancy to expose that which is demonic. There are numerous references to evil spirits including: "a spirit of jealousy" (Numbers 5:14, 30); "a spirit of heaviness" (Isaiah 61:3); "spirit of harlotry" (Hosea 4:12); "familiar spirits" (Leviticus 20:6); "unclean spirits" (Matthew 10:1); "deaf and dumb spirit" (Mark 9:25); "mute spirit" (Mark 9:17); "spirit of infirmity" (Luke 13:11); "spirit of divination" (Acts 16:16) and "spirit of fear" (2 Timothy 1:7). All of these are evil spirits that are working to kill, steal and destroy life.

Have you ever had the thought *out-of-nowhere*, "Just run your car off the road?" That thought did not originate with you. That thought is a flaming arrow that was just shot your way.

The word flaming (as in flaming arrow) is the same word used in Corinthians for *lust.* Evil spirits will try to give you sexual thoughts that are wrongly directed. Then the same evil spirit will turn around and accuse you for having evil thoughts.

Unless we are spiritually minded, we will not even know where the thought came from and *logically* believe that it originated in our own miserable self and go down the drain with condemnation.

Being Spiritually Minded

Many people I talk with complain that they feel alone, isolated, left out, and invisible. These *feelings* are flaming arrows that need to be extinguished by holding up the shield of faith (Ephesians 6:16). The problem is, the individuals who is feeling these emotions believes that his or her feelings are true. It is difficult to explain to a person who has given power to these lies that they have given power to lies! Many don't see this as a spiritual battle, instead viewing it as their own hopeless situation.

This current issue is so prevalent that, in all of my years in ministry, I have never heard so many people tell me that they are left out, alone, and invisible. As spiritually minded people, we know that when there is a temptation bothering so many individuals at once, it is a *flood* of spiritual attacks.

A new *bug* that is now epidemic, and recognized by the medical community as a disease, is called: "FoMO - Fear of Missing Out." This epidemic is primarily shown as caused by social media. FoMO refers to the apprehension that a person feels when they think they are either not in-the-know, or that they are out of touch with some social events, experiences, or interactions. People who grapple with FoMO might not know exactly what they are missing out on but can still hold a fear that others are having a much better time or enjoying a better life than they are. The temptation of FoMO could be inflamed through viewing pictures on social media which depict activities in which one feels absent, such as: a conversation, a TV show, a wedding, a party, or pictures of food from a restaurant.

When there is something loosed across our land (like this new so-called *disease*, FoMO), we, as believers, must not allow ourselves to be influenced by that spirit.

Loneliness can be a spirit, outside of a person, which tries to take advantage of his or her circumstances. To counter the attack, we must recognize that even though the feelings are actual, the truth of *God with us*, can be accessed in Scripture, through prayer, and through serving others.

I suggest copying Scripture verses and words from the Lord on paper and carrying them with you. When tempted to pull out your phone and randomly scroll social media, instead, pull out strengthening Scripture and help yourself feel God's power. Read Scripture aloud if possible, and believe what God says about you. As you meditate on God's ways, you will realize that evil spirits have no power over you - even though the lies feel accurate, the Word of God will flash through with truth. Grab the light and resist corrupt darkness!

Let us realize that we cannot trust our emotions to be accurate since we are in a spiritual battle, and evil spirits can affect our emotions. Submit to God, resist the devil and he WILL flee (James 4:7). God's Word chases away the servants of evil!

Remember that battles come in waves and floods, and they do not last forever. (And don't say that the devil can't talk to you - he talked to Jesus.)

How do you know when the thoughts you are having are from evil spirits? Joy Dawson said this: "How do we know when evil thoughts come into our minds if they are satanic in origin or from our own hearts? The answer is very simple - by our immediate reaction to these thoughts. If we have an immediate reaction of hatred to them, we know they never came from our hearts. The thoughts came, therefore from satanic activity upon our minds. If we do not have an immediate reaction of hatred to some critical, evil, unforgiving, lustful, or unbelieving thought, then we know there is still a love for that sin in our hearts."[2]

It is possible to walk in victory in our personal thought lives. It will require paying attention and doing what is needed at the moment of conflict. Let us call upon the Holy Spirit for understanding of spiritual things and welcome Him to teach us the mind of Christ.

New Territory

Spiritual conflicts often occur when we advance into new territory that has been inhabited by evil spirits. As Doctors of the Cross, we are willing to advance, regardless of the price. Although no one wants to encounter demons, the compelling love that God has for people will enlist your best effort for Him. He wants people free, and He wants you to help bring the deliverance!

I carry out 'deliverance sessions' for people all the time. Many individuals are secretly harassed by a demon and haven't told anyone else about it. Many children and teens have a dark presence in their bedrooms at night and think that it is just the way it is and that there is nothing they can do about it (or that no one would believe them if they told about it).

Recently, I helped bring freedom to a teen who was terrorized by a demon whispering her name in the night. When we pinpointed the time it began and saw that it coincided with a trauma in her life, we were able to dislodge it. his came through forgiving an individual who had sinned against her, pleading the Blood of Christ Jesus over the traumatic moment, closing a door that had given the evil one access, and commanding the evil spirit to leave. The teenager slept that night with no harassment!

It is not uncommon for me to *see* a demon leave someone. (Whether this is a privilege or a peril, it is often a benefit to be able to confirm the deliverance.) Recently, I prayed for a woman who was being harassed by a spirit of death. I knew that it was a spirit of death because of what the woman told me it was saying to her (she believed the thoughts were her own). I have seen that suicide spirit before, cloaked as a huge black bird of prey. Often its claws are deeply imbedded in a person and it refuses to let go.

That evil spirit had to take flight and leave that woman when she agreed to ask Father to forgive her for giving a place in her soul to a death wish. When the demon left her, she felt light and was filled with joy!

If a person who has been freed, refuses to allow the evil spirit to come back in and deceive them again, freedom will grow and grow. This means that when the old thoughts, such as, 'I wish I could die" are heard, one must refuse to agree with those thoughts. It is work to refuse the lying spirit; but, is completely worth the work it takes to form new thoughts.

"Greater is He who is within you then he who is in the world" (1 John 4:4).

"Finally, be strong in the Lord and in his mighty strength. Put on the whole armor of God so that you may be able to stand firm against the devil's strategies. For our struggle is not against a human opponent, but against rulers, against authorities, against cosmic powers in the darkness around us, against evil spiritual forces in the heavenly realm. For this reason, take up the whole armor of God so that you may be able to take a stand in that evil day. And when you have done everything you could, you will be able to stand firm. Stand firm, therefore, having fastened the belt of truth

around your waist, and having put on the breastplate of righteousness. And having put shoes on your feet so that you are ready to proclaim the gospel of peace. In addition (above all), to all of these, having taken up the shield of faith, with which you will be able to put out all the flaming arrows of the evil one. Also, take the helmet of salvation and the sword of the Spirit, which is the word of God. Pray in the Spirit at all times with every kind of prayer and request there is. For the same reason be alert with every kind of effort and request for all the saints" (Ephesians 6:10-18).

The "Greater One" lives right here, within YOU. So, take authority over your circumstances, wage spiritual warfare, and go on the offensive. Remember, winning spiritual battles is something we will need to do until the Lord returns. And don't forget that we win!

In the next chapter we will continue with the acquisition of a sound mind.

Spiritual Warfare Swords to Copy and Carry

If you haven't already, begin today to carry your weapons with you. The Sword of the Spirit will spread light onto your path as you wield it decisively. Here are some great weapons to copy and carry with you:

"The Lord will go forth like a warrior; He will arouse His zeal like a man of war. He will utter a shout, yes, He will raise a war cry. He will prevail against His enemies" (Isaiah 42:13).

"Upon this rock I will build My church; and the gates of Hades will not overpower it" (Matthew16:18).

"For though we walk in the flesh, we do not war according to the flesh, for the weapons of our warfare are not of the flesh, but divinely powerful for the destruction of fortresses. We are destroying speculations and every lofty thing raised up against the knowledge of God, and we are taking every thought captive to the obedience of Christ" (2 Corinthians 10:3-5).

"Behold, I have given you authority to tread on serpents and scorpions, and over all the power of the enemy, and nothing will injure you" (Luke 10:19).

"You will tread upon the lion and cobra, the young lion and the serpent you will trample down" (Psalm 91:13).

"But thanks be to God, who always leads us in triumph in Christ, and manifests through us the sweet aroma of the knowledge of Him in every place" (2 Corinthians 2:14).

"Whatever you bind on earth shall be bound in heaven: and whatever you loose on earth shall be loosed in heaven" (Matthew 18:18).

"And take the helmet of salvation, and the sword of the Spirit, which is the word of God" (Ephesians 6:17).

"The Son of God appeared for this purpose, to destroy the works of the devil" (1 John 3:8).

Prayer

Lord of Hosts, You, who have innumerable angel armies at Your disposal, thank You for protecting me. Please forgive me for the times that I have been unwilling to engage in spiritual warfare and thereby capitulated. I cry out for discernment to know what to do! Speak to me, O God, and I will obey You in Jesus' name, amen.

Reflection

1. Do you think that Jesus was surprised by Nicodemus' lack of understanding about spiritual things (see John 3:10)? What would Jesus say to you about your understanding?

2. With what tool did the Lord defeat the devil's lies (Matthew 4:1-11)?

3. Is our warfare against flesh and blood people (Ephesians 6:12)?

4. How do we win a wrestling match against the powers of darkness (Ephesians 6:13)?

12

A SOUND MIND – AGREEING WITH GOD

Be careful with your thoughts; make sure that you resist adopting the attitudes of people who, through their negative outlook and lack of self-esteem, neutralize your faith-filled viewpoint. This includes the devil, the author of negativity and insecurity. Remember, God has given you a sound mind.

Since we opened a Healing Rooms in our region, we have been seeing wonderful miracles! But what we are seeing is only a trickle of what we are about to see. I believe we are right on the threshold of remarkable things! We are taking territory for the Kingdom of God.

Just like when land is taken in a physical war (consider the ongoing struggle for land of Israel), there is a strategy employed - often with tanks, bombs, and other weapons. When spiritual territory is taken for the Kingdom of God, there is also strategy needed to wage and win the battle.

Smith Wigglesworth wrote, *"You must not think that these gifts fall on you like ripe cherries. You pay a price for everything you get from God. There is nothing worth having that you do not pay for, either temporally or spiritually."*[1]

The cost for bringing salvation, deliverance, and healing to people is worth it. But what does this cost mean? As we have seen, there is a battle to win in our own personal thought lives. With that victory, we able to help others.

As I write this chapter, I am thinking about a post that I saw on social media. The post exposed a problem that I hear from the mouths of Christians often.

The post was in reference to my husband's Sunday message and accurately quoted Tom as saying, "You can't skirt the Cross!" Then, the person posting the quote, invited responses to his own questions: "1. Who do you say [Jesus] is? 2. Who does He say you are?"

Under these questions, most of the responses were based on human thinking and not on the true love of God we find in Jesus Christ. One responder stated, "He is Almighty; me, I am stupid."

How would you respond to these questions - if you truly gave attention to your answers without responding with pat answers? Do you know who God says that you are? Have you asked Him that question, listened to hear what He said until you heard the truth, and then held on with all your might to His true description of you?

Francis Frangipane opened the way to glimpse who we truly are when he said, "We know how we appear to other men but, if God truly is within us, how do we appear to angels, or devils? What light marks us in the spirit-world, what illumination surrounds us, what glory declares to the invisible realm: 'Behold and beware, here, walks a son of God!'"[2]

Many people put Jesus in a category in their own minds without knowing it; not consciously realizing that are limiting their own experiences and possibilities. The vast explosive power of His Spirit is underused and limited by one's own belief systems. And, as we learned earlier, human thinking can be sabotaged by demonic influences.

Like the responder to the questions on social media, many Christians inaccurately see God as unapproachable and themselves as 'stupid'.

A good illustration might be to use the example of math. You can see a mistake in a math problem when it is pointed out to you; but while you are making the mistake, you cannot see it. Likewise, you might read a good book like "Battlefield of the Mind" (Joyce Meyer) and say "amen" to the principles, but not notice the mistakes you are making in your own thinking.

Maybe we each need a teacher to go through a printout of our thoughts at the end of the day, so we can see the check marks next to the thoughts that are incorrect! On the other hand, maybe we each need a Teacher who we are constantly aware of and who leads us into truth moment by moment! No wonder our constant Helper, Holy Spirit, is called The Spirit of Truth! Will you allow Him to help you with every thought?

"When He, the Spirit of truth, has come, He will guide you into all truth; for He will not speak on His own authority, but whatever He hears He will speak; and He will tell you things to come" (John 16:13).

Holy Spirit has been sent to help us in every aspect of our lives and ministry. He is the key to love relationship with our Father in Heaven as well as to our success here on earth! We must lean heavily on Him.

SOUND-MINDED

What is a "sound mind"? Strong's Concordance describes it as "safe-thinking." If you are sound-minded, you will have good judgment, disciplined thought patterns, the ability to understand and make right decisions. In other words, a sound mind promotes a life of wholeness and well-being.

For yourself, and for the people to whom you minister healing, there may need to be a cleansing of the mind. Clearing up the unknown, unseen, and the past, that may have kept sickness and disease hidden away but nonetheless, present.

All the innumerable thought-choices we make daily turn the central part of us. Taking your life, with all your innumerable choices, all your life long, you are slowly turning this central thing into something. Through what we believe, we are either becoming a sound-minded, well person, who is in harmony with God, and with other people, and with itself; or else into one that is in a state of war with God, and with others - and with itself.

WILL YOU ALLOW GOD TO BE THE CHOICE OF YOUR THOUGHTS?

Earlier in this book, I wrote about disease - the ease that Jesus Christ died to give us, becoming dis-ed. The culprit is so often a mind that is not sound - destructive thoughts that drain from the mind into the body.

Today, as with most days, I ministered to several people who are (or were!) sick, and some who have been diagnosed with a disease. In response to a woman to whom the medical community spoke the words "Lupus" and "Multiple Sclerosis," I wrote the following:

> *After I got your email early this morning, I spent quite a bit of time asking the Lord about your immune system. Having it turn on your body is totally unacceptable, and I want the root cause flushed out! I know that Jesus wants this most and then, of course, you desperately want this! We have to nip this thing before it becomes "Lupus" or "MS." Even the medical community knows that the body attacking itself and damaging its own tissue causes autoimmune diseases. And I have found that autoimmune diseases have a spiritual root of self-hatred, self-bitterness, and guilt.*

Somewhere in this woman's thoughts, she had turned on herself and her body responded in like manner. How can she, or any one of us, find the open door which gave access to disease; and then how does one close that door? Obviously, we turn to the One who loves us and knows every moment of our lives intimately. Nothing is hidden from God! We decide to fight the good fight of faith in the soul (mind, will and emotions) with the power of Jesus Christ, the Deliverer.

Why Thoughts Are Susceptible to Demonic Influence

Paul explained to his pupil, Timothy, that God did not give him an evil spirit (spirit of fear), but that God did give him a sound mind, love, and power. Do you see the whole soul in this equation? The mind is mentioned, the will is mentioned (power), and the emotions (love).

> *"For God has not given us a spirit of fear, but of power and of love and of a sound mind"* (2 Timothy 1:7).

Since God did not give the spirit of fear, who did give it? Wisdom sees beyond the obvious. The Apostle Paul knew that there was a spirit-realm, with demonic powers, which have evil intentions and who will try to manipulate our thoughts.

Unwelcome Guests

When any evil spirit takes territory in our bodies, it begins with a suggestion that grows into an action. The action is often shrouded in shame - a power spirit that keeps it hidden away. Confession is a golden key to rooting out demons.

"Confess your trespasses to one another, and pray for one another, that you may be healed" (James 5:16).

There are many cases where demons have influence over the mind, and few of them are obvious. However, wisdom sees beyond the obvious.

One night after ministering at His Way Women's Bible Study, a woman came and asked me to pray for her. Courtney* was a beautiful woman with a seemingly blessed life. She had a loving husband and sweet children but was ready to leave her family to fulfill a fantasy which had taken over her mind. As her story unfolded, she explained that she was tormented to the point that she had to tell me about her issue. She didn't want to leave her children but was being driven away because of her thought life. Courtney said that she had been involved in a relationship with a boyfriend before she was married to her husband, and that the boyfriend had been her first love. One day, 'out of the blue', she began to remember his kisses and compare them with her husband's lovemaking. The next thing she knew, she had become dissatisfied with her husband and was thinking about her previous boyfriend all the time, including during times of sexual intimacy with her husband. Soon she found that the only way she could respond physically to her husband was by pretending (fanaticizing) that she was with her old boyfriend. This was eventually followed by refusing to submit to any intimacy with her husband and entertaining thoughts of leaving him.

Clearly, Courtney needed deliverance from a demon who had found a place of residence in her mind and was affecting her actions in her body. I asked Holy Spirit to show me what to do and immediately, the Lord showed me that a demon was masquerading as her old boyfriend in her fantasy world. It was a grotesque monster with claws, drooling and snarling. I carefully explained to Courtney that her old boyfriend didn't look like she fantasized he looked; and I asked her if she wanted to see what he really looked like. Not really believing that anything would happen, Courtney said, "Sure, okay." I then asked God to open Courtney's eyes to see the one she was embracing, and I commanded the demon to show itself. Suddenly Courtney screamed and jumped to her feet in horror as the demonic being was revealed before her. She began to scream, "Get it away from me, make it go away!" Then the demon was no longer visible.

As Courtney calmed down enough to listen to me, I asked her if she was ready to repent. And of course, she was! I led her through a prayer of repentance, asking God to forgive her for giving place to lustful thoughts about her old boyfriend. Then I instructed her to command the demon to leave her. She was one of the most contrite people I have ever prayed with.

We closed the door that Courtney had opened to the demonic, through her thought life, which was trying to destroy her marriage and family. Through repentance and forgiveness, we applied the righteous blood of Jesus Christ to the door she had opened in her mind. Then Courtney invited Holy Spirit to fill her up and take residence in her mind and body! Courtney got completely free that night and has now been happily married for over twenty years! Her children are walking with the Lord, and her family is blessed. Jesus Christ is the Almighty Deliverer who is always willing to conquer the demonic as we agree with Him!

Since Jesus Christ has given us authority to drive out demons, you might ask why I didn't drive the demon out and bring deliverance to Courtney as soon as the demon was revealed to me. Let us take seriously the words of God, found in Matthew 12:43-45 and Luke 11:24-26: *"When an unclean spirit goes out of a man, he goes through dry places, seeking rest, and finds none. Then he says, 'I will return to my house from which I came.' And when he comes, he finds it empty, swept, and put in order. Then he goes and takes with him seven other spirits more wicked than himself, and they enter and dwell there; and the last state of that man is worse than the first."*

If Courtney had not understood what her thoughts really were, and if she had only been half-willing to be rid of the demon, she would have been in danger of being swept clean but stationary.

A person can have an evil power swept out of him or her and their life *put in order*. But when the Lord heals you, you dare not remain in a stationary position. You must take authority continually for a period of time (and this timeframe varies according to how effective you wage the war in your thought-life). You see, the demon will come back knocking to get back in with thought patterns that you were in the habit of accepting before. In the case of Courtney, there was no way she would allow that horrific being back into her life ever again. She was determined to keep it away.

Minister the Baptism of Holy Spirit

Someone who receives deliverance while at Healing Rooms may be upset if you even suggest that a demon is present. Or, as is often the case, the demon is so familiar that the person believes it to be their friend, or part of their personality.

Therefore, it is possible that when you have driven out a demon (because you do have authority to do so), that it will return after the person leaves your presence. Consider this scenario: You discern a spirit of infirmity in a person (Luke 13:11). The infirmity leaves when you command it to do so in the Name of the Lord Jesus. But when the infirmity comes knocking the next day with symptoms of sickness, the 'logical' thing is to think, "I must not be healed." With this acquiesce, the next thought is, "I am so disappointed;" and the next, "God doesn't love me;" "I won't go to Healing Rooms again;" and so on and on.

What are these thoughts: disappointment, hopelessness, deception, fear, cynicism, complaint, anger? Perhaps they are a few of the *seven spirits* that came in, as Jesus said could happen. And the last state of the person is worse than the first. I have seen this happen.

As Doctors of the Cross, with a mandate from the King to cast out demons, what do we do? A person who is delivered of a demon must be filled with Holy Spirit and stay filled through love which brings obedience. People want to know how to be kept by the power of God, and you have the answer - the Almighty Holy Spirit! Minister the baptism of Holy Spirit to those you pray for. If the person is unwilling, issue a warning to them and let the individual know that they must submit to God!

God has a million ways of helping anyone who will submit to Him!

He has deliverance for every captive. He loves us so much that He even says, *"Before they call, I will answer"* (Isaiah 65:24).

Dry Places

When a demon leaves a person, according to the Lord Himself, "it goes through dry places." What are dry places and what does this mean?

Although I do not know very much about *dry places,* as I have only been asking Holy Spirit about this for a few years (sometimes God answers my questions decades into the searching), I know a little.

I will illustrate some insight into the dry places through a message I sent to an individual who had been diagnosed with a disease and who was seeking healing. I wrote, "The Holy Spirit is showing me that your bone marrow needs healing. Healthy bone marrow is a major contributor to a strong immune system. It serves an active function in the body by producing all three types of blood cells, as well as lymphocytes, which support the immune system. Holy Spirit directed me to encourage you to read Ezekiel 37. In this passage of Scripture, you will see that a prophetic proclamation brought life into dry bones. The bones were dry because of lost hope (verse 11). The remedy is the River of God! Get in the Spirit and He will pour refreshing into your bones and the breath of God will bring life into your bones! Read Ezekiel 37:1-14 and proclaim the Living Word of God into your bones."

A Sound Mind Requires Diligence, But is Well Worth the Effort

To walk in love, power, and a sound mind is about choosing well. Deciding in the random details of life to submit to God and conform to His ways. He is never stingy, scared, mean, verbally abusive, self-incriminating, cynical, or powerless! He who is love hopes all things, believes all things, and endures all things (1 Corinthians 13:4-7).

To love entails forgiveness, openness, and affection. Consider what Frances Frangipane wrote about this: *"Is your love growing and becoming softer, brighter, more daring and more visible? Or is it becoming more discriminating, more calculating, less vulnerable and less available? This is an important issue, for your Christianity is only as real as your love is. A measurable decrease in your ability to love is evidence that a stronghold of cold love is developing within you."*[3]

What is the remedy for *cold love*? The Lord told us in Matthew 24:9-13! *". . . The love of many will grow cold. But he who endures to the end shall be saved."* Endurance is a cure for cold love! Loving with tenacious determination, no matter how one is treated! I often tell a woman who loves her husband no matter how she is treated, that she is accomplishing something great. When there is no reason to love except for Love, we push back the demonic kingdom and the Kingdom of Light goes forth. Of course, there is no way to love like this without spending time with God, forgiving others, and receiving His love in place of the hurt and pain.

Choosing a well soul is about power. Many people struggle with feelings of powerlessness because their situations seem out of control. Long ago, Holy Spirit convicted me for saying that I felt powerless. He said that if I want Him living in me, I have all power and need to believe that I do.

Do you feel powerless in your job, in your marriage, your children's choices, or in your finances? Another word for this is hopelessness. Is there any area in your life that feels hopeless? Perhaps you need to repent of your thinking and agree with God that you have His power in you. Then ask Him to help you to change your thinking - to convict you for every thought that doesn't agree with His power in you.

If you were drowning, you would be gasping for air! In a similar way, we are living in turbulent waters in life and must depend absolutely upon the ministry and power of Holy Spirit to carry us through these times. Our lives depend on it. We must know His power!

> *"Every area in your thinking that glistens with hope in God is an area which is being liberated by Christ. But any system of thinking that does not have hope, which feels hopeless, is a stronghold which must be pulled down."* Francis Frangipane[4]

I do not pretend that I never have thoughts of jealousy, anger, fear, or condemnation. Everyone is tempted with the devil's negative and toxic thoughts. But I no longer own the devil's thoughts as my own. I do not have time to play with insecurity, offence, or fear. I need a clear and sound mind; I need power and love; I am determined to walk in the Spirit of the Living God who brings life to my mortal body (Romans 8:11), and peace to my soul.

Some examples of decisions, which I have made about how to guard my thoughts include:

- With God's Holy Spirit power working in me, I will not bolster up my own case against anyone else through negative thinking in my head about them
- I refuse to prop up any bad attitude through rationalization
- I will not sympathize with anyone who is playing the victim or wallowing in self-pity
- I refuse to make any deal with the devil as the only way out (lying, cheating, running away or stealing)
- I will not hide or be ashamed of my shortcomings and mistakes
- I will not create 'what if' scenarios in my mind nor give place to fear of future calamity or trouble
- I refuse to be disloyal to God by giving thought to what other people think without asking God what He says I invite you to join me in these mandates, and to seek the Lord for your own.

"For though we walk in the flesh, we do not war according to the flesh. For the weapons of our warfare are not carnal but mighty in God for pulling down strongholds, casting down arguments and every high thing that exalts itself against the knowledge of God, bringing every thought into captivity to the obedience of Christ, and being ready to punish all disobedience when your obedience is fulfilled" (2 Corinthians 10:3-6).

You may believe that it is impossible for you to get to the place in your life where you submit every thought to Jesus Christ and keep yourself in His truth moment by moment. However, if you will continue to ask Holy Spirit to change you, and help you to change, eventually you will become a person who possesses a sound mind continually. The unbelieving thought, which tells you that you cannot conquer your thought-life, is **not** in agreement with God's Word.

My husband, Tom, and I attended a concert, which featured a famous cellist. His music was so beautiful and captivating that at times the entire audience was awestruck. Toward the end of the concert, the cellist addressed the children in the audience who played an instrument. He encouraged them not to quit, keep practicing, and to not give up, even though it is hard and though it may seem like all they do is play the same thing over and over. He said, "Keep going. Because one day it will all change!" He went on to say that even though it is a process over a long period of time and practice, there will come a moment when it will feel like a 'suddenly' because 'you will fly!' And then everything has changed, and you from then on, fly with your instrument!

We can apply this principle to gaining a sound mind. There will come a time of crossing over as we practice tuning our thoughts to God's Word, His voice, and His ways. In the next chapter, we shall see more of the ways in which the Lord searches out and delivers people from hidden thoughts and demonic oppression.

Let us be willing to welcome Holy Spirit to occupy our thoughts, our homes, our lives, and our churches. Let us go through the transformational process that is necessary for Holy Spirit to have full reign in our lives, and for His ministry to have full expression in our city! We are no longer living in normal days; we can no longer do things in a normal, limited, human way. We need the ministry and power of Holy Spirit to bring forth great fruitfulness in our lives.

Prayer

Let us be in one accord in this prayer: Holy Spirit, we need You; We can't do anything without You. We're thirsty for more of your presence. We don't care about the other things we've been focusing on; we just want to know You.

Reflection

1. Who do you say [Jesus] is? Who does He say you are?

2. What does it mean to possess a sound mind?

3. What happens when a person drains toxic thoughts into their body?

4. What enlists seven more demons to enter into a person?

Memorize the following Scripture: "*You are of God, little children, and have overcome them, because He who is in you is greater than he who is in the world*" (1 John 4:4).

13

PURE SPEECH

"For then I will restore to the peoples a pure language, that they all may call on the name of the Lord" (Zephaniah 3:9).

Many people condemn themselves with their own voices without realizing what they are doing. Maybe you have said some of these things to yourself: "I never get it right", "I can't remember anything", "I am a failure", "I am sick and tired of what is happening", "I can't handle one more thing". This kind of common self-talk appears to have some dastardly affects.

New discoveries in medical science now show that our brains are greatly influenced by a small member: the tongue. Whereas, throughout history (and not until the 1970s), science insisted that our brains remain the same all of our adult lives, we now know that our brains have the ability to change and adapt as a result of experience. "The brain is, in fact, quite malleable and influenced throughout life, especially by the tongue."[1]

Science is once again confirming what the Bible has taught all along: the tongue has tremendous power to bring death or life (Proverbs 18:21, Matthew 12:36). The latest research proves the connection between the tongue and the brain stem. Much of the information coming out of this current research is phenomenal, for example, the fascinating article: "Is Your Tongue The Key To A Neuroscience Breakthrough?"[2] This piece (one of many on this subject), shows the tongue's influence on the brain: "Knowing that there is such a rich nerve connection to the brain, scientists and doctors are turning to the tongue as a way to possibly stimulate the brain for neural retraining and rehabilitation after traumatic injuries or disease."[2]

Why the tongue? Our tongues have a plethora of nerve endings which connect directly to the brain stem. Is it possible that we are influencing our own brains by the words we say with our own tongues?

In the middle of writing this chapter, I left to take a counseling appointment with a person who was stressed about his career.* Although his struggle would probably not be apparent to an observer, for he is very successful, nonetheless, he felt that he was failing at his job. Since there were absolutely no signs that he was failing, why would he believe the illusion of failure?

As we saw in the previous chapter, lies often come in the form of suggestions, which come from outside of us. In the case of the aforementioned counselee, he had heard the suggestion that he was a failure during a vulnerable moment while dealing with a difficult client. Instead of countering the suggestion with Scripture (see Joshua 1:8), he bought the lie, and began to speak it to himself. He actually thought that if he spoke that he was a failure, it would keep him vigilant and make him work harder, ensuring success. But of course, speaking words in agreement with a lying spirit, empowers the lie and creates more turmoil.

As the truth of the agreement he had made with the lie was understood, the man repented and then resisted the devil (James 4:7). And, as Scripture declares, the devil left. The man was liberated from the feelings of failure and left the counseling session with complete freedom from the weight he came in with. He felt a physical change, as comfort replaced pain in his back and shoulders.

A thought we agree with may seem harmless, but when that thought is counter to God's truth, it must be brought into submission to the truth. Even when the thought feels true, if it doesn't agree with God's Word, it is not true. Believing the enemy's suggestions can eventually become one's own words that become destructive self-talk.

Take good care of your tongue! It has been proven to have influence on your brain. Don't harm yourself by using your tongue to form destructive words; do not use your tongue to tell lies. The commandment of Jesus, *"You shall not bear false witness"* (Matthew 19:18), was given for your good, and obeying this command will protect your tongue and your life!

The Power of Words

If anyone doubts the power of spoken words, they need merely to hear the words "you have cancer" spoken from a doctor's mouth. When those words hit my ears, my knees turned to water and my heart began to beat like a drum in my chest. Here is my personal story with insight into the relationship between cancer and self-condemning words.

I was 39 years old when I found a lump in my breast and made an appointment for a mammogram. Of course, I was concerned but not overly fearful. I assumed that it would not be a big deal and I would do whatever test was needed to be assured that I was fine.

After the mammogram test, my doctor's office called me with some concerns and asked me to schedule an appointment with my doctor for a biopsy as soon as possible. Of course, my alarm increased but I continued to assume that the results would be favorable. I scheduled that next appointment and looked forward to being done with the test.

Meanwhile, I asked for prayer from friends and family, and was of course, praying for myself! I knew that God heals and had experienced His healing touch in my body many times before.

The next test seemed routine as the biopsy was accomplished at the doctor's office. But the thought of *routine* faded with the phone call that came a couple days later: further tests would be needed.

I was scheduled for more tests at a radiology center and this time my husband, Tom, would go with me to the appointment. I was so glad that Tom was there that afternoon, especially when the radiologist expressed that he needed to bring in the oncologist and a couple of others who were experts on . . . cancer.

It was shocking to hear the hushed voices of the doctors who gathered in that room, all looking at a screen which showed my body, all very concerned and troubled. They were not talking to me or to Tom, but just to one another.

Eventually I was told to get dressed and that one of the doctors would talk with me. I will never forget that conversation for there was no conversing back and forth. The doctor simply put his hand on my back and said something like, "we know that you have had a good life and we are so sorry." Then he ushered us out the door and into the night.

Tom and I were stunned. What did this mean? The next afternoon we received the phone call that turned my knees to water, as the doctor spoke the words, "you have cancer." I remember asking if the cancer was throughout my body and the doctor telling me that it was probable.

A surgery date was scheduled for me and we called our kids who were away at college to come home. The surgeon made no promises for the outcome of the surgery and our family gathered in close, knowing that my life was in danger.

The Sunday before the surgery, as I was kneeling in prayer in our living room at home, I heard a rustling in the leaves of a large house plant that was nearby. The leaves were moving as if by an invisible wind inside my house! I thought it very strange but then the next thing that happened made me forget about the plant. I heard these words very clearly, "I will heal you."

I have to say I was not entirely encouraged by what I heard and saw but was actually frightened by this occurrence. When one is living in the middle of a trauma, it is difficult to respond with any kind of normalcy. I didn't tell anyone about what I had heard. But in the days leading up to surgery, I noticed a calm inside of me that had not been there before.

It was a few days later that I was taken to the hospital and prepared for exploratory surgery. Friends and family gathered around me and prayed for me before I was taken into the surgery room. None of us knew what the outcome would be, but we knew that I was in God's hands.

If you have ever woken up in a recovery room after surgery, you know that it is not usually a pleasant experience. But that day when I awoke, I felt such a joy that was completely unexplainable except for God's presence! Therefore, I wasn't entirely surprised when my doctor came in to tell me, to the confounding of the surgeons, that the tests they had performed during my surgery, had shown no trace of cancer in my body at all! God had performed a miracle for me and there was no denying it!

With the good news, my kids returned to college, normal life ensued and it was as if I had never been given a deadly diagnosis. Except that I was now on a quest to find out from Holy Spirit what had happened to me and why! Understandably, my faith was high and my hearing acute after such a mighty miracle!

The Protective Covering of Light

God began to show me some things about sickness and how it can find a place in the bosom of a person. He led me to Scripture about anger hiding in the bosom: *"Do not hasten in your spirit to be angry, for anger rests in the bosom of fools"* (Ecclesiastes 7:9).

Since I did not think of myself as an angry person, I did not understand why I would be subject to destructive anger in my bosom.

As I sought to find out more about the dangers of unresolved anger, I came upon a Scripture that is quoted fairly often in church, but for some reason the impact of its truth not always recognized. *"Do not let the sun go down while you are still angry, and do not give the devil a foothold"* (Ephesians 4:26). Giving a foothold to the devil means that he who is fully evil has a foot inside of a person. Had I somehow given the devil a foothold in me through unresolved anger?

I asked God and He answered me with revelation from my childhood. Having grown up in a church, which put the main emphasis on being holy, I had been taught that if I was not righteous *enough*, I would go to Hell. Consequently, I was hyper-vigilant to keep myself perfect in what I did, where I went, what I looked at, and in time spent in prayer and reading the Bible. I was attempting to earn my own righteousness by what I did and didn't do, and when I failed to be perfect (which, of course, was all the time), I would condemn myself. **Condemnation is self-anger!** Anger toward myself had been wreaking havoc in my bosom.

I was convicted to the heart! I had been trying to be righteous enough so that God would accept me and in so doing, I was trying to put on my own righteousness. In essence, I had rejected HIS righteous covering! The words of condemnation which I had used to motivate me to do better (telling myself that I was a failure and needed to shape up) were directed anger against myself. The revelation was staggering.

I also saw that I had come into agreement with the devil's accusations when I spoke against myself. The accuser had been accusing me and I had echoed his words at myself, giving him a foothold in my life.

God gently reminded me about the piece of armor which He provides for my protection - the breastplate of HIS righteousness; the breast-covering which protects the bosom of a person with God's holy light! What a tremendous gift God has given each one of us who will put it on.

"Put on the breastplate of righteousness" (Ephesians 6:14).

That very day I began to conquer the spirit of condemnation that had shadowed me all my life. I did this through forgiving those who had taught me that I had to be righteous through my own merit; I repented for trying to earn my own salvation through good works; I proclaimed with my mouth (many times a day), "Lord, you are righteous enough for both of us and I take your righteousness as my covering breastplate." I began to take Communion daily, holding up the cup of salvation as the only payment for my sins; I accepted God's grace for me; I spoke His grace over me!

I memorized Romans 8:1 and used it as my sword when the condemnation tried to come back in: *"There is therefore now no condemnation to those who are in Christ Jesus, who do not walk according to the flesh, but according to the Spirit."* Guarding my thought-life with the word of truth, I began to walk and continue to walk, in freedom and in health!

The fruit of my healing has been that I have been able to tell hundreds of women my story and help set them free from self-condemnation! I have proclaimed the good news about the protective covering of light which is the righteousness of Jesus Christ alone. I have also prayed for many women who have been miraculously healed from breast cancer!

Mine is but one story of how Father God will heal and set a captive free. Why did He come to me that day in my living room and promise to heal me? Why not me?! Father God will reach to the farthest star and last grain of sand to help anyone who will cry out to Him! He will bring any person into deep revelation and give anyone what they need as they pursue Him with all their heart! I am not an exception - I am an example of going after God with all of my heart and receiving His light!

"Call to Me, and I will answer you, and show you great and mighty things, which you do not know" (Jeremiah 33:3).

Your Mouth Holds a Miracle

Just as Holy Spirit showed me a key to my healing, you also have a key. Your own tongue may be the key to your breakthrough. But please don't take this idea in the wrong direction.

We have all known people who speak what seems to be the right words, yet the words sound hollow. Yes, the tongue has been proven to have a great influence on the brain but there is more to be considered. The body, soul and spirit are all interconnected. Jesus said that it is from out of the heart that the mouth forms words (Matthew 12:34). When the heart is in agreement with God's Word and our thoughts are lined up with His thoughts, and we verbalize true words, health flows into the body.

As we saw in the chapter, *Hold onto Your Healing*, many people who go to Healing Rooms, are touched by God but relapse into destructive and unbelieving self-talk. How can we help ourselves and others stop that kind of self-talk?

Understand that neglecting God's Word will lead to deception. Submit to God's Word and follow it fully, daily, and above all else.

We set ourselves to meditate on Scripture until it is the way we think and speak. "I know that the tongue of the wise is health and pleasant words are like a honeycomb, sweet to the soul, and health to the bones. And if I would love life and see good days, I must refrain my tongue from speaking deceit" (Proverbs 12:18;16:24; 1 Peter 3:10). *"I will give attention to the LORD'S words; and I will incline my ear to His sayings. I will not let them depart from my eyes; I will keep them in the midst of my heart; for they are life unto me when I find them. And health to all my flesh"* (Proverbs 4:20-22).

The tongue is the part of the body that can deceive the heart (James 1:26), defile the whole body (James 3:6), and can be set on fire by Hell (verse 6). The tongue affects the heart and the heart affects the tongue. The tongue is also the part of the body that can speak blessing, life, and faith! The choice is ours but the good choice will require tenacity, patience, and grace.

Pause and ask the Holy Spirit to give you power to speak as He wants you to. Invite Him to convict you every time you speak destructive words - His definition of destructive words, not your own.

The Edifying Gift of Tongues

I also highly recommend that we do as Paul spoke of in 1 Corinthians 14:4-5, *"[Speaking in] Tongues edifies [oneself]. . ." "I wish you all spoke in tongues."* Using one's tongue to edify yourself may mean that moving your tongue in that way - speaking in the supernatural and pure language of tongues, actually brings health to you!

The "pure language" spoken of in Zephaniah 3:9, may be, as some scholars believe, the gift of tongues.

Jack Hayford states this about that *pure language*: "The gift of tongues was used to bring believing Gentiles and astonished Jews together in unity of faith and purpose during Peter's reluctant visit to the home of Cornelius (Acts 10:44-48). It is this pure language, this gift of tongues, that has also served to merge believers of widely divergent theological persuasions into the modern charismatic movement. They have been enabled to transcend boundaries of tradition and nationality and serve the Lord together in the unity of the Spirit."[3]

The documented research about the value of the gift of tongues is indisputable. Oh, that we would all speak in a pure language!

Also, remember that Isaiah experienced revival when he was touched on his **mouth** with the burning coal (Isaiah 9:6). Purified in speech, Isaiah went forward with great power and authority!

Practice by Saying: "I Have a Great Memory"

Let us, who minister healing, be assured of the groundbreaking science that reinforces the ancient truth of Scripture: **the tongue is a key to healing miracles**.

And just one more example for now: how many times have you heard someone say with their tongue, "I can't memorize Scripture"? Neural science tests show that by stimulating the nerves in the tongue, the areas of dysfunction in the brain, get the stimulation that is needed to fire up the neurons in the area that weren't working. In other words, speak with your tongue the words, "I have a great memory" and your brain will develop new ways to remember, through the stimulation of the words on your tongue! Incredible!

Although we may not be able to convince the people around us, including our family members, about the health found in the power of their own tongues, let us be convinced in ourselves, and act on what we are convinced of! As we minister the gospel to people, we will meet varying levels of success in the human hearts. But may the truth we speak with our tongues bring health and healing to our own bodies and to as many as will listen to the words of truth formed with our tongues!

Prayer

Holy Spirit, please show me any secret sins in my own attitudes that could give place to the enemy. Reveal where I have given satan a foothold through agreement with his accusations. Heal me and make me like You! I give You my tongue and so, it now belongs to you, Holy Spirit. In Jesus' name, amen.

Reflection

1. Ponder this statement: It is the holiness of Jesus that makes you holy.

2. Do you believe that the righteousness of Christ Jesus covers you? What is your part in this?

3. How does satan get a foothold into a person's life?

4. Do you desire for Holy Spirit to show you the secret things which you do not know?

14

THE GREAT EXCHANGE

"Those who enter into Christ's being-here-for-us no longer have to live under a continuous, low-lying black cloud. A new power is in operation. The Spirit of life in Christ, like a strong wind, has magnificently cleared the air, freeing you from a fated lifetime of brutal tyranny at the hands of sin and death" (Romans 8:1-2, TMB).

Wherever I travel, I find people who have a desire for personal breakthrough in their lives. Whether it be a promotion at work, a cure for illness, or the desire for satisfying relationships, the hope for something better is real. But many people feel stuck as victims of their heritage, gender, or circumstances.

Today, more than ever before, we have evidence of the place that DNA plays in our physical makeup. The ancient people of God knew the importance of inheritance and spiritual bloodline but did not have the technology to show the actual physical proof.

The discoveries in our lifetime are amazing! Medical scientists can actually look into a person's genes and find out if that person has a propensity toward a certain disease. For some people, these tests create a crisis for them as decisions are presented that rely on genetic testing being infallible and unchangeable. Reports show that many men and women have actually had *at risk* parts of their bodies amputated to eliminate the possibility of cancer occurring in those places.

We can access numerous websites that promise to give us *simple, secure, and easy* DNA testing that will provide the information we think we need to know to become healthy. I vote that we use this new technology as a tool to find out what in our bloodline that needs to be cleansed by the Blood of the Lamb!

DNA Testing

Companies, which offer the new DNA testing, claim that you can find out your personal ethnic mix by sending them a saliva sample. "Learn about the genetic code within us all and how it unlocks your story," one company advertises. One website has a bright picture of a woman on its homepage with these percentages next to her picture: "39% Scandinavian, 24% Europe East, 16% Caucasus, 8% Asian East, 7% Great Britain." A leading company claims to tie into over 90 million family trees and billions of records on ancestry.

Many people I know have used these online services and have shared their findings with me. Usually, a person who is telling me about their roots will refer to a country of their origin; for example, a person might say, "I am from Italy and found out that I am 35% Italian." But what does this really mean?

To find out that you are originally (in part) from Italy means that there was a real person in your past, a man or a woman who was Italian, who carried you in his or her seed as a future person to be born. That is why you have a part of their code inside you.

It is now possible to find out if there is something sinister lurking in your past. What if that Italian ancestor, who you celebrate as being your Italian heritage, was a pirate? Could he have any bearing on your life now? If we look a little deeper at what this could mean, it may be a little threatening to find out that a person you never met and know nothing about has a connection not just to you, but also in you.

The Biblical View

Scripture teaches that people, who would be born centuries after Abraham died, were in his loins while he lived (Hebrews 7:5, 9-10). Do you have a little bit of Abraham in you?

If you grew up in church, you might have sung the children's song,

"Father Abraham" in Sunday School. The words went something like this, "Father Abraham had many sons, many sons had Father Abraham, you are one of them and so am I, so let's just praise the Lord!"

Scripture shows us that we receive God's seed when we are born again: *"Whoever has been born of God does not sin, for His seed remains in him . . . because he has been born of God"* (1 John 3:9).

We know from reading Genesis 3:15, that God called Eve's Seed (ancient writers called both the male sperm and the female egg "seed") the One who would crush the serpent's head thousands of years after Eve died. That One, who was to come, is the Lord Jesus Christ, the "Seed of the woman" Eve.

A New Bloodline for Abram

Does it still sound exciting to find out about the mixture of people who carried you in their body's decades and centuries ago? What else did you inherit from these individuals and what kind of people were they anyway? No wonder we must, as Jesus said, "be born again!" We need a clean bloodline!

Abram (Abraham's name before God changed his name), received a new inheritance and bloodline from God. Genesis 12 opens with these words to Abram from God, *"Get out of your country, from your family and from your father's house, to a land that I will show you"* (Genesis 12:1). Evidently, even Abram needed a new family tree. And he was about to get one, as God had planned a great exchange to happen between Himself and Father Abraham!

If Abram would obey God and leave his father's house and his family behind, God promised, *"I will make you a great nation; I will bless you and make your name great; and you shall be a blessing. I will bless those who bless you, and I will curse him who curses you; and in you all the families of the earth shall be blessed"* (Genesis 12:2-3).

A Principle for Prosperity

Herein lies a principle of prosperity that has never changed. If we will bless the Hebrews (the Jews, the Israelites), God will bless us.

While visiting our network church, The Father's House, in Vacaville, CA, we were reminded of an important directive and given greater insight into how to obtain blessing. At the time, we were walking through an especially challenging time with the finances of Horizon Church. Our network leader, Pastor David Patterson, spoke about how when The Father's House began to bless Israel financially each month, their finances took a giant leap forward.

This corresponded with something that Holy Spirit had shown me years earlier in regard to prayer. Whenever I would enter into my morning time of intercession, I would hear Holy Spirit say, "Israel first!" Consequently, it has been my practice for many years to pray for blessing, protection, and peace for Israel, before I pray for other things. Since Israel is present throughout the Bible and on God's mind, of course He cares that we support His people through prayer and the giving of financial gifts.

When we got home from Vacaville, we immediately began to support Israel through the church and through our own personal finances. There was a shift almost immediately and there has been abundance since this decision!

By blessing Abraham's descendants, we bless Abraham and receive blessing.

Let Us Also Understand a Curse

Scripture teaches that those who curse Abraham are cursed. How do we know that curses, words spoken by one person against another person, have an impact? We know through the accounts of this happening in the Bible as we read in the Scripture about Abraham. We also recognize the impact of a curse through personal experience.

Curses are mentioned in the Bible (NKJV) more than 60 times. Remember that Jesus Christ cursed a fig tree and it dried up overnight (Mark 11:21)?

A biblical account of a curse that continues to this day is the curse, which Noah spoke about his dishonoring son, Ham. The people groups who make war against Israel today are descendants of Ham (Genesis 9:25)!

We see current examples of the impact of curses around us. Here is one true story about a ministry that was being cursed by its opposition: *"Steven Johnson, president of World Indigenous Missions wrote, 'As president of a world-wide church planting ministry I found myself under severe spiritual attack. This resulted in extreme fatigue, the vexing of my soul, as well as spiritual attacks on my family.' So, Steven formed a team of prayer partners for the first time. 'Results of this were overwhelming,' Johnson reports. 'Within days of sending the letter, I sensed a tremendous lifting of spiritual oppressions. I sensed a freedom concerning a warfare that was attacking my family as well as my personal ministry.'"*[1]

As we saw in the previous chapter, we know that our words have power to bring life or death. Jesus Christ put the power of words into a very substantial category when He said, *"I say to you that for every idle word men may speak, they will give account of it in the day of judgment. For by your words you will be justified, and by your words you will be condemned"* (Matthew 12:34-37).

Our words have great power to kill or to heal, to bind up and to loose. *"Death and life are in the power of the tongue"* (Proverbs 18:21).

What we say with our mouths can actually grieve Holy Spirit: *"Do not let any unwholesome talk come out of your mouths, but only what is helpful for building others up according to their needs, that it may benefit those who listen. And do not grieve the Holy Spirit of God"* (Ephesians 4:29-30). We certainly don't want to do anything that will grieve our Helper, Holy Spirit!

Symptoms of a Curse

Derek Prince wrote, *"A curse is like a dark shadow from the past. You probably do not know where it comes from; perhaps it did not even originate in your lifetime. It may have something to do with your family background. It stretches out over your life and shuts out the sunshine of God's blessing. You can see other people around you in the sunlight, but rarely do you ever enjoy the sunshine yourself. You may have no idea what it is from the past that is the cause."*[2]

Symptoms of a curse may include mental or emotional breakdown;

repeated or chronic sickness, especially if it is hereditary (which is the nature of a curse); female problems (barrenness, etc.); breakdown of marriage, family alienation; financial insufficiency; being accident-prone; a history of suicide or unnatural deaths in a family.

Why should you be susceptible to a curse spoken from another person, or a curse that has been carried in your family line?

One meaning of the word "curse" in Scripture is to *notice slightly* or *make light of.* Almighty God said to Abram, *"I will bless those who bless you, and I will curse him who curses you"* (Genesis 12:3). "I will curse" in this context, means to give "small weight" to those people. This shows that all protection and every good thing comes from God's attention and favor. To be cursed may mean to be overlooked and not regarded as relevant or significant. *"Every good gift and every perfect gift is from above, and comes down from the Father of lights, with whom there is no variation or shadow of turning"* (James 1:17).

Have you ever felt passed over for a promotion or other benefit? Have you ever felt that you carried small weight (not bodily!), but in influence? Entire family lines have been passed by. Why? Not because God isn't calling - He is calling (Mathew 22:14). But is He being chosen? A blessing can come through a family member choosing God above all else like Abraham did. Then God's eyes will be drawn to that family line and His eyes bring honor and healing! *"For the eyes of the Lord run to and fro throughout the whole earth, to show Himself strong on behalf of those whose heart is loyal to Him"* (2 Chronicles 16:9)!

Get Noticed by God!

Have you ever been in a church service when the pastor asked people to raise their hands to acknowledge that they gave their lives to the Lord? You might have heard a preacher say, "I see that hand!" Maybe God is saying, "I see that hand!"

Consider what Abram said: *"I have raised my hand to the LORD, God Most High, the Possessor of heaven and earth"* (Genesis 14:22). Think about a child in a class at school - who is the one called on by the teacher to ask or answer a question? That child is the one who had his or her hand raised. You want God to take notice of you? Raise your hands to Him in worship, call upon His name in prayer, and support Israel in words and in money. (Notice that Abram also paid his tithe - Genesis 14, the end of verse 20.) Get out from under a curse and get blessed like Abraham! The great exchange that God gave Abram is available to you too!

Trading

Several years ago, we sang a song in church by Matt Redman, "Trading My Sorrows." The words state: *"I'm trading my sorrows, I'm trading my shame, I'm laying them down for the joy of the Lord . . . I'm trading my sickness, I'm trading my pain, I'm laying them down for the joy of the Lord."*

What wise trades those are!

With man's effort, it is impossible to trade-in your bloodline (like trading in your used car) for a new one. But with God, all things are possible!

"The Spirit of God who raised Jesus from the dead lives in you" (Romans 8:11).

The Ancient Covenant-Making Ceremony

My all-time favorite sermon which my husband, Tom, has preached through the years is "The Covenant." No matter how many times I hear this message, I am always overwhelmed by the exchange that took place between Almighty God and Abraham! The beauty of the message and the love which is expressed is magnificent!

To demonstrate the exchange that took place during the Covenant that God made with Abraham (Genesis 15:1-12, 17-18), Tom always chooses another man to help him. With that other man standing next to him, Tom gives instruction about the way a covenant was "cut" in the Mesopotamia Valley where Abram (Abraham's name before God changed it) lived at the time.

During a Covenant-Making Ceremony, two men would go out into the middle of an open field, surrounded by witnesses. Then they would begin the blood covenant that would be forever binding with no way out, until death. As a symbol of the exchange of the men's identities, first, the two men would exchange robes.

At this time, Tom, and the other man (let's call him Bob), take off their coats, and help the other man put his own on the other. Then Tom would announce, "When anyone sees me, they will say, 'here comes Bob,' and whenever anyone now sees Bob, they will say, 'here comes Tom.' If someone wants to push me around, it is hereby known from now on that he is also pushing Bob around and not messing with just one man!"

The second thing that would happen in the Covenant-Making Ceremony was that there would be an exchange of strength. The ones making the covenant would say something like, "Every strength I have, every asset I have, I give to you - they are now yours."

At this time, Tom and Bob would exchange belts, as a symbol of their strength being doubled, as they stand together.

The third exchange was the exchange of weapons, words, shields, and all military equipment would be exchanged. This signified the fact that the other man's enemies "are now my enemies."

At this point, Tom hands Bob his wallet and Bob gives Tom his wallet. They have given each other all of their assets.

The next part of the Covenant-Making Ceremony is the blood walk. A heifer, a goat and a ram are brought as sacrificial animals; each one is cut exactly in half and laid open. Each man would stand on each side of the animal and literally do a blood walk, called "the walk of death." One at a time, the men would walk through and around and back through the sacrificial animal. This blood covenant was all sufficient. This was the way of making a covenant - always with blood.

Of course, Tom and Bob did not demonstrate this part in church - but remember that this type of ceremony, with real animals, actually took place hundreds of times in the Middle East (and still does in some places).

Next came the striking of hands. Usually, an incision was made on the wrist of each of those making the covenant. Both men would then intermingle their blood together as a sign of oneness. This established a permanent covenant.

At this point, Tom would bring out a huge knife and the congregation would laugh. But Bob would not laugh! Tom would pretend to cut Bob's wrist and then his own. Then the two men would strike their wrists together.

The next part of the Covenant-Making Ceremony took place as each man stood across from the other inside the two halves of the heifer and said, "So long as you keep the covenant, blessed be your coming and going; blessed shall your wife and children be; blessed shall your lands be, your herds, your crops; blessed shall you be." Then they would each state: "However, if you violate the terms of the covenant, cursed shall you be, cursed shall your wife and children be, cursed shall your coming and going be, cursed shall your crops, lands and herds be. And if you violate the terms of this covenant, may it be to you as it is to this heifer, may you be slaughtered and cut in half."

Then the two men would walk through the animals again, followed by a covenant meal, out in the same field, and surrounded by a cloud of witnesses. Each one would feed the other man the first few bites. This signified the consuming of each other forever, pledged and committed to each other with a promise to never forget each other.

After the meal came the exchange of names. Standing facing each other, the two men would take each other's name and announce that the other man's name would forever be in the middle of their own name. This last action finalized the Covenant-Making Ceremony.

These ceremonies were very common in the ancient Middle East and you might notice some similarities to our current wedding ceremonies. However, for the most part - in this age, we do not know the depth of meaning of a true covenant or commitment like the one Abraham experienced with God.

Abram and Father God Take Part in a Great Exchange

Let us now see how Covenant-Making Ceremony applied to Abram, and how it applies to us and our need for a new bloodline.

Father God told Abram to leave his own bloodline behind, *"Get out of your country, from your family and from your father's house"* (Genesis 12:1). In so doing, God invited Abram to enter into Covenant relationship with Him!

The words of God to Abram *"Bring Me a three-year-old heifer, a three-year-old female goat, a three-year-old ram . . ."* (Genesis 15:9) must have struck sheer terror into Abram; for Abram knew that these words meant that God was wanting to cut a covenant with him! No wonder Scripture states four verses later, *"Now when the sun was going down, a deep sleep fell upon Abram; and behold, horror and great darkness fell upon him"* (verse 12).

Almighty God was initiating a blood covenant with a man, Abram, which could never be broken. (Are you seeing a foreshadowing of the Cross?)

Abram, in fear, knew that Almighty God was coming into his presence to make a Covenant with him. No wonder Abram was laid out prone on the ground unable to move. Then God appeared in the form of a torch fire, a smoking fire pot and with clouds - symbols of Almighty, Awesome God.

In the usual covenant between men, the lesser party always went first with the more important person going last. Abram knew this and yet he was unable to move. Undoubtedly, Abram knew in his heart that he could not keep a covenant with God and realized the seriousness of what the consequences would be. He was terrified!

Yet God became the servant and expressed His love by showing Abram, "It is ok, I will walk for you. I will go first and last and I will bear the consequences for you." God always initiates His love to us first!

Almighty God promised Abram that he and all his decedents would possess that land, and that this Covenant would extend to all generations. Including you and me.

During the Covenant that God established with Abram, He changed his name to "Abraham", putting the "ah" of Yahweh's name into Abraham's name! It may not sound like a big difference to you, but it was an important change! When God added the "ah" to Abram's name, He was saying that He was putting His breath into Abram! "Ah" means the "breath of God"! Abraham became a new man; a man breathed into by God!

The Covenant is Also for Every Believer

What does this event have to do with us? God's Covenant, spoken of in Scripture countless times, is for each believer today. God is for us like He was for Abraham.

As you know, the Israelites continued to break God's Covenant; and

God took the failures of His Covenant People on Himself when He sent His Son Jesus to make a new and better covenant with us.

Today we have the benefits of Abraham's Covenant, and the joy of the New Covenant in Jesus Christ. All who live by faith and trust in Jesus Christ are saved. This New Covenant has similarities to the old:

When Jesus and I entered into the New Covenant, there were witnesses. Jesus swapped robes with me - He took my sin and gave me His righteousness. Jesus traded belts with me - He gave me His strength, His very Spirit, and I gave Him all that I am. We exchanged weapons. Jesus took on my enemies; my greatest enemy is death and Jesus defeated death. Jesus' enemy is satan and I was given power to defeat him. Jesus sacrificed His life for me; His blood covers my sins. I, in return, have willingly sacrificed my life to Him. I've taken His name - I am a Christian. He has taken my name to Father God and written it in the Lamb's Book of Life! Now, all that He has is mine - His peace, presence, salvation, eternal life, guidance, support, and love. This is the GREAT EXCHANGE!

"[Jesus] breathed on them, and said to them 'Receive the Holy Spirit'" (John 20:22).

The Power of the New Covenant

"They overcame him because of the blood of the Lamb and because of the word of their testimony, and they did not love their lives even when faced with death." (Revelation 12:11)

"He made you alive together with Him, having forgiven us all our transgressions, having canceled out the certificate of debt consisting of decrees against us, which was hostile to us; and He has taken it out of the way, having nailed it to the cross." (Colossians 2:13-14)

"When He had taken a cup and given thanks, He gave it to them, saying, 'Drink from it, all of you; for this is My blood of the covenant, which is poured out for many for forgiveness of sins'" (Matthew 26:27-28).

"As for you also, because of the blood of My covenant with you, I have set your prisoners free from the waterless pit. Return to the stronghold, O prisoners who have the hope; this very day I am declaring that I will restore double to you" (Zechariah 9:11-12).

Deliverance is Not Automatic

A good question at this point might be to ask how a Christian could still be in poverty, or any other bondage, when that person has entered into such a fantastic covenant relationship with God.

You might wonder why you did not automatically get your entire bloodline cleaned out when you were born again. After all, being born all over again should mean that your first birth is now null and void, shouldn't it?

Obviously, we have two births. The Lord Jesus said, *"Unless one is born of water and the Spirit, he cannot enter the kingdom of God. That which is born of the flesh is flesh, and that which is born of the Spirit is spirit"* (John 3:5-6).

"Having been born again, not of corruptible seed but incorruptible, through the word of God which lives and abides forever" (1 Peter 1:23).

Physical birth is an amazing thing, but even more amazing, is spiritual birth. In the natural, you see the miracle of a newborn baby. But at salvation - the supernatural birth, there is the miracle of a soul being transformed and a spirit coming alive in Christ! Through new birth, we enter a new realm, opening up the possibilities of our whole being to the supernatural dimension of life, to Holy Spirit!

When you were born again, a renewed order was established. Your purpose was restarted - you are now a worshipper of God! New birth has not reversed the loss of man's original dominion on earth - you still live on a fallen planet. But you are now a recipient of all the benefits of being a child of God. At salvation, a cleansed realm for seeking God's Kingdom first - was opened and became newly available to you! Being born from above didn't neutralize freewill or cancel the devil's onslaught of temptation. But you now have absolute access to the power of Holy Spirit!

And His power is dynamite, supernatural, power that can reach into the past and cancel out every personal and generational sin!

Read what author Tony Evans says about this: *"When the Spirit takes over, a lot of our excuses are nullified. We say, 'Well, that's my personality.' But the Spirit can change our personalities. 'But this is just how I was raised.' Well, when the Spirit takes over, He can change the way you were raised into the way you ought to be. 'I've always been like this.' That's because you have not always been under the control of the Spirit of God. The Spirit transforms us supernaturally. That's why I say rather than spending our time, energy, and effort trying to change, we need to spend our time getting filled. A sober man doesn't have to try to stagger. All he has to do is get drunk. The alcohol will take care of the staggering. He doesn't have to change his personality. He just has to get drunk."*[3]

Holy Spirit is the One who comes into our lives and brings with Him every good thing that we need to access God's Kingdom. The possibilities with the help and power of Holy Spirit are unlimited!

It is up to each one of us, individually, to go after the secret things that God promises to reveal - including our own deliverance from generational curses. As we are free, we are a conduit to bring freedom to other people.

Uncomplicate the Process

My wonderful Christian mom suffered from migraines and several other infirmities, which had access to her body due to the fear that had residence in her soul. One day. Holy Spirit asked me this question, "Linda, do you need to be tied to the torment that fear causes because your mom was, and her mom was, and her mom was?" I was stunned! Since Holy Spirit doesn't ask questions to gain information, I knew this question had the potential to change my life! So instead of filing away this amazing communication with Holy Spirit with a "wow, what an encounter I had" moment, I decided to do whatever it took to get free from the fear that brought torment. (You can read more about my deliverance in my book, Freedom From Fear.)

Let us simplify and specify one way to clear your bloodline of generational sin. The primary way to shut the door on someone else's sin - sin, which is affecting your life, is through forgiveness.

> *"If you forgive the sins of any, they are forgiven them; if you retain the sins of any, they are retained"* (John 20:23).

> *"I will give you the keys of the kingdom of heaven, and whatever you bind on earth will be bound in heaven, and whatever you loose on earth will be loosed in heaven."* (Matthew 16:19)

> *"Assuredly, I say to you, whatever you bind on earth will be bound in heaven, and whatever you loose on earth will be loosed in heaven"* (Matthew 18:18).

When I gained victory over the generational fear that had a place in me, the progression of freedom was this sequence of events:

I asked God to show me why I was suffering with feelings of irrational fear (fear of what other people thought of me, fear of calamity in my family, fear of failure, etc.). This is when Holy Spirit showed me that my mother suffered from fear, and that her mother had suffered from fear (and continuing back in my family line).

I scheduled a time when I could pray, read God's Word, listen for His instruction, and not be interrupted.

As I waited on God in prayer, Holy Spirit showed me that I needed to forgive my mother for not dealing with the fear. I didn't have any idea that I had resentment in my heart toward my mother for being fearful. My resentment was because I didn't want to have to do the work myself. I saw my selfishness.

I repented for resentment and asked Holy Spirit to forgive me and to help me to forgive my mom. Eventually, I received the grace to forgive her from my heart. Then I went through the same process about my Grandma's fear and I forgave her. I then asked God how many generations this went back. As the Lord showed me the roots of the fear, I asked God to forgive each of the generations and keep this sin from being visited on me or my children. Then I forgave all the people in my bloodline who enlisted and allowed fear to rule in their lives. After I forgave, I applied the righteous Blood of the Lamb, Jesus Christ, to the doors that my ancestors had opened to a spirit of fear. Then I commanded the spirit of fear to leave me and go to the Cross of Jesus Christ.

Then, knowing that God's Word states, *"perfect love casts out fear"* (1 John 4:18), I asked God to fill the place where fear used to reside with His perfect love.

Yes, it is a lot of work; and it takes time. But there is nothing I would trade for the freedom that I received by asking God to clean fear out of my bloodline! The time and effort it took is nothing compared to the freedom I now walk in! Father God exchanged my fear for His perfect love!

You can use this method of deliverance for inherited sin in your own life. It is not difficult to bring this exchange into your bloodline; but it does require time with God, and obedience to His Word.

Whatever you are struggling with, whether it be fear, poverty, anger, disease . . . God has freedom for YOU!

Hidden Things

I ask God all the time to reveal the hidden things that He wants me to know, and to show me secret things. When I forget to ask Him about something, Holy Spirit will wake me up at 3:33 in the morning to remind me! One of my life verses, Jeremiah 33:3, invites, *"Call to Me, and I will answer you, and show you great and mighty things, which you do not know."*

Be assured that God will orchestrate situations in your life so that you can see what is truly in your heart. These issues will always surface.

The devil wants to remain hidden in the soul of a person, subtly controlling. The Lord could have ripped him by force from the soul of a person when he or she was born again. But that would not change their heart. The surfacing of darkness in a person (after being born again) may not be by the power of satan, but by his defeat. Until Holy Spirit comes in, a person can play-act by determination and appear to be a good person. Satan does not want to disturb a phony-front. He has a secure hiding place there. So, when Holy Spirit comes in, an individual can no longer be the "nice guy" he or she thought they were. This is because Holy Spirit causes the enemy to surface and to be revealed-pushed up and out! But some

Christians believe that the surfacing evil must be avoided at all costs. Not so! It is the mercy of God to reveal sin - it is the work of the devil to conceal it. This can be a humbling experience. When God begins to expose the little lies that we tell, or the cold love that we have toward another person, or any number of 'little' things that we discount, it is humbling.

Are you willing to trade-in your "righteousness before men" for the love of God? The Lord said, *"You are those who justify yourselves before men, but God knows your hearts. For what is highly esteemed among men is an abomination in the sight of God"* (Luke 16:15).

So, we see that it takes humility, a desperate pursuit of God, and time to root out the issues. As Doctors of the Cross, we are willing to do whatever it takes because we love God and we love other people.

You Have What You Need to be Whole - You Have Jesus!

"The Spirit of God who raised Jesus from the dead lives in you" (Romans 8:11).

Have you underestimated the power of Jesus Christ? Have you read the words of Jesus: *"All authority has been given to Me in heaven and on earth"* (Matthew 28:18) and discounted the words to fit into your commonsense?

The almightiness and the power to save, heal, and deliver that Jesus Christ has, no other human in all the world possesses. Only Jesus Christ has the laser power of the Spirit of God that dissolves sin and sickness out of a life and makes that person free! In the very heart of God, there is a dynamic, a power, which is great enough to save every person in the world, to heal every sick person in the world-to heal anyone of anything, of any degree of sin and any degree of sickness!

I just read a legend about the name of Jesus that might help give you greater perspective as to the enormous power of His name, and the lengths satan goes to in order to keep us from remembering God's name.

This legend is told in the book, Legends of the Jews: *"The ineffable Name [Jesus] was engraved on this stone [the stone which the foundation of the world was laid on], whose power checks the Tehom [Abyss] from overflowing the earth. Since the knowledge of this name enabled anyone to accomplish all one desired, a device was necessary to prevent misuse. At the gate of the temple, two brazen dogs were placed so that whenever a person who had acquired the Knowledge of the Name would pass, they began to bark. Frightened by this sound, the person would forget the knowledge of the Name."*[4]

Isn't that what often happens when us when we are trying to pray? You know that the Lord Jesus said that *"If you ask anything in My name, I will do it"* (John 14:14), but when you go to ask, the "dogs" start barking, and you forget that God hears, answers, wants to hear from you, and that you are His beloved child. Besides all of that, the noise of the devil's distractions can cause you to become completely sidetracked with barks of work, sleep, food, people, and maybe even your pet dog. Dogs barking.

Believing the Great Exchange

Recently, I had the opportunity of visiting one of the places that Horizon City Ministries has taken under its' wing: a senior housing facility. As I went around visiting with many of the residents, I talked with a woman who said that her back "was killing her." I asked her if she wanted me to pray for her, and she told me that she didn't have any faith. I explained that I had plenty for both of us and then shared some testimonies of healing that I have witnessed. Then I put my hand on her back and began to ask Jesus Christ to take her pain upon Himself on the Cross, to exchange her hurting back for His well back. I could sense God's love for her and knew that God was healing her.

About half an hour later this same woman came to find me. She said, "I just have to tell you that my back feels better!" I replied, "God loves you so much!" to which she replied, "Well, I don't know about that!"

In my healing ministry, one of the biggest problems that I see is that people do not understand the *Great Exchange* because they really don't believe the depth of God's love for them. Jesus took our sin upon Himself so that we may take His righteousness in ourselves. He took our griefs and sorrows so that we can have His joy. Jesus took our sickness on His own body at the Cross, and now there is no point in both of us continuing to carry it. This is the truth and it needs to be believed.

I Took a DNA Test . . . God is My Father

When Jesus Christ died upon the Cross, He actually BECAME my sin so that I could become His righteousness. Then my sin died with Him! It was the great exchange! Oh, glorious truth!

"For He made Him who knew no sin to be sin for us, that we might become the righteousness of God in Him" (2 Corinthians 5:21).

Have you waited on God, meditating on the Cross of Christ, asking for a revelation of the great exchange? Have you seen Jesus Christ hanging on the Cross AS your sin? Have you seen your sin swallowed up in victory as the King conquered death?! Have you witnessed the transference of righteousness into your whole being? This vision, this encounter, this glory is available to you; for it is written in the Scripture of Truth that this is what really happens to a person when they are born again! Therefore, this revelation of what Christ did is available to you and all who desire to give Jesus Christ all He died to gain - He wants you to see and accept this exchange!

In the next chapter, we will see how a segment of your earth-time can be cursed and the remedy for any *curses on time* which you may have experienced.

Prayer

O God, what You did for me is so awesome - I am in awe of YOU! May I know the strength of my new bloodline, day by day, until I am completely taken over by Your love!! I know that You, Lord God, will do what You have promised. You have not forgotten me for I am constantly in Your thoughts. You are waiting to fulfill Your Word through me. I know that You, oh Lord, cannot lie; You will not change Your mind. Please reveal to me an area of my life in which You want to bring in the Great Exchange. I will do whatever it takes to be delivered, free, and will help others find deliverance and freedom. In Jesus' name, amen.

Reflection

1. What traits do you have in your earthly heritage that affect your outlook on life?

2. Is there a category in which you have underestimated the power of Jesus Christ to redeem something about you?

3. After being born again, how can there still be a propensity to have cancer (or another malady) and how does one overcome a particular weakness in their bloodline?

4. How might generational sin be broken in your own life?

15

THE REDEEMER OF TIME

"See then that you walk circumspectly, not as fools but as wise, redeeming the time, because the days are evil" (Ephesians 5:16).

Upon rising on a recent spring morning, I was surprised to open the blinds and see snow pouring down outside in great big heavy flakes of beauty! As usual, my husband opened the door to let our black-backed, collie-heeler mix dog go outside. Just a minute later I called her in and saw that her back was white with snow. She couldn't have gone out into heavy snowfall like that without snow clinging to her fur.

It reminded me of what I had prayed fervently at our Friday morning prayer gathering the day before: *Father, let every person who walks on to the church property be touched by Your Spirit!*

Just as our dog didn't go out into the snowfall without it touching her, I greatly desire that every person who walks into the environment of God's presence will become different - look different (whiter/purer) and feel whole.

It would be a great thing if only pure things touched each of us throughout our days. But we know that we are subject to the conditions on our planet, which can include weather conditions, sickness, and curses. Without meaning to let it happen, and not even realizing that something got attached to us, we may be walking around with something on our backs.

One Sunday as I was getting ready to lead a prayer time at church, Holy Spirit spoke these words to me, "Tell the people that they cannot stop the birds from flying over their heads, but that they can stop them from building a nest in their hair." I was surprised by these words and began to ask the Lord what this meant. Then I understood that Father God wanted me to let the people know that even though there were germs everywhere (it was during what the news called "flu season"), that His people didn't have to let sickness have a place inside of them. Just telling this word from the Lord gave people hope that they could avoid sickness and helped to eradicate fear.

It is interesting to note that during World War II, newspapers in Europe published tips about how to avoid sickness during those dark days. One of the items on a newspaper list stated, "Keep yourself from giving into fear." I read this newspaper article while at a museum in Bucharest, Romania, and recognized how important that advice was. Bombs were falling around the people of Romania, but letting fear take them over would make them more susceptible to sickness.

Redeeming

In Scripture, the Apostle Paul instructs believers to redeem time because the days are evil (Ephesians 5:16). I have been asking Holy Spirit to explain this instruction to me for many years. It always seemed to me that there was more to understand in this word than to simply make sure I was a good steward of my schedule or at worst, to complain about living in evil days. I propose that we take this word at face value and learn how to buy back time that was stolen away by evil.

To *redeem* means to buy back, or to purchase with a price. I believe this is the true meaning for what Paul instructed - take back time that was stolen due to the devil's trespassing. I purpose that we believe that time can be bought back with the payment of the Redeemer's sacrificial death on the Cross; we act in faith according to that belief. This does not mean that we will transport back in time, but that the things in the past that harmed us will stop repeating!

How does a person go about taking back the elusive commodity called time, sanctify it, and possess it again? We learned in chapter 7 that *Healing is Circumspect* - it has many aspects and facets to consider. To redeem time will call for walking out the days of our lives circumspectly, as Scripture advises, not as fools, but by paying attention to our personal timelines.

A Battle to Win

Mentioned in the Bible over one hundred times, curses are real - stumbling blocks that can affect our lives. The Bible says that before we were born again, that we were under a curse. Jesus Christ died to free us from the curse, and to take authority over all the power of the evil one. Refusing to believe that curses are real and staying in ignorance can wreak havoc. We must do something to stop the curses from building nests in our hair!

Let us once again consider the good fight of faith (1 Timothy 6:12). We are in a battle against the forces of evil. We live in a world where the Lord said we will have trouble, but to take heart, for He has overcome the world. *Take heart* can also mean to take courage and do what is needed (John 16:33).

Years ago, Tom and I planned to have a wonderful vacation on a cruise ship. I say planned to have because there is an analogy here for life. We want a smooth sail and an easy way. So, Tom and I boarded the ship for our long-planned vacation. The first night on the ship, I began to have symptoms of the flu. That night I went to bed early and had an encounter with the Lord of Hosts. These are the words I wrote in my journal about the battle taking place:

> *The Captain of the hosts is Almighty to save!! On a cruise ship, throat so sore that it wakes me every time I try to swallow, I hurt all over and have fever. In the night, the temptation was huge to give in and be sick. But Jesus gave me the determination to fight. I put on the armor and began to battle. The words coming out of my mouth and thoughts were amazing. Clearly, I was being instructed by the Holy Spirit. I battled for a long time. Then I fell asleep and in a "dream" I saw the Powers of Light - wind and fire - servants of God most high-battling the darkness and evil. I saw the war room and the multi-level plans and strategies of God's servants. I heard the discussion about the ways of combat. It was amazing! Then I saw the flashing of swords, heard the crashing of weapons, and felt the intensity of the conflict.*

Suddenly the Captain's voice broke through to me, "The battle is a mixture of set-backs and victories." Immediately, there was silence and I awoke on the ship. I swallowed and although my throat still felt swollen and clogged, the pain was gone! Gratitude rose all through me and the echo of the Captain's voice was like liquid peace!!

Although we were on a luxury cruise, there was a battle raging in the spiritual realm. Just like in each of our everyday lives. If we forget about the battle and close our eyes to the fight, we will not win. There is sickness to overcome, curses to overturn, and territory to take for the Kingdom! God has given us the power to rise up and stand against those powers that would kill, steal, and destroy.

On that cruise ship, the sickness did not take me over and I was able to enjoy the cruise while I fought the symptoms of sickness. That was victory!

Curses on Time

Kris Vallotton said, "A curse can be defined as "doing the right thing and getting the wrong results."[1]

A person who is under the shadow of a curse may feel as though other people are blessed, but that blessing is only fleeting for themselves. A curse may affect health, finances, time, and relationships.

One of the most difficult issues that I deal with in my counseling ministry is ministering to children who are sick due to a generational curse that was put on them. No matter how many children I have helped set free, nor how many healings have occurred, I still struggle every time a new case comes into my office, because that case is an innocent child.

There are various reasons as to why a curse is activated at a certain time or season in a child's or an adult's life. As we will see, a person's own personal timeline, and family line, may have certain aspects that are susceptible to time-curses. These stumbling blocks often continue from generation to generation until something is done to terminate them.

Your Personal Timeline

Each person has a month in which he or she was conceived and became a person. In the United States, most people know when their birthday is - the day that they left their mother's womb, but few people calculate the moment when their life actually began.

I had never calculated the time in which my life began until a series of events happened that caused me to wonder why April was always a month of trouble. Year after year, there was an accident, injury, serious illness, or other calamity that would occur during the same month. When I finally noticed the pattern, I began to seek God's answer and remedy.

In the 50s, the time when I was born, birth control was hit or miss, and newlyweds often had a baby in their first year of marriage. My parents were married just one year when my brother was born and when he was less than a year old, my mom was pregnant again, with me.

Many children in the 50s were told that he or she "was an accident."

From the moment of conception, my mom was very sick, and not at all happy about being pregnant. There was no celebration that APRIL when an unwanted pregnancy was discovered. I was born in January, nine months later.

To say that I was cursed at conception may seem like an exaggeration or a judgment against my parents. But I was actually so relieved when Holy Spirit began to show me what was wrong that I rejoiced! Now I knew what my responsibility entailed; I must forgive all who spoke words against my being. The primary way in which curses are broken is when forgiveness is given and received, in the name of Jesus.

Were my parents to blame for my April-troubles? Not any more than I am to blame for taking so long to pay attention. Once I understood why there were cyclic problems that took place at the same time each year, I was able to redeem the time. After many years of troubled Aprils, we have not had a single issue in April for decades! The Redeemer reached back in time and bought back time (the month of April) that was stolen from me. There are no accidents with God!

Do you believe that the words your parents spoke (or others who had authority over your life) had impact on you before you were born?

When Elizabeth, the mother of John the Baptist, was pregnant with him, he was aware of things happening around his mother. The Bible says that the child (John), while still in the womb, reacted to the approach and greeting of Mary (Luke 1:39-40). When John heard Mary's greeting, he leapt for joy!

Since a fetus can leap for joy in his mother's womb (as when Mary walked up to Elizabeth), it is likely that an unborn child is also susceptible to negative emotions. Pause and ask God if there is anything that you need to know about your conception and birth that needs His redeeming touch.

Curses are Broken When Forgiveness is Applied

Breaking a curse off time is not rocket science! To think that you cannot reverse a curse is to underestimate the immense power of the High King of Heaven who died on the Cross to redeem you - and lives in you now! Nothing is too difficult for God! Taking your authority, in the Name of Jesus, can move the mountain. So, let us do what Jesus said and "say to this mountain 'Move from here to there,' and it will move; and nothing will be impossible for you" (Matthew 17:20).

The basic way in which I went about breaking the negative words (curses) that were spoken against my life will follow. But please understand that there are entire books written on the subject of breaking curses and this one chapter cannot contain all that you may need to know. The bottom line is always: God knows all there is to know; so, *ask God*. He knows if you need help from a counselor, a book, or a Christian friend. And His Holy Spirit Helper is ready to aid you every moment.

The following is the short version of the course of action I took to receive freedom:

- I reaffirmed my faith in Jesus Christ as the One who died to set me free from sin and death. Then I asked Jesus to stand up for me as my Advocate (1 John 2:1) in the Court of Heaven (see Job 1-2).
- I acknowledged that satan had been given a legal right to interject evil into my life because of words spoken by those who had authority over my life. But I readily affirmed that I have a higher legal right because of the blood of the Lord Jesus Christ.

- From my heart, I forgave those who rejected me. Then I asked God to completely forgive them. I continued, forgiving family members, back several generations in my family line, as Holy Spirit led me. Then I asked Father God to forgive the people I named, and to close the door on their sins with the righteous blood of Jesus Christ.
- I spoke out loud, "I receive the timeline of my life, from conception forward, as a gift from God; I accept my life as a gift from Him" (according to Psalm 139). I severed the agreement that people entered into with the demonic realm and annulled those agreements by the purifying blood of Christ. I placed the Cross of Jesus between my ancestors and me and commanded the curses to be halted at the Cross of Jesus Christ (Galatians 3:13)!
- I believed the work was done; and then, I praised the Lord with great thanksgiving!

Insight

Armed with the insight of my own experience and the very real victory, I began to notice patterns in the lives of the people who came to me for counseling. I would ask questions about reoccurring issues and maladies and find out that quite often the issues were cyclical - related to a certain timeframe in a person's life. The curse was not necessarily on where a person lived, or on his or her physical health, but was attached to a certain time in their family history that had become susceptible to the devil's foothold (Ephesians 4:27). Sometime in a past generation, satan had obtained a legal right to cause problems at a certain time because of a human ancestor's sin.

Thinking about the possibility of a certain timeframe in the timeline of your life being cursed may be a new concept to you. So, let us begin with a question that may bring an aha moment. Is there a certain time of the year when you feel sadness with no understanding as to why? You may look at your life and be unable to determine a single cause for your feelings, yet you feel inexplicably depressed.

Another example that you may identify with could be that there are specific weeks of the year when your finances seem to dry up. There may be unforeseen car repairs or medical bills that seem to happen at the same time each year. And for some reason, even though you are doing everything right, money is not covering your bills like normal.

As a Christian, you may fight a spirit of infirmity to no avail because the curse is not on health but is attached to time. Maybe you have experienced a physical problem that doesn't seem to budge by addressing the physical symptoms. (And why I often hear that medical tests are performed but the cause of the malady is not found.)

We had friends who became sick every time they planned a vacation. No matter how much they prayed and battled, it would happen again. When they realized that the stumbling block they were tripping over was a curse on their travel-time and not on their health, they were able to break the curse and move into a time of blessed vacationing! This particular family had ancestors who migrated to the USA from another nation. When they left their parents and their home country behind, the family angrily cursed their departure and travel. When this was revealed, our friends sought help for deliverance from the curse. After the curses were broken, they were free from sickness and received God's blessing on their coming and going (see Numbers 28:6).

Coincidence? hat is a possibility. But there is also the possibility that someone back in a family line made a trade that is affecting the present.

Trading

When I was a child, the church my family worshipped and served at did not believe in being part of secret societies. Although I didn't know why secret societies were "against my religion," I did know that for some reason they were bad. It wasn't until (as a pastor) I had too many teens and children in my office for counseling who had similar experiences, that I went looking for an answer.

The common account that I heard over and over was about a dark figure standing in a child's room at night. The figure did not move to touch the child, nor did it speak. It was simply present in the room and terrifying to the child.

While speaking at a youth conference, I paused and asked the teenagers how many of them experienced a dark presence in their rooms at night. I am sorry to say that many, many hands went up.

It is not uncommon for a person who is being initiated into a secret society (or when climbing to the next level in one), to utter curses on a descendant in a future generation. The person uttering the curse receives a reward of some kind for giving away authority in their family line - and that person traded away may be the child coming into my office in need of deliverance.

When oaths made in a secret society (like Freemasonry) are exposed, repented of, and the door is closed on those curses that traveled through time to a certain descendant, remarkable freedom ensues! Time is redeemed by the righteous blood of the Redeemer, who reaches into the past and heals forward. I have seen remarkable freedom come to a child, teen, or adult when the curses associated with Freemasonry were broken!

Lest you think that an ancestor who traded with the devil was an evil person, consider the following. One night I was speaking at a meeting where I was giving instruction on how to help children become free from night terrors. I paused and exhorted the people to make sure that they did not make any deals with the devil that would specifically affect their children. I went on to explain some of those deals. At the end of the meeting, I had several upright people come to me privately and say that they had made a deal with the devil without realizing what they had done. There was great conviction and sorrow, but the good news is that any such deals can be completely broken by the power of the blood of Jesus Christ!

To further explain the concept of making a deal with the devil, let me illustrate with a very current scenario from my own life.

While writing this chapter, I asked Holy Spirit to give me a great illustration to explain how the devil makes deals. Let me begin by saying that satan is a terrorist. Making a deal with the devil is agreeing with his intimidation.

Freemasonry is a power spirit and stays hidden under the covering of good deeds. To expose this spirit (as I have done in this chapter) is to anger the devil. After writing the words about children being tormented because an ancestor who was part of Freemasonry traded that child for something he or she wanted, the enemy brought an onslaught. I kept hearing him say that if I didn't erase the words about Freemasonry, my family would be in danger. Not only was I hearing this threat, I was experiencing extremely painful jabs in my physical body. I knew what was happening, but I was still tempted to delete the part in this chapter about secret societies. However, I also knew that this would be making a deal with the devil. I would be giving satan authority over my family's "protection" as a tradeoff for erasing the words about Freemasonry.

As I sought the Lord for strength to stand against the temptation, the God of Angel Armies rose up in me and I proclaimed out loud, "The Lord God of Hosts is my protector and the protector of my family and I will not give that place to any other!"

The relief and freedom were immediate, and I felt great victory that has continued! There will be no making deals with the lying devil nor fearing his threats.

Have you ever backed off from witnessing for the Lord or being honest in a work situation (etc.), in order to protect yourself from the spiritual warfare it would cause? What kind of deal is that?

An Old Testament prophet named Balaam was paid by an enemy to curse Israel (Numbers 22). Balaam's name and story became infamous, and he is referred to several times in the New Testament. Peter said of Balaam, "[he] loved the wages of wickedness" (2 Peter 2:15). Jude echoes this estimation, associating Balaam with the selling of one's soul for financial gain (Jude 1:11). Jesus speaks of Balaam when He warns the church to not be like Balaam (Revelation 2:14). The story of Balaam is a sobering reminder from Scripture that we must never trade with the devil to further our own comfort.

Had I put the protection of my family in the hands of the devil, because I was intimidated by fear and because of physical pain, I would have been trading with a terrorist.

Let the reader understand and beware of the devil's traps. And may each of us break the curses which our ancestors (who may have traded with the devil in some way or another) set up that effect our time. We are called to pay attention, to walk as wise, not as fools, and to redeem the time from evil! *"See then that you walk circumspectly, not as fools but as wise, redeeming the time, because the days are evil"* (Ephesians 5:16).

Other Examples of Cyclic Troubles

Recently I asked a man who suffers with reoccurring migraine headaches if he could spot a pattern in the migraine's occurrence. He thought for a moment and then said that he didn't know. But then his wife who was listening identified a definite pattern of timing. I expect freedom for this man as the time is redeemed through forgiveness.

Another case in which a pattern was observed and then dealt with, was a young man who had his heart broken during a certain month every year for several years consecutively. For seemingly no reason, he would be rejected at the very same time each year. When we dissected the timing (instead of only praying for healing from rejection), he was freed from a time-curse and his life was changed!

Arthur Burke, of Plumbline Ministries[2], has several good tools that help bring healing for wounds that may have taken place in a person while in their mother's womb. One provoking statistic that he cites is that an adult who survived an abortion attempt while in the womb is susceptible to a suicide attempt on that day each year. A secular researcher gave Burke a piece of information that showed the tracking of a number of people who committed suicide as adults on the exact day that their mother intended or attempted to abort them (the victim did not know about the attempted abortion). After the suicide, the mother acknowledged that on that particular day of the year, 10, 20, 30, or more years earlier, there had been either the intent or attempt to abort that child. And without the child's conscious memory of that date, there was a defilement, a death curse that attached to that day of the year. Although I do not have access to the research group that reported these statistics, it is worthy to mention in case the reader of this book has experienced an annual strange compulsion to end his or her life.

On the other side, there have been numerous publications describing individual cases of completed suicide of the mother or father after aborting their child. In many cases, the attempted or completed suicides were intentionally or subconsciously timed to coincide with the anniversary date of the abortion, or the expected due date of the aborted child, years later.

Suicide has increased in our nation, as well as globally. Death curses on timelines need to be identified and brought to the Redeemer of time, Jesus Christ!

Patterns

If you have already identified a pattern in your life (the month of February, the third week in August, the first part of September) when there is some kind of repeating trouble, the first place to look for a problem is when your life began. Curses may have been placed on your life in the womb.

Was there defilement when you were conceived (adultery, fornication, pornography, or other sexual sin)? If not, move forward four weeks to when your mother found out she was pregnant. Often there is rejection there. Or, more commonly, a wrong response from the dad and rejection of the gift which God had given. Either one can cause a defilement of time.

If there were none of these sins, you can then begin to ask our timeless God, the One who has the books about all the days of your life, to look back at the generations in your history and show you what you need to know. Listen to hear the furthest generation that Holy Spirit brings to mind. Then ask the Lord what happened there. He will give a word or a picture. Then take your legal right, as a child of God, and as a born-again descendant in your human family line and renounce those sins. Ask God to forgive the offender; and then you also must forgive him or her. In this way, you cover the sin with the blood of Christ and close the door that was left open into your own life. Continue with each thing which Holy Spirit shows you.

There are things that only Holy Spirit knows, and He will reveal them to you. For example, if the sin which brought defilement was adultery, there isn't just confession of adultery but there is also the sin of covenant breaking, betrayal, deception, cover-up, and shame. Don't worry that you might confess something that didn't happen as there is no harm in this - Holy Spirit will bring your prayers on target (Romans 8:26).

Where There is a Curse, Is There Always a Demon?

Curses are always a sin issue; a curse has power because someone did something somewhere. Demons are not the most relevant factor (although of course we do not want a demon's evil influence in our lives). But a demon will leave quickly if he is just an intruder with no legal right to stay. By confessing the sins that God reveals, you disempower the demon and are then able to command the demon to release its hold on time and leave. In so doing, you have broken a demon's legal right from your timeline.

When a pattern that makes no sense begins to be noticed, we should do our part to bring it up with the Lord. Frequently, curses continue from generation to generation until someone does something to terminate them.

Postscript

Upon finishing this chapter and then teaching some of the main points at our Healing School, I received a question from one of the students. With his permission, we will call him Andrew* and tell a little of his story. Andrew has a special needs child and wanted to know if generational curses could be the cause of his child's problems and if he and his wife could break those curses.

I asked Andrew to read this chapter through and then we would dialogue about the possibility of generational curses being the culprit for the problems in his family line. After reading he wrote me again with the following account: "My grandpa, in China, sold his babies into slavery to pay off his gambling and alcohol debts. My grandma kept track of where one of my aunts was sold to and my dad was next to be sold and he ran and went into hiding."

Andrew shared this heartbreaking account of a man, his own grandfather, trading his children away in order to pay for his sinful actions. Could this past sin have given the adversary the right to bring affliction on the future children in his family line?

Our responsibility as parents is to go before Father God on behalf of our forefather's sins and get those sins cleared out through forgiveness, closing the door that had been opened into our children's lives. Will this action bring Andrew's special needs child into complete health?

My reply to Andrew was this: "As far as you being able to clear out all of the generational stuff and see your child healed - remember that we are changing things for the generations to come in our family line, and not always for what we will see in our own children or lifetime. But we pray and hope, knowing our prayers will be answered."

Regardless of what we see in our own temporary lives as we battle for our children and the generations to come, let us do the good we can. Let us do the work of breaking all curses in prayer and faithfulness. Your work will not be in vain.

Establish Blessing

The wonderful news of the Kingdom of God is that you are fully able to break the generational curses from your generational line, and, you are fully able to establish blessings that will continue for many generations!

Time can be cursed; but the good news is that time can be blessed. The very first thing that God ever set apart and made holy was time. We read in Genesis 2:3, *"God blessed the seventh day and sanctified it,"* a timeframe!

Giving God the first fruits of your time each day will sanctify your time (make it holy). Throughout Scripture we read that the first born, the first fruits, the first everything belonged to God. How much better would your day be if you gave God the first part and made the whole day holy!

The first part of your week can be blessed. It is common for people to complain about Monday mornings because the weekend is over and its back to school or work. If you have joined in the common groan over Monday mornings, you can change the way Mondays feel by beginning to bless Monday mornings. Death and life are in the power of the tongue (Proverbs 18:2) and you can use your tongue to pronounce blessing on Monday and have a better week.

Many families have chaotic Sunday mornings and argue on the way to church. Ahead of time, bless the family-time that you will have on the way to church. Speak blessings over the timeframe.

You are fully able to establish blessing upon your own life and upon the generations to come! This fact is seen in Scripture as we find that the blessings God promised to His servant, David, continued for three hundred thirteen years following David's death. Throughout that time, the Lord reiterated to the people in David's bloodline that He would defend them for the sake of the promise He made to their forefather, David (2 Kings 20:5-6)!

You can redeem time for your children and your children's children. You can make a difference in time starting today. The Redeemer of time lives in you; He is happy to help you redeem time!

Prayer

Great Redeeming God! I look to you for my deliverance and the cleansing of my family line. I want to make an appointment with You, Lord, to do the work that is needed. I will get my calendar and set aside a day or days, whatever You want, and keep this appointment. I know that You will show up! I look forward to experiencing greater blessing upon my life and upon the generations to come. In Jesus' name, amen.

Reflection

1. Has there been a time when you prayed that a disease or sickness would be healed and wondered why your prayer was seemingly not answered? Could the cause be a curse on your personal timeline and be manifesting as a sickness in your body?

2. Is it difficult to break a curse on time? What does it take to do so?

3. What does it mean to make a deal with the devil?

4. Where are curses halted?

16

TIME-WARP HEALING – HEAVEN'S TIME

"It's nothing short of miraculous, which is impossible in the mind of science. Meaning maybe all the claims of spontaneous healings and other miraculous events that have been recorded in history really did happen. Someone, somewhere, activated a higher power beyond space and time, and that power changed matter within time." Ted Dekker[1]

While visiting friends in another city, some of them were sick with bad colds the entire week. Being just a few days until our big Extraordinary Women's Conference (which I host and was one of the main speakers), I didn't have time to be sick!

On the last day of the time with our friends, I felt my throat become sore. Then, the next morning as my husband, Tom, and I got on the road to leave, I had full-blown cold symptoms. Being such a short time until conference, I was doubly upset. I cried out to the Lord for healing and asked Tom to pray for me. As he does often, Tom prayed "Let it be the same here as in Heaven, for Linda". One hour later I was completely well!

As I rejoiced and praised God for healing me, He began to speak to me about how He sped up the sickness and packed the full duration of it into one hour. With this insight, I began to remember other times when I had experienced or witnessed accelerated healing.

One of the very first times when I was jarred into God's swift and immense healing power was when I was a young mom. We'd had only one vehicle; and I was often home with our two young children without transportation, as Tom drove the car to his workplace.

It was a regular day of taking care of the kids at home when something terrible and incredible happened. Our four-year-old son, Gregg, was playing in the family room; while our two-year-old daughter, Tamarah, was standing by the sliding glass door and teasing the dog who was outside. The dog was becoming agitated; so, I walked over and opened the slider to let him in. I had no idea just how upset he was until the door opened and the dog rushed in, leapt up on Tamarah, and bit her hard around her eye. Blood instantly began to gush out as her skin was torn and mangled and she was screaming in pain. It was clearly an emergency situation; yet, I had no car to rush Tamarah to the hospital.

I immediately put my hand over the torn place on Tamarah's face and called our son to come and help me pray. We prayed for her for a minute or two when I suddenly realized that she had completely quieted. I removed my hand from her face and was stunned to see that the wound had already healed! There was nothing but a scar (which she still carries today as a reminder of the miracle)! To say the least, I was astonished, overjoyed, in awe, & praising Jesus! To this day, no one but me knows the extent of the injury because it was healed in the blink of an eye!

As I prayed for Tamarah to be healed on earth as she was in Heaven, the injury was removed out of earth-time and put into Heaven-time. The injury was healed as the healing accelerated, leaving only a scar to tell the story of the terrible injury. As my son and I called to the Lord from our small place on earth, He answered us in the freedom of infinite-timeless-Heaven!

Although God has given each one of us the possibility of the miraculous happening at any time, most people don't flow in the miraculous because they are tethered to earthly structures. Most hardly know when they are earthly-minded and in agreement with the collective observation of the majority, simply because that shared agreement is accepted as normal. My little four-year-old son, who had agreed with me in prayer for Tamarah's healing, had no earthly laws of physics in his soul, nor any collective agreement with unbelievers. Children are often able to access the faith-realm and break the constraints of time!

More Than One Place

If this book were a fiction book, the concept of *sped-up healing* might be viewed as *cool* or, "I wish we could do that." But to truly believe that we can pray for people and see them instantly healed takes real faith. The miracles found in the ministry of Jesus Christ, and the way in which He represented the Kingdom of God, are not fictional ideas. Therefore, to comprehend the teaching of Jesus Christ in regard to *time and space* could be challenging if you are using a mind wired with old programming and a collection of secular viewpoints.

For years, I read Scripture from the viewpoint of the denomination in which I was raised. When I read the following words of Jesus Christ, I always missed that He was talking while simultaneously being in two places, on earth and in Heaven: *"Now I am no longer in the world, but these are in the world, and I come to You, Holy Father, keep through Your name those whom You have given Me, that they may be one as We are. While I was with them in the world, I kept them in Your name. Father, I desire that they also whom You gave Me may be with Me where I am, that they may behold My glory which You have given Me; for You loved Me before the foundation of the world"* (John 17:10-12, 24). Jesus Christ was right now in Heaven and right now on the earth; Jesus wanted His disciples to be able to be, and to see, like Him. The Lord didn't say, "Where I will be", the Lord said, in present tense, *"Where I am!"*

Throughout the book of John, we find the Lord speaking of being in two places at once. For example, where was Jesus when He said, ". . . *the Son of Man who is in heaven"* (John 3:12-13)? He was sitting talking with a leader in Israel! Jesus Christ was always walking in both realities and helping people come with Him. That leader (and we also, who are sons and daughters of God), should know about heavenly things. "If I have told you earthly things and you do not believe, how will you believe if I tell you heavenly things?"

As we study the words of Jesus in the Bible, we find that He taught obsessively about perception. Consider these words from Jesus about the unseen-seen harvest: *"Do you not say, 'There are still four months and then comes the harvest'? Behold, I say to you, lift up your eyes and look at the fields, for they are already white for harvest"* (John 4:35).

Lift up your eyes to look where?

The Lord told His disciples that they were stuck seeing things in earth-time; He desired for them to see in heaven-time. Jesus might have said it like this: *"You say four months until the harvest, but I say . . ."* (picture Him lifting His hand and sweeping it across the desert landscape), "Lift your eyes - change your perception - and in that perception you will see a realm beyond time in which the harvest is already ripe, now, not in four months." He wasn't looking at the unripe fields, Jesus was looking above and beyond!

Jesus called this seeing realm the Kingdom of Heaven and eternal life. He says it is now, not in some distant future, as many suppose. Through a shift in perception, our entire lives can change. This is the basis for all that is miraculous: the shifting of our perception of the material world beyond time and space, and up to Almighty God.

The harvest is plentiful (already ripe) but the workers are few; because few see above, they do not know that the harvest is already ripe. Most people see below and view the field that appears to be filled with tiny plants. The Lord wants us to see what He sees; therefore, ask the Lord of the harvest to send out workers into his harvest field who see the Kingdom that is now present.

I was recently talking with a woman who is a missionary overseas. She stated that workers were desperately needed, just as Jesus had said, *"The workers are few."* I encouraged her that Jesus was wanting us to pray for workers who see, not just more people to do a job. The Lord of the harvest desires seers who see what He sees (in this case, a ripe harvest)!

There are two worlds to see in this breadth of existence. At any given moment, you have in mind one or the other, depending on how you choose to see. The Lord said that we can step beyond the common explanation of time and space and see what cannot be seen with earthly eyes.

The blockage in seeing as Jesus desires for us to see could be ignorance. For example: for those of us who are western believers, we may not understand the magnitude of the significance of the timeframe of the harvest. There is no doubt that the disciples of Jesus knew the facts about seedtime and harvest. For them the barley was sown in the ground, and four months later the harvest came. But even more important was the fact that the barley harvest was the time of one of the four major feasts on the Jewish calendar - it was the time of Passover! During that sacred and holy season every year, the Jews would gather to meet with God. In fact, the Jews designed their entire life around this calendar. Their devotion to God was that they would meet with Him on holy and sacred days - such as Feast of Tabernacles, Pentecost, Passover; their lives were structured in a way to say, "We meet with God on these certain days and times."

When the Lord Jesus declared to His disciples that the harvest was already ripe, it must have been incredibly upsetting to their mindsets. Families all over Israel were anticipating the harvest-time festival like we anticipate Christmas coming in December (not the end of August!). Listen to what He says, *"Don't you say four more months and then the harvest? I tell you, LIFT UP YOUR EYES, and see the fields are already white for harvest!"* Right NOW!

Jesus was speaking to the fact that He is the fulfillment: *You don't have to wait for the barley harvest to celebrate Passover; I am your Passover! You don't have to wait for seven more weeks after Passover to celebrate Pentecost; I am your Pentecost! I am your feast of Tabernacle; I am your harvest; I am your holiday; I am your festival; I am your feast! THAT DAY IS TODAY! I am what you are looking for NOW!*

The Now God Sees

Most cannot comprehend that the timeline of a person's life is all *now* to God. A parent who is worried about their wayward son is caught in the moment, anxious whether that son will turn to God. But if that same parent could see their son at 35 years of age (or 50, or even 85 years) bowing his knee in repentance, that parent's present would be liberated.

I often encourage worried parents to ask God for prophetic vision into the future of their son or daughter. Many times, Holy Spirit has given such a parent a picture of their child coming to Christ at a future time. This picture is in heaven-time, bringing comfort, peace, and patience to the present earth-time.

We can believe that we can see things to come because we have examples of this happening in Scripture. Just as the Apostle John, a good friend of Jesus, was in the Spirit (as recorded in Revelation), while he was on Earth; he saw things that were past, present, and future. In the Spirit of God, there are no earth-time constraints: only heaven-time; which is, of course, outside of time.

> *"Immediately I was in the Spirit; and behold, a throne set in heaven, and One sat on the throne"* (Revelation 4:2).

REWIRING

To help with rewiring your mind, try reading the following Scripture from Colossians 3:1-3 and Ephesians 2:4-6 (comments interspersed), with no preprogrammed mindset or limitation. You will need the help of Holy Spirit. Invite Him to rewire your thinking as you read the passage, out loud, a couple of times. Be sure to ask Holy Spirit to set you free from every thought that tethers you to earthly thinking! Then read it out loud again.

> *Since, then, I have been raised with Christ (already above), I set my heart on things above (on the spiritual dimension), where Christ is, seated at the right hand of God (right now). I set my mind on things above (on the Kingdom of God), not on earthly things. For I died, and my life is now hidden with Christ in God (in union with God, which is my true state of being right now in this moment). God, who is rich in mercy . . . raised me up together (with Him) and made me sit together in the heavenly places in Christ Jesus (I in Him, He in me) at this moment.*

Now, with your rewired mind (or at least a mind that is open to God's transforming truth) you are ready to read about earth-time and heaven-time, without automatically conforming to the old patterns of this world.

> *"Do not be conformed to this world, but be transformed by the renewing of your mind, that you may prove what is that good and acceptable and perfect will of God."*
> (Romans 12:2)

In God, all things are possible (Matthew 19:26). God is beyond space and time, as is our identity in Him as citizens of Heaven (Philippians 3:20).

Miraculous manifestation in space and time is possible in His identity, in His name.

Earth-Time

Time is a created measurement that is a product of created light. God said, *"Let there be lights in the firmament of the heaven to divide the day from the night; and let them be for signs, and for seasons, and for days, and years"* (Genesis 1:14-18). Without light, there would be no way to measure earth-time. Earth-time is a measurement confined to earth and therefore one of earth's characteristics. All of earth is subject to the rule of mankind (as we learned earlier in this book). Therefore, as those who have been called by God to subdue the earth, does it not follow that *we* hold jurisdiction over the creation called *time*?

Time was made to serve man, not the other way around.

Insights About Earth-Time

As humans, we know that we live in the measurement called *time* on earth. Why did God create it for us, being as He is not caught in it, as we would be and often are? (Or are we who are created in God's image *caught in time*? Are we able to overcome time as children of our timeless Father God?)

Recently Holy Spirit convicted me for something I have said many times (in complaint): "I am caught in time and space." Caught: limited by, and in captivity to, time. As the Lord convicted me, He showed me the following examples in the Bible of His people who were not caught in time and space:

- Paul wrote in 2 Corinthians 12:2-14, *"Such a one was caught up to the third heaven ... he was caught up into Paradise."*
- John wrote in Revelation 17:3, 21:10, *"He carried me away in the Spirit into the wilderness ... He carried me away in the Spirit to a great and high mountain ..."*
- Ezekiel said in Ezekiel 2:12-14, *"The Spirit lifted me up ... lifted me up and took me away..."*

As I read these examples, I repented and asked Father God to deliver me from my own tethering thoughts that held me captive. After all, I know by experience that being caught up into the glory of God's presence supersedes *time* and brings me into a place of blessed timelessness!

According to Science

According to those who speak as authorities on earthly knowledge, a literal definition of *time* is illusive. Various scientists have described *time* by calling it a taskmaster, an illusion, a dimension, or just an innovation of man to help us keep track of ourselves. Time is an observed phenomenon, by means of which human beings' sense and record changes in the environment and in the universe.

Most of us know that time was measured in larger segments (parts of the day) in early history. A sundial (or shadow clock) certainly didn't show hours, minutes, or seconds like we live by today. Life was *slower* back then. Which also brings us to the relative slipperiness of time. At times, time seems to move very s-l-o-w-l-y; and at other times, it evaporates. One's perception appears to play a major role in how they experience time.

The earth has been divided into what humans have established and named, 'time zones,' and according to which I have been able fly *back in time* while flying west on an airplane!

Time is a Useful God-Created Measurement

Living in the realm of clocks is normal for our modern times, and these instruments can be helpful tools. Clocks are a relatively new invention, created to help people coordinate events and, in general, keep their lives in order (getting to work *on time*, etc.)

Our century is not far removed from the time when individuals first began to strap a device on an arm and measure every minute of their lives! The very first wristwatch was worn in the 17th century by a Frenchman who used a piece of string to attach his pocket watch to his wrist. That watch registered the increments of an hour and called greater attention to time, as time was watched on his watch.

Can you imagine the freedom our early ancestors lived in with no exact time constraints of clocking in and out? No stress of being late until the sun went down (remember Joseph and Mary didn't look for Jesus until they had traveled an entire day without Him (Luke 2:44-46)? There was no train to leave on the dot or bus schedule, only donkeys and walkers with lots of time.

It is interesting to note that in the middle ages, church life, and specifically monks calling others to prayer, made timekeeping devices a necessity in daily life. The earliest medieval European clockmakers were Christian monks. A clock's purpose was to unite people in prayer at a certain time. Now that is certainly a good use of time!

Calculating Time

On Earth, we measure the motion of the moon to calculate a month; and, we measure the motion of earth's rotation to calculate a day. Without the planetary system, there would be no calendar.

For a normal three-day-cold, we expect the earth to rotate on its axis three times and then we will feel better (Be glad we don't live on Venus where one day is 243 earth-days!). So, with a cold we expect to feel pretty miserable for three days and then kind of lousy for a week (seven 1000 miles per hour spins of the earth as we see the sun rise and set seven times). Is it possible to speed up sickness without speeding up the earth's rotation? I believe it is.

On Earth, gravity trumps time. Time doesn't move at the same speed everywhere because it is subject to the gravitational pull. Time, as Einstein discovered, is affected by gravity. If you place extremely accurate clocks on every floor of a skyscraper, they will all tick at different rates. The clocks on the lower floors (closer to the center of the earth where gravity is stronger), will tick a little slower than the ones on the top floors. Gravity pulls on time. As we go higher, time moves faster.

How can we, as Doctors of the Cross, who have been called by Jesus to heal people, pull the sick up and out of the slow-pull of the gravity of earth-time and put them into the higher heaven-time?

Lifting People Up to God

No wonder Scripture instructs us to set our minds on things above (Colossians 3:1-3), where gravity does not slow down healing! Miracles happen in a higher realm than earth-time.

In preparing for the ministry of Healing Rooms at Horizon Church, Holy Spirit instructed me to exhort the Doctors of the Cross to lift the patients up before the Throne of Grace (Hebrews 4:16). Father God wants us to help the sick come up into God's restorative presence (heaven-time), the place where they are already well.

Remember that the Lord Jesus Christ often lifted His eyes to talk to His Father who is above in Heaven: *"[Jesus] took the five loaves and the two fish, and looking up to heaven, He blessed...the loaves"* (Matthew 14:19); *"Looking up to heaven, [Jesus] sighed, and said to him, 'Ephphatha,' that is, 'Be opened'"* (Mark 7:34); *"Jesus lifted up His eyes and said, 'Father, I thank You that You have heard Me'"* (John 11:41); *"Jesus spoke these words, lifted up His eyes to heaven, and said: 'Father, the hour has come. Glorify Your Son, that Your Son also may glorify You'"* (John 17:1). Clearly, the Lord looked up at Heaven; that place above determined how He ministered!

I have been waiting to write this chapter until Holy Spirit gave me further understanding. You see, I had a question. If God sped up the sickness, did that mean that one's whole life sped up too? Did it mean that a person aged quicker because time sped up in his or her body?

The Lord showed me that since Heaven has no disease, no sickness, and no pain (see Revelation 21:4), heaven-time has none of these either. Praying for a person, according to Jesus Christ's way, *"Your Kingdom come; Your will be done on earth as it is in heaven"* (Matthew 6:10), on behalf of an individual, is lifting them up into God's heavenly place. We can lift people to God in prayer and bring them up into the atmosphere of heaven, where there is no time or entropy.

In the 1870s, an Austrian physicist first coined the term *entropy*. Entropy is just a measure of how disorderly things are; this theory states that things move forward into greater disorder (the second law of thermodynamics). But, the theory of entropy does not take faith into account. Faith is a higher law than entropy; faith is outside of time.

Since there is no deterioration in Heaven, no entropy at all, everything improves there, always! And since there is no deterioration (ageing) in Heaven, sickness can speed up and disappear from an individual without speeding up his or her age. The changes that happen in the atmosphere of God's heaven are all good! The bad (sickness, disease, death) cannot stay in heaven's atmosphere, while the good (wholeness) thrives there.

Therefore, let us with full confidence lift the sick up to the timeless One who heals! How do we lift them up? Remember that the Lord instructed His ministers to tell the sick that *"the Kingdom of God has come near you"* (Luke 10:9). We help people to believe that God is near them with healing. We cannot force individuals to receive the Kingdom; yet we can certainly use our vocal cords to try and pry them from the earth with our faith!

While writing this chapter, I was reminded of a phenomenon which C.S. Lewis spoke of in his fictional work, *Out of the Silent Planet*[2], and to which astronauts attest. Lewis wrote of a fictional character, Ransom, who was abducted from earth and carried into space. After the initial shock of the kidnapping, Ransom began to experience euphoria. Having left the Earth's atmosphere and traveled high above the enemy's rule (*"the whole world is under the sway of the evil one"*, 1 John 5:19), Ransom "became aware of another and more spiritual cause for his lightening and exultation of heart. A nightmare, long engendered in the modern mind by the mythology that follows in the wake of science, was falling off him. He had read of space [and] at the back of his thinking for years had lurked the dismal fancy of the black, cold vacuity, the utter deadness, which was supposed to separate the worlds. He had not known how it affected him until now-now that the very name 'Space' seemed a blasphemous libel for this empyrean ocean of radiance . . . he felt life pouring into him from it every moment. . .Space was the wrong name. Older thinkers had been wiser when they named it simply the heavens."

What Lewis described in his fictional writing is verified in the testimonies of real-life astronauts who have experienced "Space Euphoria" upon leaving the Earth's atmosphere. According to astronaut, Ed White, he experienced "an out-of-this-world happiness, only accessible beyond the atmosphere."

We can and must lift people up in prayer; for when they rise above the pull of earth, where the enemy has sway, they receive a measure of healing.

This is possible since the King instructed that we ask for His Kingdom to meet us, *"on earth as it is in heaven"* (Matthew 6:10)!

As we lift people to heaven in prayer, remember that healing often comes as a seed, and a seed can be stolen (Luke 8:12). We cannot force people to have receptive soil. We can only do our part to hoist them up and expect miracles. May we not become weary or discouraged due to a patient's receptivity, but may we continue to plant seeds that spring up into life!

Earth-Time is a Measurement That Can Build Faith

Receiving many prayer requests daily, I have the opportunity to "send the healing word" out at God-speed toward individuals I always expect miracles. I often picture in my mind the name of Jesus going to the person in need, as I lift him or her to the Lord and speak His name. I know that the wind of His Spirit goes forth to the individual and lifts him or her up. Of course, I can't control the person's response to that wind. Their perception and acceptance play a role. But I can do my part to echo what God has said: *"He sent His word and healed them and delivered them from their destructions"* (Psalm 107:20).

When I hear back from an individual that peace flowed in at the very hour I prayed, I am always encouraged. Taking note of time can build faith, as in the account of the nobleman's son: *"The nobleman said to [Jesus], 'Sir, come down before my child dies!' Jesus said to him, 'Go your way; your son lives.' So the man believed the word that Jesus spoke to him, and he went his way. And as he was now going down, his servants met him and told him, saying, 'Your son lives!' Then he inquired of them the hour when he got better. And they said to him, 'Yesterday at the seventh hour the fever left him.' So the father knew that it was at the same hour in which Jesus said to him, 'Your son lives.' And he himself believed, and his whole household"* (John 449-53). Now that's a Healing Revival!

Prayer:

Father in Heaven, even as You said to Your servant, John, "Come up here" (Revelation 4:1), I greatly desire to come up higher with You! Teach me to live in the atmospheres of heaven where You are. Change my old pathways into new pathways in You. And may I lift many people up to that healing place where You are. Heal me, Oh God, and heal many people through me! In the name of Jesus, amen!

Reflection

1. What was the reason for the expansion of time-keeping devices, according to our church fathers?
   How are individuals called to prayer in this age?

2. While talking with His Father in prayer, Jesus stated that He was *"no longer in the world"* (John 17:11). Where was the Lord Jesus and what do you think He meant by what He said?

3. When Jesus Christ spoke of the harvest being ripe, He stood with His disciples, looking at a harvest that was months away from full growth. Why did He tell them that the barley was ready to pick *right now*?

4. How do we lift a person up to God in prayer and what happens to time at that moment?

   Are you ready for a transformation of your mind and are you willing to see as Jesus sees?

17

HEALING REVIVAL!

A Healing Revival is here and this time we will not cycle around in a circle of hope, disappointment, hope, disappointment . . . This time, we are flying off the top of that circle in full-force-faith. May each one of us fan into flame the gift of God and may our corporate fire burn brighter and brighter!

The environment was ripe for a visitation from Heaven. Worship had been dynamic with a stream of God's present presence, and worshippers with lifted hands had been crying out for revival. Communion elements had been given out and the atmosphere had been cleared, as individuals collectively ate and drank the symbols representing the Lord's body and blood. As worship rose up again, I called out to the Lord of Hosts to send His angels to touch each present person with a hot coal of revived love. Expectant, I looked out across the congregation and could see fires lit in several people - many dim and a few bright.

I moved forward to the platform to address the people and to share with them my request of Father God during the worship a few moments earlier. I told about the coals of fire that had been distributed to them by the hosts of heaven. I explained that this happened in the Bible when Isaiah was touched by a hot coal which an angel brought to him from the altar of heaven (Isaiah 6:6). Then I enlisted the people to form groups and pray for one another to receive the revival fire of God into their lives. Across the sanctuary the cries rose up for "Revival!"

After this impassioned prayer-time and the heard cry of God's people, we closed the doors, turned off the lights, and headed to our homes. But the coals of revival continue to burn in individual hearts; we must each continue to fan them into flame daily.

Healing Revival

How does revival come to a particular location? Being a student of revival and having read numerous books about the details of what happened when revival occurred, the pre-revival *formula* still alluded me. Apart from the expected components (passionate prayer, hunger for God's Word, love for people, and a desperation for *more of God*), I didn't know the way to breakthrough into in a true Holy Spirit ignited outpouring.

The statement, "Healing Revival" is not one that I can remember ever hearing in my lifetime. When Holy Spirit conveyed that short phrase to me one day during prayer, I was dramatically impacted. I have prayed for, and looked for, revival most of my adult life; yet I never thought of it coming through manifest healing. With that short phrase, I had revelation and understood that individuals could be awakened (revived) into the greatness of God's love for them *personally* through His kind curing touch!

One obstacle to be cleared out in order to usher in a healing revival is: a mind that disputes with God. This can also be a major roadblock to an individual experiencing their own miraculous healing. Remember the account of the Lord Jesus teaching in the synagogue in Nazareth where many people believed His words (Mark 6:1-6)? But then the people's minds took over their hearts and they began to question Jesus' qualifications and dispute about His heritage. Due to the way those people consciously *thought*, the story ends with the words, "Now He could do no mighty work there except that He laid His hands on a few sick people and healed them" (verse 5). The next thing that happened was that Jesus left that place - a location where revival could have taken place because the Reviver Himself, Jesus Christ, had been right there at that appointed moment.

No doubt many of the people felt disappointed as Jesus left Nazareth that day. The Savior of the world had gone from them and so had their hope. Isn't it interesting that disappointment can stifle hope; and without hope, revival, which restores hope and revives life, "could do no mighty work there"?

The Problem with Disappointment

A key insight about the harmful influence of disappointment is found in Proverbs 11:12, "Hope differed makes the heart sick". **Hope deferred** is referencing disappointments in life. Where there had been hope - an expectation for something good, it had been delayed, suspended, and lost. The progression in this Scripture shows us that this loss of hope can actually make one's heart sick and can also explain why there is sickness - even in the body of Christ.

Since disappointments are common in every person's life, we may accept them as 'just part of life' and not grasp the impact which a pile of disappointments can have on our faith. *It is often disappointment that takes away our passion, hope and our fire.*

We have all had many disappointments in one way or another, some worse than others. For some there has been terrible loss in family - tragic divorce, abuse, or wayward kids. Maybe you fasted, prayed, and cried out to God for restoration, and what you prayed for did not happen in the way you had hoped.

Over the years of our ministry, Tom and I have talked with many disappointed people who have come to us for help. Ironically, the very promises in the Bible and the prophetic words that were received from God, became the subject of an individual's complaint. The bright hope which came through a prophetic word was lost as time went by - hope deferred made the heart sick.

One such person, a disappointed woman, came to see me, asking for help. She began with the words, "God did not come through for me," and then she told me her story. Years earlier, she and her husband had been prophesied over that they would have a powerful ministry together. But her husband had been unfaithful to her and now she was walking around under a dark cloud of disappointment. She did not understand why God gave this prophesy and it did not come about. She had anticipated something good that did not happen. With her mouth, she refused to blame God; but underneath, frustration and cynicism were evident. Her diminished trust level manifested in an unwillingness to take risks any longer as she expressed that 'things just don't work out for her.' She had become like a wounded soldier who had fallen into a ditch along the side of the road of life. When I asked her if she believed that God is good, she replied, "Yes, God is good *to some.*"

As we worked through her disappointment before the Lord, in open honesty, she began to see differently. She saw that the Lord had been working to draw her husband into a place of integrity and draw him into the purpose for his life - but God gave him a choice. God brought the prophetic word to call them to another level. The wife was willing, but the husband was not.

She also saw that her husband's poor choices did not remove her from a place of significance in the Kingdom. No one else's sin could remove her from significance or a place in ministry. It was time for her to let go of the disappointment, step out in faith, and be brave again. God healed her heart that day and her health began to improve. Today she has a burning heart for God instead of a sick heart!

The stories of disappointment's smothering influence are common in the lives of good people who don't understand that disappointment can be a fire-quencher. Disappointment must be dealt with continually in order to keep the coal of revival fire burning in our hearts.

The disciples of Jesus burned with a steady, internal, fire. They were enthusiastic to the point of complete abandon. How did they persevere through all of the trials and persecutions which they endured? I believe that the love that burned in their hearts compelled them to keep going.

A Burning Heart Versus a Sick Heart

What Does a burning heart look like? One of the Doctors of the Cross, Bill*, who ministers at our Healing Rooms, had a recent situation, which revealed a heart that burns for Jesus.

Bill had an older brother, Frank*, who had never submitted his life to God. This brother (who lives in another state) was diagnosed with a very serious disease a few months ago. Upon hearing this news, Bill, and his wife, Kari*, immediately rearranged their schedules and priorities in order to go and visit Frank. Helping his brother come to salvation through Christ Jesus was one of Bill's great hopes and prayers. Bill had encouraged Frank many times in the past to receive Jesus as his Savior and was always rebuffed.

During the hospital visit, Bill sowed more seeds in prayer as he stood in faith for his brother. Bill and Kari returned home with even greater determination to see Frank saved. They enlisted more people to pray for his salvation and continued to believe that God would bring breakthrough.

A few weeks later, Bill's brother was taken to the hospital a second time in very serious condition. Once again, Bill and Kari rearranged their schedules, and were quickly on the road to help Frank.

After arriving at the hospital, it wasn't very long before Bill was once again explaining to his brother that he needed to be ready to meet God. At that time, Frank was unable to respond, but Bill believed his brother could still hear him. Later that morning, Frank was awake and somewhat coherent; so, Bill talked to him again about God, Heaven, and receiving Jesus. Once again, Frank refused to submit to God. But Bill-of-the-burning-heart did not give up.

A little while later, as Bill was talking to his brother once again, Frank was having difficulty responding and being understood because of a breathing mask he had on and kept having to repeat himself. Finally, Frank became so irritated that he said, "why don't they take this thing off, I'm going to die anyway." In hope, Bill asked his brother a third time, "If that's how you feel then you need to pray with me and receive Jesus so you can go to Heaven." This time, wonder of wonders, Frank said "yes", and Bill led his brother in a prayer of salvation, receiving Jesus as his Savior. The Holy Spirit enabled Frank to know and understand what he had prayed. Praise God!

A few minutes later Bill's wife came in and found Bill with a shining face, full of light! His face was glowing with the fire in his heart, for his brother's salvation. It was just a few hours later that Frank walked into Heaven!

What could compel a man to persevere like Bill did, to bring a lost one to salvation? A bright hope that does not disappoint!

"Having been justified by faith, we have peace with God through our Lord Jesus Christ, through whom also we have access by faith into this grace in which we stand, and rejoice in hope of the glory of God. And not only that, but we also glory in tribulations, knowing that tribulation produces perseverance; and perseverance, character; and character, hope. Now

hope does not disappoint, because the love of God has been poured out in our hearts by the Holy Spirit who was given to us" (Romans 5:1-5).

For those of us who greatly desire to see people saved, families healed, and the Kingdom of God manifest, we must cultivate the flame of hope and resist the sway of disappointment. We cannot afford the hopelessness of a sick heart; for there is much the Savior of the world wants to do in and through us!

"Fan into flame the gift of God . . . For God did not give us a spirit of timidity, but a spirit of power, of love and a sound mind" (2 Timothy 1:6-7).

God's Goodness

Disappointments in life can form in any number of ways: not yet seeing the healing of a relative or friend; waiting for the conversion of someone you have been praying for a long time; losing hope for the restoration of a broken relationship; lack of success in business or a hoped for promotion . . . you fill in the blank. Disappointment. You prayed and believed - you had a word from God and then it didn't happen.

For some people, God wired them in such a way that they are more sensitive than others and they have experienced disappointments in ways others discount. This sensitivity compounds the dilemma as such a person may become disappointed in themselves and in the way God made them.

Whether your disappointment is toward God, yourself, life in general, or toward other people, disappointment is something that must be addressed with God. Unless it is brought to God, it will fester and eventually bring harm to you. A pile of hopeless experiences creates soil that the tempter will attempt to plant lies into. As those lies take root, they draw us into a position to question the goodness of God for us personally. When we start breaking down in our concept of who God is, we are vulnerable to the father of lies, the deceiver himself (John 8:44). A lie comes to be established in an individual's thought life, so that the personification of that lie can take it to a supernatural level of bondage. No wonder hope deferred makes the heart sick.

Lost hope usually comes after some sort of disappointment or trauma and can bring someone to a place of vulnerability. At the end of every disappointment we are in a brief season of extreme vulnerability. If we could take this into the natural, it's as if our immune system is broken down. Whereas we are not usually prone to becoming sick, there seems to be one illness after another.

Hope is the spiritual immune system of the soul. When a person walks in the joyful anticipation of good things happening, there is prosperity and strength in the soul. But when there is a loss of hopeful expectation, there can also be a loss of immunity. To strengthen ourselves, both during and after times of disappointment, we need to recognize our need and take steps to be healed.

Losing Heart

A few years ago, I was invited to travel to Turkey where I was one of the main speakers at a missionary conference. Missionaries from all across the Middle East and Northern Africa gathered for connection and encouragement. Can you imagine the caliber of these selfless ministers of the Kingdom? These people who ministered in the most dangerous of circumstances were, to me, the cream of the crop: people who suffered persecution and persevered.

I remember one specific missionary who attended the conference and ministered in Iran. Right before the conference, he'd been beaten for his testimony of Jesus Christ. He had been thrown over a wall at the border between Iran and Iraq and left for dead. Revived by the Lord and rescued by a stranger, he had found a way to get to the conference in Turkey (north of Iraq). As he told me this story, his face shown with the light and love of Jesus. All he wanted was to get back into Iran and continue preaching the gospel of Jesus.

You might be able to imagine the intimidation and humility I felt as I prepared to address such amazing saints of God. What could I say to them?

It was on the second day of the conference, as I was teaching for the second time, that something supernatural happened. I was speaking on the subject of guarding the thought life, when my eyes were suddenly opened to the spiritual dimension in the room. What I saw, all across the crowd of people, were heavy and oppressive spirits sitting on individuals. I was momentarily shaken and shocked. Then I heard the prompting of Holy Spirit, "Bring deliverance, many have lost heart."

I paused right in the middle of the message and told the crowd that Holy Spirit had just spoken to me that many of them had lost heart. Led by Holy Spirit's prompting, I turned to 2 Corinthians 4:1 and spoke these words from the Scripture, *"Therefore, since we have this ministry, as we have received mercy, we do not lose heart."* Looking up, I asked, "Have you lost heart?"

You could've heard a pin drop as the words pierced the atmosphere and hit home. It was clear that the majority of those wonderful people had lost heart (become disappointed) and had grown weary in well doing. I turned to Galatians 6:9 and read out loud, *"Let us not grow weary while doing good, for in due season we shall reap if we do not lose heart."* Then I asked, "Have you lost heart while waiting for God to move in your ministry?" The conviction in the room was tangible.

I led those cream-of-the-crop missionaries in a prayer of repentance and encouraged them to express to God that they were sorry for giving place to disappointment and weariness. Because the conviction of Holy Spirit was so thick, voices were raised in heartfelt prayer all across the meeting room.

The next thing that happened was amazing! The enemy lost territory and deliverance began to take place. I commanded the spirit of weariness to go to the Cross; I told the spirit of heaviness to go with it; I told disappointment that it was bound, and I proclaimed that the spirit of infirmity was finished and could not stay - all in the Name of Jesus Christ and His shed blood! Unclean spirits began to leave individuals! It was like a mass exodus of shadows going up and out of the room! Then rivers of joy flooded that place and the transformation was utterly remarkable!

During the remaining three days of that conference, many, many people gave testimony of renewed joy, strength, and freedom! It looked like revival!

> *". . . [God gave] them beauty for ashes, The oil of joy for mourning, The garment of praise for the spirit of heaviness . . ."* (Isaiah 61:3).

If God's missionary workers were in need of deliverance from disappointment, it is safe to say that we all need help from time to time.

How to be Clear

In whatever arena disappointment is currently trying to take over your hope, stop and recognize that this is a temptation. If you prayed for someone to be healed and that person died, the natural way of thinking would be to decide that you are not as willing to pray for anyone again. This kind of thinking may lead you to deflect opportunities to pray for healing. You might even put a religious covering over your disappointment and rationalize that another person has a stronger anointing and recommend they pray instead of you. The more honest answer would be, "I no longer have hope that God will heal a serious illness since *so and so* died." When you hear your disappointment come out of your mouth, repent, and take the steps toward getting free. If we continue to let disappointment influence our actions, the only outcome is sin.

The number one reason why people stop taking risks and going after the miraculous is disappointment. We cannot reach our destiny without risk; we cannot help others without stepping out in faith.

If you have noticed yourself deflecting ministry opportunities, this is an alert that you may have lost hope someplace along the way. Remember that hope deferred *makes the heart sick.* Loss of hope opens the door to spiritual disease and often results in infirmity within the physical body. If this is you, take heart; the problem has been pinpointed and you have the Healer available!

Before we look at the steps toward freedom from disappointment, let us address one more area of disappointment - one that results in great loss. We all have questions as to why one person was healed and why the next person we prayed for was not. Could it be that a person who was healed and did not continue to contend for his or her healing, ended up worse off for the healing?

Individuals who come into our Healing Rooms are sometimes carried on the wings of the faith of the house. This can happen, as we see in the man, Saul (1 Samuel 10:11). United with a company of prophets, while with them, Saul had their gifts operating in himself. But when he left that company, Saul eventually reverted back to be an insecure man.

So, we see that being among people of God who operate in His gifts can carry a person for a while. Then it is up to the individual to choose to have faith of their own.

Might it be possible that Father God, in all His wisdom, knows that healing a certain individual will bring harm in the long run? Might the blessing of healing, bestowed upon a person who does not have the fortitude to walk it out, open that person to disappointments that may fester? Would it have been better to not have been healed in the first place? Might this be part of what Jesus meant when He said, "When an unclean spirit goes out of a man, he goes through dry places, seeking rest, and finds none. Then he says, 'I will return to **my** house from which I came.' And when he comes, he finds it empty, swept, and put in order. Then he goes and takes with him seven other spirits more wicked than himself, and they enter and dwell there; and the last state of that man is worse than the first" (Matthew 12:43-45).

If it was a spirit of infirmity that was cast out of the person in an atmosphere of faith, and then that person goes back into their normal lifestyle, without guarding against that spirit coming back through waging spiritual warfare, what might happen? The spirit of infirmity comes back in with disappointment, self-pity, anger, and others. Remember, it was God who warned us about this; He does not want a man to be in a worse state than before, due to blessing.

As a minister of healing, let us never question God's goodness because of what we see, nor blame ourselves when someone walks out "unhealed." It is our job to heal and God's job to do what is best with the person in the long run.

What to do When Disappointed

When you recognize that you are disappointed, this is the time to cut down the busyness. Restored hope is vital to your life and well-being! Deliverance from disappointment must be pursued. This is not the time to clutter your life with busyness. You have got to make time to sit with "the God of all hope" (Romans 15:13).

As you talk with God, be honest - not in accusation, but in pouring out your heart to Him. "Lord, I don't understand, we prayed all the prayers and did everything we could. I realize I am vulnerable, and I come to You for help."

- Be patient with God, because impatience is a form of unbelief. Impatience is what we begin to feel when we doubt the wisdom of God's timing or the goodness of His direction. Therefore, determine to wait on God and *believe* He will answer you.
- Choose to believe that God is good and that He will reward you: "He is a rewarder of those who diligently seek Him." Stir up your expectation to receive God's reward in the way He chooses, knowing He will be good to you (Hebrews 11:6).
- Make room for Holy Spirit to help you abound in hope through His power, not yours.

"Now may the God of hope fill you with all joy and peace in believing, that you may abound in hope by the power of the Holy Spirit" (Romans 15:13).

Use the promises of God to persuade your heart that God is always good and that His way is perfect (Psalm 18:30). Fill your mouth and use your vocal cords to read words from the Psalms - there is healing in the Word. The Psalms contain every emotion for life. Keep reading until you identify your issue. As you read *out loud*, you may find yourself weeping and not have a clue as to why. Look at what you just read, and you will see the cause of the hidden pain that has just surfaced. Then you can talk openly and honestly with God about your disappointment.

This may take a lot of time in the Word. Be careful to guard against thinking that you can't afford the time; because if you want to be whole, you will have to take time eventually. Living with a sick heart invites disease as a normal course of life and would require your time, later, to deal with it.

If we don't take care of the issues of the heart, we will remove ourselves from the umbrella of Divine protection. This loss is not the Lord's plan for His people, nor is it okay with Him. But when we remove ourselves because of our own unwillingness to deal with the disappointments and issues of the heart, there are consequences.

Camp in the Psalms until you are healed! You may stay before God for several hours or even days but persevere as you pray and pour through them. You will find your word, your promise, and you will find that thing that brings you peace beyond your understanding.

"Do not be sluggish but imitators of those who through faith and patience inherit the promises" (Hebrews 6:12).

Receive peace from the Lord. The peace that passes understanding will invade your life if you are willing to wait for answers - even if this means waiting until Eternity. To know the answer to 'why' concerning your disappointment is not the real necessity for your freedom. Dropping your complaint and fear into the crystal sea of God's peace will bring you peace. If you will not allow that peace beyond your understanding to come to you, you will probably not gain the understanding you are asking for.

It is vital that we know how to receive the peace of the Lord! We must learn how to not only perceive with our understanding (mind), but to receive the peace that bypasses understanding. The Spirit of God works so deeply and profoundly. Often, I go into my time of prayer troubled about something. And then, although the outside circumstances haven't changed, I emerge transformed and happy because I received peace from God that I cannot explain to you. God has given me a peace that has settled on me which is beyond my understanding; I am at ease. Why is this so important? "Dis-ease" brings disease. But peace brings me to a place of ease and a place of trust.

We must all guard ourselves against allowing the power of disappointment to have influence over us; we must not embrace disappointment as a legitimate companion. Remind yourself that disappointment can take away your passion, hope, and fire. Remind yourself, and believe, that you are part of bringing a Healing Revival and that your burning heart makes a difference for everyone around you.

Lamps Burning

You may wonder why this chapter, *Healing Revival,* is focused on staying free from disappointment. The primary ignition for revival is the fiery coal of hope. When we greatly desire a Holy Spirit awakening among us, we burn with hope every day, and we are always on the lookout for any sign of revival. We look for revival and we celebrate even small indicators of breakthrough.

The Lord Jesus wants your lamp to burn: *"Let your waist be girded and your lamps burning"* (Luke 12:35). The oil of Holy Spirit is our fuel; it is imperative that we always have a full supply. Lost hope brings a gray perspective on life and puts out the bright flame - the very flame we must fan. We will fan the flame if it is our desire to keep it burning. Disappointment diminishes the flame and takes away the willingness to take risks of faith. If God's people do not step out, miracles lay dormant.

Gathering with other people of hope and faith spurs us on. It is important to attend fire lighting events - such as church, conferences, Christian camps, and prayer meetings, where God is moving in power.

> *"Let us hold unswervingly to the hope we profess, for he who promised is faithful. And let us consider how we may spur one another on toward love and good deeds, not giving up meeting together . . ."* (Hebrews 10:23-25).

Some people give up on meeting together because of disappointment. At Horizon Church, we often have testimonies of God's goodness as we see many people healed, delivered, and blessed financially. These kinds of testimonies can elicit varied responses from the listeners. Some people are inspired to hope for miracles of their own, while others may be frustrated in waiting. If disappointment gains a foothold during the wait, this can cause individuals to give up attending church or other revival events.

Recently, I heard a podcast from a healing conference where many of the nation's foremost faith-healers had ministered. At one point, three testimonies in a row were of healing and all three had one thing in common - perseverance. The first two testimonies were from women who had been disabled by disease for 30 years before healing flowed in. The third testimony was from a man who had an infirmity for 21 years. All three were completely healed at that event. Even after so many years of praying and expecting, each of the three persevered, attended yet another healing conference, and each one was healed! Such great examples of pressing forward into healing with hope!

When a Person is Healed

At the Healing Rooms here in Reno-Sparks, Nevada, God is bringing a Healing Revival! If you could look in on the prayer gatherings, you would see Doctors of the Cross preparing for the healing ministry, praying with fervor passion, and love! Seeing people revived by God in body and soul is what revival is about. It is what is on God's heart.

Every month we record the many healings that happen around us. A woman who was healed of stage-four cancer is well and is telling everyone what God did for her! A man who was in constant pain from the waist down was freed and is astonished. The reports are amazing: intestinal issues healed, anxiety healed, joint pain healed, a neck *strangely warmed* and pain gone, fibromyalgia healed, arthritis gone, tumors vanishing, and many more! People who were starving for the reality of God's personal love for them, felt His touch and experienced a healing revival!

At the beginning of this chapter, I shared that I saw some people at church who had burning hearts. How did certain individuals acquire a heart that is on fire for God? One answer is found in the words of some of Jesus' disciples, *"Did not our hearts burn within us while He talked with us on the road, and while He opened the Scriptures to us?"* (Luke 24:32). When the Lord speaks to us through His Word, and through Holy Spirit, we are touched by fire! Almighty God is a passionate God, and He Himself burns with Holy fire: *"Our God is a consuming fire"* (Hebrews 12:29). With Him inside of us, we can't help but burn with His love!

All around us people are bound and in need of a Savior. Where will they go to find healing, forgiveness, and deliverance? May there be a burning heart in you, and may you be a channel for the supernatural power of Holy Spirit to bring healing revival to many people!

"Do not put out the Spirit's fire" (1 Thessalonians 5:19).

An Unquenchable Fire

The natural temperament of a person is prone to ebbs and flows of passion. But the supernatural temperament of a revivalist is subject to a continual blaze, because it is fed by the reality of God's presence, and the ceaselessness of His love! It is Holy Spirit fire, which ignites us and continually regenerates us with the flame of God's eternal love.

Of course, we will have challenges and troubles in this world. But we are those who follow Jesus' promise, *"Take heart, I have overcome the world"* (John 16:33).

Let us call upon God now for that flame of light and life; let us occupy our minds with the wonder of God's love; let us depend on Holy Spirit to keep us in that inexhaustible flame!

Prayer

O Lord, I know that Your compassion for the world has never exhausted itself. I join with you today, and for the rest of my life - in Your pure flame of love for me and for the world. Ignite me in Your love! You have captivated my heart and You are my King and dearest friend. In the name of Jesus, amen.

Reflection

1. Read the following statement from Proverbs 13:12: "Hope deferred makes the heart sick." Take a few moments to ponder the way in which a heart can become sick. What does this warning mean to you personally?

2. Do you have a pile of disappointments in your life? Pause and ask Holy Spirit to show you if you do. Wait on Him to speak.

3. What must you do to become free when disappointments come in your life?

4. Turn to Isaiah 9:6 and read about the burning coal with which an angel touched Isaiah. Are you ready to burn with the fire of God? Will you take that fire and, like Isaiah, say, "here I am, Lord, send me"? Will you help usher in a Healing Revival?

STUDY GUIDE FOR PERSONAL AND GROUP BIBLE STUDY

Chapter 1: Becoming a Doctor of the Cross

1. According to James 5:13-14, what is the cure or relief for suffering?

   What is the directive for the cheerful?

   What is the course of action for the one who is sick?

2. What will this prayer of faith accomplish (James 5:15)?

- Ask the Holy Spirit to expose any unbelief or doubt that you have because of your life experiences. Invite God to give you new revelation about healing.

3. What else may be needed to bring about healing (James 5:16)? What "avails much"?

4. What do you and Elijah have in common (James 5:17)?

- Miracle-producing prayer is not limited to a select few prophets and apostles! You can have the same kind of results that Elijah had (read the story in 1 Kings 17:1; 18:41-46). **The key is faith**. Do you need increased faith? The Word of God instructs us in how to increase our faith. Read Romans 10:17 and then write it here:

5. The instruction about healing in James, turns from physical affliction to spiritual sickness. How can you save a soul from death and cover a multitude of sins (James 5:19-20)?

- Invite God to put someone on your heart who has wandered from the faith. Pause and wait for instruction from the Holy Spirit as to what you need to do to help. What did the Lord say? What will you do?

Chapter 2: How to Receive
Bible Study

Open your Bible to John 11, and get ready to receive deep revelation of who Jesus Christ truly is. Welcome Holy Spirit to change your thinking and to heal your Love Receiver.

1. Who was sick, according to John 11:1?
   Did Jesus Christ care about this man (verse 3)?

2. Did the Lord rush right over to His friend's house to heal him (verse 6)? Are you willing to wait for God to perform a bigger miracle *later* instead of the small one you are asking for today? What are you asking God to do for you?

3. What was Lazarus' sickness *for* according to verse 4?
   Who else had a sickness for this purpose (John 9:2-3)?
   It is easy to forget that we were made for God and not He for us. Are you willing to tell God that He can do whatever will bring Him the most glory with your own life?

4. How many days had Lazarus already been dead and, in a tomb (verses 17 and 39)?
   Did this interval stop the purposes of God from being fulfilled?
   Who is Jesus Christ according to the declaration found in John 11:25?
   What is your answer to the question Jesus asks in the last line of verse 26?

5. Read about the way Martha and Mary approached Jesus, about the delay in His coming to help them (verse 21 and verse 32)? Have you ever talked to God in this way? When?

Did Jesus care about how Martha and Mary felt (verses 33-35 and 38)?
Does God care about your heartaches, worries and fears?
Take a few moments and bring your troubles to God. As you do, let Him know that you trust Him and that you know He will answer in the best possible way.
Read John 11:40, and as you do, commit to memorizing this amazing promise!

6. Jesus Christ said that Father God always hears Him! Why did He tell us this according to John 11:42?

7. What did Jesus Christ say to the dead man (verse 43)? What happened next?
Who did Jesus command to loose the man (verse 44)?
The Lord Almighty, Jesus Christ, is always calling people forth into life. But it is our job, as His earthly agents, to loose people from their bondages. Who has helped you get free from oppression? Who will you help?

Chapter 3: Healing Rooms - The Dream
Bible Study

At Healing Rooms, oil is often used to activate healing (see James 5:14). Oil is a very important element in the Bible. It is spoken of many times to symbolize the Holy Spirit. Oil is also used concretely as a substance which is applied to people or objects for various spiritual reasons. The word "anoint" describes the procedure of rubbing a person or thing with oil.

1. If you were God and you got to pick the substance you would make special use of on earth (like God picked oil), what would you pick and why?

2. Almighty God chose the scent of several different spices, roots, and plants to be His favorites.
What did He choose to compose His favorite incense according to Exodus 30:34?

3. What were three of God's preferred elements, which He put on earth when He created it, in order that the wise men could bring them to His Beloved Son, Baby Jesus (Matthew 2:11)?

4. What components did God choose for the holy anointing oil according to Exodus 30:22-25?
   What else did the Lord enjoy smelling like (Mark 14:3)?

5. We as people, continually and simultaneously inhabit two realms. We are endeavoring to live in these earthly bodies while walking in the Spirit and interacting with a Supernatural God. Some decide to believe that Jesus is God in the flesh, and others hold onto the ways of the world and close their eyes to the spiritual. As you invite the spiritual to invade your physical world, ask Holy Spirit to help you believe that a "common" element of life, oil, can have the following spiritual benefits. Read the following Scripture and describe the spiritual benefit of the oil:

   - Isaiah 10:27
   - James 5:14
   - Ruth 3:3
   - Leviticus 8:10
   - Exodus 29:7
   - Hebrews 1:9
   - Exodus 40:9
   - Mark 6:13
   - Psalm 23:5
   - Isaiah 61:3

   Which one or two of these benefits (of the anointing oil) do you desire for God to make real for you? Tell Father God about your desire.

Chapter 4: Friendship With God
Bible Study

1. Read each of the following passages about Jesus taking His friends up on a mountain with Him. Pay attention to the change in Jesus' appearance.

   - Matthew 17:1-8 (verse 2)
   - Mark 9:2-8 (verse 3)

- Luke 9:28-36 (verse 29)
- 2 Peter 1:16-18

Mount of Transfiguration: Transfiguration means a change in form or appearance (metamorphosis); a change of physical form, structure, or substance especially by supernatural means.

2. Turn to Revelation 1:13-17, and read about the Lord's current appearance! Pause and ask Holy Spirit to confirm to you the beauty of Jesus' reality (feel free to ask God if you can see Him like John, the writer of Revelation did).

3. Who did the Lord Jesus Christ take with Him on the hike up the mountain (Matthew 17:1)?

4. What kind of emotion did the disciples experience when the glory cloud covered them on the mountain (Luke 9:34)?

   A cloud appearing on a mountaintop was a privileged experience in Jewish history, signifying the presence and activity of God. When Moses was establishing the covenant between God and His people and was summoned by God up the mountain, 'the glory of the Lord settled on Mount Sinai, and the cloud covered it for six days,' and on the seventh day God addressed Moses out of the cloud (Exodus 24:15-16).

5. What did Moses and Elijah converse with Jesus about (Luke 9:31)? In contrast, what did Jesus' disciples talk about when they were with Jesus (Luke 9:46, 49, 54)? Note the Lord's answer to each dispute.

6. Turn to Job 38 and ascertain some of the things that God likes to talk about:
   In Job 38:1, who is the Person who is speaking? Did God want Job to answer Him (verse 3)?
   Have you ever had God ask you a question? Pause and ask Holy Spirit to remind you of a question God has asked you in the past (what is one of the Holy Spirit's jobs - see John 14:26)?
   What has God asked you (ask Him what He wants to ask you)?

Do you want God to reveal His interests to you? Why or why not?
What happened to Job after he received revelation of who God really is (Job 40:3-5, 42:1-6)?
Then what happened to Job (Job 42:10-12)?

7. What was the question that Jesus Christ asked a Jewish leader in John 3:12?
Are you ready for God to talk to you about the things that He is interested in?

Chapter 5: The Living Substance
Bible Study

Since faith grows through love, let us review what the Word of God teaches about loving God, loving our neighbors, friends, and enemies. Let us grow in the substance of faith through love!

1. According to 1 John 2:3:11, what is the test of whether a person knows God or not?

2. What commandment does all the Law and Prophets hang on, according to Matthew 22:36-40?

3. Every time that the Word of God commands us to love God, it always states "heart" first (see Matthew 22:37). We are always instructed to relate to God with our hearts first. The sequence is as divinely inspired as the words used. God has a priority list for how to relate to Him. Is your heart first in loving God or have you altered the equation and put your mind first or your will first? Pause and ask Holy Spirit to show you if you are in His sequence. What did He show you?

4. After loving God, we must love other people. In the Bible, Joseph is a great example of loving others no matter what they did. Why did Joseph's ten brothers hate him (Genesis 37:3-5)?

5. What were Joseph's older brothers doing in Shechem when he went to see them (verse 12)?
   What were the big brothers talking to each other about (verse 18)?
   Have you had a sibling or other family member hate you without cause?
   Do you have love for that person still?
   Do you believe that God can bring transformation to your relationship?
   Pause and talk to God about how you feel. What did God say?

6. How was Joseph transported to the nation of Egypt (Genesis 37:27-28, 36 and 39:1)?
   God wanted Joseph in the land of Egypt because He had a great destiny for Joseph there. What do you think about God allowing Joseph such hardship?
   Is God working on bringing you into YOUR destiny? How?

7. Was God with Joseph in Egypt (Genesis 39:2-5)?

8. Joseph was thrown into prison for something he didn't do. Did he still have enough grace (Genesis 39:21)? Did Joseph have it easy in prison? Please find the answer in Psalms 105:17-18.

9. God gave Joseph the gift of knowing the meaning of dreams. In prison Joseph helped fellow prisoners understand their dreams. He was caring about others, even in prison! Eventually, the ruler of Egypt needed someone to tell him what a dream of his meant. Someone mentioned the prisoner, Joseph! God had a plan! Overnight everything changed as Joseph went from a prison to a palace because he could interpret dreams. Do you want this gift? Ask God!

Chapter 6: Basic Reasons for Sickness
Bible Study

1. Read John 9. Through the ages, people have asked the same question that the disciples asked the Lord in John 9:2. We all want to know what causes sickness and suffering, hoping to somehow avoid affliction

through knowledge. What reason did Jesus Christ give for the man's blindness (verse 3)?
Does this seem fair to you? Ask the Holy Spirit to reveal any complaint you have against God in your own life for the way He does things. Repent, receive forgiveness and then renew your mind with the truth found in Romans 8:28!

2. What method did the Lord use in giving the blind man sight (John 9:6-7)? Did the healing stir up a lot of conversation from neighbors and others (John 9:8-10 and 18)?
What was the task of the blind beggar to receive his sight?

3. The Jewish leaders totally missed the revelation of who Jesus was by continually asking "how" instead of "who" (verses 10, 15, 19, and 26)! If only they had eyes to see the Light!
What did the "blind" man say in verse 30?
What did the formerly blind man say in verse 33?
Who do you say that Jesus Christ is? (If He is your Lord, with Him inside of you, you can also spit healing light on others and bring healing! Do you believe this?)
Memorize Romans 15:29 to use to strengthen yourself in the truth!

4. The Lord did something so loving for the healed man! After being excommunicated from the temple, the Lord sought to find the man. What did Jesus reveal to the man (verse 37)?!

   When you are persecuted for your testimony of Jesus, you can be sure that He is looking for you to give you deeper revelation of who He is!!! What does Matthew 5:11 say about this?

5. Once again, enlist the help of the Holy Spirit as you read the account of another healing found in 2 Kings 5!

   In order to get well, Naaman (the leper) had to SUBMIT. Naaman had to listen to and believe a foreign servant girl, request an audience with the king of Syria and Israel too, pack up lots of gifts (and his own stuff), choose people to go with him to Israel, kiss his wife good-bye, travel a distance of over 100 miles to find a prophet he didn't know, and then get miserable instruction from a servant he didn't like. Then Naaman had to decide if he would listen, vent his frustration, humble himself, travel to what he felt was an inferior river, take off his clothes, and find a spot to wade in. Then, Naaman had to go under water once, twice, three times and decide if he would keep it up, go under water four times, five times, six times and, do it one more (seventh) time. Wow!

What kind of man was Naaman, the man who needed healing (2 Kings 5:1)?

Who was used to bring healing to this powerful man (verses 2-4)?

What do you suppose caused Naaman to be willing to act on the testimony of a servant girl?

Have you ever been given a word of hope from a person who was not of your *class* or *rank*?

What steps did Naaman have to take in order to walk toward his healing?

6. Naaman could have held onto his sickness because of pride or anger (verses 11-13). Who helped him pursue healing?
   Do you have any friends who encourage you on to good?
   Who are you encouraging this week?

7. Allowing anger or any other sin can give the devil a foothold, causing sickness to become worse. What does Ephesians 4:27 state about this?
   Pause and ask the Holy Spirit if you have anger that needs to be dealt with.
   What did He say to you?

8. Naaman's healing was progressive as he continued to submit (even though the result of dipping seven times in the Jordan River was not certain or logical)!

- Humility and repentance will not earn healing, but they will free the way for God's mercy to be laid open!
- Washing in the Jordan River. Jordan means: "Descending", which equals low and slow.

"Many lepers were in Israel in the time of Elisha the prophet, and none of them was cleansed except Naaman the Syrian" (Luke 4:27).

Do you have need of healing in your body? Where? What will you do? Take time to ask God for instruction about what to do to gain and give healing.

Chapter 7: Healing is Circumspect
Bible Study

In the book of 1 Corinthians, chapter 11, there is a phrase, *"For this reason many are weak and sick among you and, and many sleep [die]"* (1 Corinthians 11:30). Are you curious what the reason for sickness, weakness and death was? Read the important instruction found in 1 Corinthians 11:17-34

1. Were the people of the church gathering together for good according to verse 18?
   What was supposed to be the purpose of taking Communion (the bread and the wine)?

2. What do people who wrongly participate in the Lord's Supper bring on themselves (29-30)?
   What is the remedy for this judgment according to verse 31?

3. Why do you think the Corinthian people were participating in the tradition of Holy Communion without the right heart attitude or actions?
   Have you ever tried to appear holy or spiritual in front of other people?

4. The Scripture in 1 Corinthians 11, gives us insight into things that cause people to be sick or die. Look at the following (other) biblical reasons for sickness and jot the cause beside each one.

   a. Exodus 20:5
   b. Proverbs 13:12
   c. Matthew 8:16-17
   d. John 9:2-3
   e. Luke 13:16

5. According to 1 Thessalonians 5:23, what are the three parts of a human being?
   Therefore, healing may need to be any combination of one or more of these: Spiritual healing, emotional healing, physical healing, demonic deliverance healing.
   Is there an area of your life that you would like for God to bring healing?

6. What does God's Word tell us that His will is regarding healing?

   - Exodus 15:25-26
   - Exodus 23:25
   - Psalm 103:1-3
   - Matthew 8:2-3

Chapter 8: Hold onto Your Healing
Bible Study

1. What proof did Luke state that he had about the resurrection of Jesus Christ (Acts 1:3)?
   Our faith in Jesus is based on "many infallible proofs" and not on myth, speculation, prejudice, family religion, or gullibility. God knew the gospel faith would be challenged, and we would need convincing evidence that it is true. So, He has provided us with solid eyewitness testimony that would stand up in any court!
   "There will always be those who openly doubt your faith. They challenge, 'What if what you believe doesn't come to pass?' Listen, it's not our job to fulfill God's promises. Our task is to believe them." Francis Frangipane[1]

2. To whom did Jesus show Himself alive, and for how long Acts 1:2-3?
   Pause and ponder whether you REALLY believe this happened. What do you believe?

3. In order for you to get the greatest empowerment and deepest revelation from the study of God's Word, you will need to believe that it is a true account and that it will benefit you.

Read Matthew 17:19-20. The disciples asked Jesus, "Why couldn't we...?" What's the answer?

4. Most of us have some unbelief in our systems, due to choices, environment, heritage, and experience. It is important that we deal with unbelief throughout each day as it surfaces!
   Below is a simple prayer that you can pray when you recognize doubts, fears, or distrust that you need to deal with (ask Holy Spirit to make you aware of hidden unbelief).

   "Father, I renounce unbelief and doubt as sin, and ask You to forgive me. I ask You, Father, to replace them with great confidence in Your Word and great faith and trust in You."

5. Now that you have made a fresh decision to believe fully in the Lord Jesus Christ, what do you need for Him to do for you?
   Open your Bible, find a promise, write it on a piece of paper, and carry it with you.

Chapter 9: The Vast Importance of the Only Begotten Bible Study

1. In the following Scripture, find out how (where, when) Jesus Christ is the Divine Totality, Uniting Principle of the Universe, Sovereign and Sufficient Potentate, Creator and Sustainer, Life and Leader, Alpha and Omega, Center and Circumference . . . !

   - John 1:3
   - Revelation 22:13
   - Mark 13:23
   - Hebrews 1:2-3
   - Psalm 57:2
   - Matthew 19:26
   - Colossians 1:16

2. Jesus holds all things together, but He has given people free-will and consequently, individuals can cause disruption (division). Read Philippians 4:3. What problem is Paul addressing?

3. It is a very serious matter to cause division among God's people. According to the following Scripture, what kinds of things cause trouble in a church?

- Ephesians 5:3
- 2 Thessalonians 3:11
- James 1:26
- James 3:13
- James 4:1

4. What happens when people come into agreement with God and each other, according to the very words of Jesus (found in Matthew 18:19)?

5. Do you feel that there is any hope for agreement in the body of Christ in your city? Ask the Holy Spirit to give you a personal strategy for helping to bring His *unity of love to* your church.

6. Philippians 4:3 instructs us to do everything possible to *keep the unity of the Spirit in the bond of peace.* Is there anyone who is keeping you from being at peace right now? Pause and ask the Holy Spirit His opinion (Truth!)!

7. Before Jesus went to the cross (to die for our sins), there was something very important on His mind. According to John 17:11, 21, 22, what was His passion?
   Why do you think that Jesus Christ cared so much about this?

8. Will God ultimately have a unified people who speak the same words (see Revelation 5:9)?
   What will everyone say (Philippians 2:11)?

Pause and ask God to fill your heart with love for His people and the church that He loves. If you feel resistant to this prayer, ask God to reveal the root of this struggle. The unity of God's Spirit is based in love and that love is poured out through YOU!

Chapter 10: Seeking Medical Attention
Bible Study

Christians often complain that they can't hear God's voice. Yet, the Bible declares that His people are invited to hear Him. Please ask the Holy Spirit to speak to you as you open your Bible. **Expect** to hear from God!

1. In the following Scripture, who did the Lord Jesus state could hear His voice?

   - John 10:27
   - John 18:37
   - Revelation 3:20

2. Whose voice should we never follow, according to John 10:5 (and who is he - verse 10)?

3. Even the great prophet, Elijah, was sucked into listening to the devil. Who did the voice of the enemy come through against Elijah (1 Kings 19:1-2)?
   What did Elijah do (verse 3)?
   Before you start criticizing Elijah for being afraid of one woman (after he had just killed 450 men), read Revelation 2:20. What kind of power did (does) the evil spirit of Jezebel have?

4. Elijah knew he had to get away alone to hear from God. He went to the very place where the Lord had revealed Himself to Moses! Where did Elijah go (1 Kings 19:8)?
   Where do you go when you feel like you just want to run away from everything?
   If your answer was not "to the Lord," you may need to ask God to forgive you for turning to other things instead of (or before) Him. Pause and ask God if there is something He wants to show you about this.

5. Was God mad at Elijah for running (1 Kings 19:5 and 7)?
   What did God send Elijah?

6. God has spoken, at various times throughout history (and especially with Moses), in the ways listed in 1 Kings 19:11-12. How did God not speak to Elijah?

7. Did Elijah pour out his complaint to God (1 Kings 19:14)? Have you ever felt like "I am the only one?"
   The Lord invites us to pour out our complaints to Him! Read Psalm 142:2.
   Is there an injustice in your life that you want to tell God about right now?
   Ask Holy Spirit to show you (since He knows more about you than you do!) What did God show you?

8. After Elijah expressed his complaints to God, the Lord did not rebuke him. God simply told Elijah the truth and then gave him the next assignment! What mission has the Lord given you? (Invite Him to give you a mission!)
   Do you have a complaint that you need to pour out to God? Take some time to get quiet before the Lord as you wait for Him to show you what is in your heart. **Listen: God is speaking**! But His voice may be so quiet that you have to get in an undisturbed place to hear Him. If you do not have time right now, get your calendar and make an appointment with God. Write it on your calendar and then keep the date! You will be so glad that you did!

There are still vacancies in the ranks of the army of the King. If you are afflicted, step out and do whatever it takes to receive healing and then get to work . . . as a Doctor of the Cross!

Chapter 11: Standing on Your Feet
Bible Study

Open God's Word to John 3, and invite Holy Spirit to speak to your heart - He will, just ask!

1. Did the man who came to Jesus have a title or place of importance (verse 1)?
   Why do you think that Nicodemus came to see Jesus in the night?
   Have you ever hidden your relationship with Jesus (for example: not blessing your food in public or with friends who don't believe)?
   Invite Holy Spirit to bring to mind any times that you have not honored Him in front of other people and then tell God you are sorry.

2. Did Nicodemus believe that Jesus was from God (verse 2)?
   Did knowing this make Nicodemus a follower of Christ or a "born-again" person (verse 11)?

3. The Lord said something very radical to Nicodemus in verse 3! What did He say?
   What kind of birth was the Lord speaking of (verse5)?
   What did Nicodemus assume that Jesus was talking about (verse 4-5)?

4. Why do you think the Lord did not want Nicodemus to marvel at the terms He used to describe the new life in the Spirit (verse 7)?
   Do you ever get stuck with your brain instead of looking at things spiritually?
   When specifically does this usually happen to you?
   Pause and ask the Lord to help you with this specific issue and give you Scripture that will help you when you face this temptation.

5. What natural illustration did Jesus give to help us all with understanding His Spirit (verse 8)?
   As with the wind, sometimes God's Spirit is gentle, soft, and sweet. Other times God's Spirit is strong, powerful, and demonstrative. Which do you prefer?
   Is it okay with you if God moves the way that is needed for the time and place?

6. Why did Jesus expect Nicodemus to know about the spiritual realm (verse 10)?
   Does the Lord also expect you to know and believe in the realm of His Spirit?

Which is easier for you to believe: Things of earth or things of the Spirit (verse 12)?

7. Verse 13 is so amazing because it shows that Jesus continuously and simultaneously inhabited both the earthly realm and the spiritual. Where did He say He was, even though He was sitting talking with Nicodemus?
   How are you doing with navigating both realms of life?

Chapter 12: A Sound Mind - Agreeing With God Bible Study

1. Luke 1: 80 and 2:40, tells us that John the Baptist and Jesus both became strong in spirit. If they had to become strong, then must we also become strong? Or did Jesus and John both have something that we don't have? Read Romans 8:11

2. Who dwells in you? The same what?

3. If the same power that raised Christ from the dead is in us, then we can also become strong in spirit! Have you believed that you cannot be like Jesus? If so, repent now and ask Holy Spirit to forgive you and give you revelation of His power in your life.

4. What are the ways we become strong in spirit? Read the following verses and make a note next to each one:

   - Luke 18:1
   - 1 Thessalonians 5:17
   - Psalm 95:6
   - Psalm 150
   - Psalm 119:50
   - Colossians 3:16
   - Revelation 22:7
   - Hebrews 10:25

A strong spirit does not happen by accident. We must feed it and exercise it to be strong. A huge temptation is to use deep introspection to try to find all the sin in our hearts in order to get clean and serve the Lord better. But this is not the best plan. There is One who really knows you and can search around in your heart and bring you deliverance and healing.

5. Read Psalm 139:23. Who is the One who searches?
   "The spirit of a person is the lamp of the Lord, searching all the inner depths of her heart" (Proverbs 20:27). The Lord's lamp shows what needs to be cleaned out and repented for - all because of His great mercy!

6. If you have spent excessive time focused on yourself and digging around instead of letting the
   Lord use his lamp to shine on your sin, ask Him now to forgive you! Pause and let Him speak to you now.

7. We CAN trust the Holy Spirit to expose the sin in us! Read Romans 2:4 (NIV uses the word "kindness", NKJV says "goodness"). Praise God for His goodness and kindness!
   In the next chapter, we shall see more of the ways in which the Lord searches out and delivers people from hidden thoughts and demonic oppression.
   Read this excerpt from My Utmost for His Highest by Oswald Chambers. Then take a time to be with the Lord. *"Come unto me" (Matthew 11:28). Do I want to get there? I can now. The questions that matter in life are remarkably few, and they are all answered by the words "Come unto Me". If I will come to Jesus, my actual life will be brought into accordance with my real desires… "and I will give you rest," i.e., I will stay you. Not I will put you to bed and hold your hand and sing you to sleep; but I will get you out of bed, out of the languor and exhaustion, out of the state of being half-dead while you are alive; I will imbue you with the spirit of life, and you will be stayed by the perfection of vital activity."*[1]

Chapter 13: Pure Speech
Bible Study

1. Disputing in the mind and speaking words of unbelief can mess-up the atmosphere. Read Mark 6:1-6. What happened when individuals began to dispute in their minds?
   The next thing the people did was speak unbelieving words to each other (verse 3). What did Jesus marvel at (verse 6)?

2. Words have great power and influence - more than most people recognize. Read Daniel 10:12 to find out what Daniel's words brought, and then finish this sentence: "Do not fear, Daniel, for from the first day that you set your heart to understand, and to humble yourself before your God, your words were heard; and I have come because of your ___________________."

3. Our words become self-fulfilling prophecies. What does Galatians 6:7 state?

   "Words are similar to seeds. By speaking them aloud, they are planted in our subconscious minds and they take on a life of their own; they take root, grow, and produce fruit of the same kind. If we speak positive words, our lives will move in that direction. Similarly, negative words will produce poor results. We can't speak words of defeat and failure yet expect to live in victory. We will reap exactly as we sow."[1]
   Joel Osteen

4. Read and then ponder Proverbs 18:21: Death and life are in the power of the tongue..." How does this apply to your tongue?

5. At creation, God spoke the world into existence. "God Said" appears ten times in Genesis 1. You are created in the image of the One who spoke things into being. What does Genesis 1:26 mean to you?

6. Read Jesus' words, found in Matthew 12:36-37. Ask God to give you a deep understanding of His instruction.

7. To help with your task of silencing unbelief, read Joshua 6:10.

   Many texts in God's Word instruct us to "wait on God," to stand still, to be silent before Him. In Joshua 6, the wise commander, Joshua, commanded the children of Israel to maintain total silence as they walked around the city of Jericho. The memory that Israel's 40-year punishment in the wilderness was a result of the people's murmuring in unbelief was doubtless in Joshua's mind. At that time, the spies had returned with a report motivated by what man sees without Holy Spirit-given vision. Their unbelief - thinking that they could take the land, had sealed their fate in the wilderness.

   "With the lessons of history in mind, Joshua's directive to keep silent is a precaution that teaches us. When facing great challenges, do not permit your lips to speak unbelieving words. Prohibit demoralizing speech from your lips. Words can bind up or set free, hence the order to silence! Later they would see the salvation of the Lord following their shout of triumph. We cannot help what we see and hear, but our refusal to speak doubt and fear will keep our hearts more inclined to what God can do, rather than to what we cannot."[2]

Chapter 14: The Great Exchange
Bible Study

1. Have you been adopted, born again into God's family? What does this adoption mean to you?

2. In the following Scriptures, find a few of the benefits of your adoption, actually transferring your bloodline from your earthly family into the family of God. (We will limit the "benefit" Scriptures to some in Ephesians-but the entire Bible is full of the HUGE advantages of being God's child!) What are some of the benefits:

   Ephesians 1:3:
   Ephesians 1:7-8:
   Ephesians 2:1:
   Ephesians 2:14:

Ephesians 2:18: Ephesians 2:19:

3. If you believe the words of Scripture, you will now have a new awareness of where you live! According to Ephesians 2:19, you are a member of the household of God! You live in God's house and He lives . . . ? Where does God live according to these verses?

Ephesians 2:20-22
2 Corinthians 6:16
1 Corinthians 3:9
1 Corinthians 6:19
John 14:23
Luke 17:21

4. As a descendant of Abraham, the Covenant that Father God made with him is also for you.

- What did Abraham do that pleased God (Romans 4:13, 16)?
- Who are the true sons of Abraham (Galatians 3:7-9)?
- How do you receive the blessing of Abraham (Galatians 3:14-18, 29)?
- Who does Father God "give aid to" (Hebrews 2:16)?

For you to pray: I know that You, Lord God, will do what You have promised. You have not forgotten me for I am constantly in Your thoughts. You are waiting to fulfill Your Word through me. know that You, oh Lord, cannot lie; You will not change Your mind. I believe what You have said in Your Word. Help me not to give in to fear and doubt. Please reveal to me an area of my life in which You want to bring in the Great Exchange. I will do whatever it takes to be delivered, free, and help others find deliverance and freedom. In Jesus' Name, I pray!

Chapter 15: The Redeemer of Time
Bible Study

Insight and Instruction: A man in the Bible, Jabez, was cursed with pain by his mother. But Jabez bypassed his mom, went to God and received his life as a gift from God! As you study Jabez' life, realize that you must also transfer your destiny into God's hands. It may be time for you to receive your life as a gift from God and be free of any curses spoken against your precious life.

1. According to 1 Chronicles 4:10, how did Jabez reverse the curse of his name?
   "Overcoming A Curse: Within the larger impact of the curse of sin on Adam's fallen race, specific instances of "cursings" still occur as evil oaths, angry words, or verbal confusions that distill into human reality. An example of facing this reality with faith and God's redemptive hope and promise is seen in Jabez, whose mother had such pain in childbirth that she named him "He Will Cause Pain." Jabez reveals insight into the negative potential of such words and interceded for God's intervention. But confessing the truth of the situation to God and renouncing evil, Jabez was granted his request. God blessed Jabez and broke the effect of the curse."[1] The Spirit Filled Life Bible

2. You have a name by which you answer. Your name is important and has meaning!
   What does your name mean?

3. How many times to you think you have been called (your name meaning) in your life?!
   Do you like your name? Why or why not?

4. Throughout the Bible, *names* are extraordinarily significant. What does God say about His name in the following Scripture (there are multiple Scriptures that refer to the *name of the Lord*!):

   - Exodus 20:7
   - Acts 2:21
   - Philippians 2:10
   - John 1:12

5. Please read I Chronicles 4:9-10 again. Why did Jabez' mom name him "Jabez"?
   (The name, Jabez literally means *"He Will Cause Pain")*
   Did Jabez take his name meaning seriously? What did he ask God?

6. Do you believe that the words that your parents spoke (or others who had authority over your life when you were young) have any effect? Read the example of a child (John) who while still in the womb, reacted to a person's approach and greeting (Luke 1:39-40). What did John do when he heard Mary's greeting?

   Since a fetus can leap for joy in his mother's womb (as when Mary walked up to Elizabeth), a child is probably also susceptible to negative emotions. Pause and ask God if there is anything that you need to know about your conception and birth that needs His redeeming touch.

7. According to Isaiah 62:2 and Revelation 2:17, 3:12, what can God give you?
   What negative thing will you ask God to reverse for you right now! God lives in timelessness, so there is no problem for Him to reach into your past and heal forward!

Chapter 16: Time-Warp Healing - Heaven's Time Bible Study

The harvest is plentiful (already ripe) but few see. Ask the Lord of the harvest, therefore, to send out workers into his harvest field who see. Jesus invites you to be one who sees the harvest now, the kingdom that is now present!

1. Read the account of the Lord Jesus (as usual) talking about real things and His disciples talking about earthly things, found in John 4:31-38.
   What were Jesus' disciples worrying about (verse 31)?
   What was Jesus' reply to His disciples (verse 32)?
   Instead of asking Jesus what He meant, what did His friends do (verse 33)?

2. Jesus had a different kind of food than that which the disciples spoke of. What was His food?

What kind of food did the Lord prefer most (verse 34)? What did the Lord instruct in Matt. 4:4?
Real Bread: *"My Father gives you the true bread from heaven. For the bread of God is He who comes down from heaven and gives life to the world"* (John 6:32-33).

3. To get one's focus off earthly things is challenging but Jesus gave the directive of where to turn our eyes (John 4:35). What must you do to see what the Lord sees?
   What does Colossians 3:1-3 instruct us to look at?

4. Jesus Christ said to the twelve, *"Don't you have a saying? Four months and then comes the harvest?"* (John 4:35). What do you think the Lord was implying about *their saying?* (Before you answer this question, please review the following paragraph from chapter sixteen in this book, and then come back to answer the question.) *As western believers we may not understand the magnitude of the significance of the timeframe of harvest. No doubt the disciples of Jesus knew the facts about seedtime and harvest. For them the barley was sown in the ground and four months later the harvest came. But even more important was the fact that the barley harvest was the time of one of the four major feasts on the Jewish calendar - it was the time of Passover! During that sacred and holy season, the Jews would gather to meet with God. In fact, the Jews designed their entire life around this holy schedule, this calendar. Their devotion to God was that they would meet with Him on holy and sacred days - such as Feast of Tabernacles, Pentecost, Passover; their whole life was set up in a way to say, "We meet with God on these certain days and times." hen the Lord Jesus declared to His disciples that the harvest was already ripe, it must have been upsetting to their mindsets. Families all over Israel were anticipating the harvest-time festival like we anticipate Christmas coming in December (not the end of August!). Listen to what He says, "Don't you say four more months and then the harvest? I tell you, LIFT UP YOUR EYES, and see the fields are already white for harvest!" Right NOW!*

5. In what area of your life are you stuck in the time of *a saying*, a tradition, a custom, or a procedure? (Pause and ask the Holy Spirit to

show you since you will not know without His help.) What did God show you?

Are you ready for a transformation of your mind and are you willing to see as Jesus sees?

Chapter 17: Healing Revival
Bible Study

Esther is a marvelous example of patience and waiting with hope. Positioned in the palace, Esther was prepared and waiting for a bigger assignment. It may have been five years between the time of the first assignment (Esther 2:19-23) and the second (Esther 3:13).

Work through the following questions, asking Father God for an impartation of Esther's kind of burning heart.

1. What was Esther's cousin, Mordecai, doing according to Esther 4:1? What was the reason for Mordecai's distress (refer to Esther 3:8-9, 13)? How serious was the plan to annihilate the Jews (was there a day and time set)?

2. What do you think Queen Esther was doing inside the palace walls while a crisis was happening outside with her people (Esther 4:4-5)? It may seem that Esther was lying around in the 'lap of luxury' for the (approximately) five years since the time that she and Mordecai saved the king's life (Esther 2:21-23). But, a self-indulgent, idle, lazy person is not prone to rise to a call to lay down their life! Pause and ask Holy Spirit if He sees complacency or lack of discipline in your life. Invite Him to search you and reveal any areas that need to change. Repent and consecrate your life to God anew!

3. The courageous character that Esther displayed points to the fact that she had probably been waiting on God, expecting her bigger purpose and destiny to be revealed. According to the following Scriptures, what gives strength during a waiting time?

Isaiah 40:31
Psalm 46:10
Romans 8:18-25
Psalm 27:14
Galatians 6:9

- What are you waiting for at this current time?
- Are you waiting with expectancy and hope? Why or why not?
- Ask God to remind you of your destiny and purpose!

4. How long had it been since Esther had been called to see the king (Esther 4:11)?
   What happened to anyone who tried to go before the king on their own initiative?

   Do you think that Esther was afraid to approach the king? Would you have been?

5. What were the people of God doing, and how far was the scope of their mourning (verse 3)?
   What did Mordecai command Esther to do (verse 8)?

6. Esther responded to Mordecai's call with a decree of her own (verse 16). What did Esther ask for? (*Esther believed in the power of prayer and fasting and the reality of action in the spiritual realm*!)

7. Please ponder and contemplate the words found in Esther 4:14. Do you think that a sense of destiny and purpose was stirred in Esther as she read Mordecai's words, *"Yet, who knows whether you have come to the kingdom for such a time as this?"*
   What do these words stir up in you?

8. What are the last six words of Esther 4:16?
   Read John 15:13: How does this Scripture apply to the details of your own life right now?

HEALING SCRIPTURE

Many people have received a Healing Card from His Way Ministries, with the following Scriptures. Testimonies abound about the miracles that have come forth through believing and proclaiming the truth of God's healing. Order the Healing Card online: www.hiswaytoday.org.

Our Lord Jesus Christ went about healing all who were sick! Proclaim the following Scriptures over your life and over your family members:

1. "I know that the tongue of the wise is health and pleasant words are like a honeycomb, sweet to the soul, and health to the bones. If I would love life and see good days, I must refrain my tongue from speaking deceit" (Proverbs 12:18;16:24; 1 Peter 3:10).
2. "You are the LORD who heals me" (Exodus 15:26).
3. "The LORD will take sickness away from the midst of me" (Exodus 23:25).
4. "The LORD will take away from me all sickness, and will not afflict me with any of the terrible diseases of Egypt" (Deuteronomy 7:15).
5. "You have heard my prayer, You have seen my tears; surely You will heal me" (2 Kings 20:15).
6. "Have mercy on me, O LORD, for I am weak; Heal me, for my bones are troubled" (Psalm 6:2).
7. "Oh LORD, my God, I cried out to You, and You healed me" (Psalm 30:2).
8. "I shall not die, but live, and declare the works of the LORD" (Psalm 118:17).
9. "The LORD will strengthen me on my bed of illness; He will sustain me on my sickbed" (Psalm 41:3).

10. "Bless the LORD, O my soul, and forget not all His benefits; Who forgives all my iniquities, Who heals all my diseases, Who redeems my life from destruction, Who crowns me with lovingkindness and with tender mercies" (Psalm 103:2-4).
11. "He was wounded for my transgressions, He was bruised for my iniquities; the chastisement of my peace was upon Him, and by His stripes I am healed" (Isaiah 53:5).
12. "Heal me O LORD, and I shall be healed; Save me, and I shall be saved, for You are my praise" (Jeremiah 17:14).
13. "The LORD will restore health to me and heal me of my wounds" (Jeremiah 30:17).
14. "I will not be wise in my own eyes; I will fear the LORD, and depart from evil. This will be health to my flesh, and marrow to my bones" (Proverbs 3:7,8).
15. "Let the weak say, 'I am strong'" (Joel 3:10).
16. "I will have a merry heart and it will do me good like a medicine" (Proverbs 17:22).
17. "I will give attention to the LORD'S words; and I will incline my ear to His sayings. I will not let them depart from my eyes; I will keep them in the midst of my heart; for they are life unto me when I find them. And health to all my flesh" (Proverbs 4:20-22).
18. "Because I have chosen the LORD'S fast, my light will spring forth as the morning, and my health will spring forth speedily" (Isaiah 58:6-8).
19. "God will bring me health and cure, and He will cure me, and will reveal unto me the abundance of peace and truth" (Jeremiah 33:6).
20. "I will return to the LORD and He will be entreated by me and heal me" (Isaiah 19:22).
21. "The LORD will bind up my bruise and heal the stroke of my wound" (Isaiah 30:26).
22. "He sent His word and healed me, and delivered me from my destructions" (Psalm 107:20).
23. "Affliction will not rise up a second time" (Nahum 1:9).
24. "The Son of Righteousness shall arise with healing in His wings" (Malachi 4:2).

25. "Only speak a word and I will be healed" (Matthew 8:8).
26. "As I have believed, so let it be done for me" (Matthew 8:13).
27. "Lord, be moved with compassion, stretch out Your hand and touch me, for I know You are willing and I can be cleansed" (Mark 1:41).
28. Jesus Himself bore my sins in His own body, that having died to sins, I might live for righteousness, by Whose stripes I was healed" (1 Peter 2:24).
29. "I know I will feel in my body when I am healed of my affliction" (Mark 5:29).
30. "The power of the Lord will be present to heal me" (Luke 5:17).
31. "God has anointed Jesus of Nazareth with the Holy Spirit and with power, who still goes about doing good and healing all who are oppressed by the devil, for Jesus Christ is the same yesterday, today and forever" (Acts 10:38; Hebrews 13:8).
32. "If the Spirit of Him who raised Jesus from the dead dwells in me, then He who raised Christ from the dead will also give life to my mortal body through His Spirit who dwells in me" (Romans 8:11).
33. "The prayer of faith will save me when I am sick, and the Lord will raise me up" (James 5:13-16).

BIBLIOGRAPHY

Chapter One: Becoming a Doctor of the Cross

1. SI McMillen, MD, None of these Diseases, page 9
2. John G. Lake, Healing, page 7
3. Reno held the title as the Divorce Capital of the World for six decades: thisisreno.com/2016/reno-a-history-of-divorce

Chapter Two: How to Receive

1. Smith Wigglesworth, Smith Wigglesworth Devotional, May 15

Chapter Four: Friendship With God

1. Testimony used with permission
2. Linda Anderson, The Prayer Team Handbook, page 31
3. SLUG Magazine, Healing Ways, February 2016
4. Cal Pierce, Preparing The Way

Chapter Five: The Living Substance

1. 7 Great Examples of Scientific Discoveries Made in Dreams, www.famousscientists.org
2. dreamsocial.co/famous-dreams-sewing-machines/
3. www.dreaminterpretation-dictionary.com/famous-dreams-jack-nicklaus.htm
4. R.J. Davidson, Alterations in Brain and Immune Function
5. Jonathan Edwards, The Religious Affections, page 288

Chapter Six: Basic Reasons for Sickness

[1] Zachary Bercovitz Quotes - allgreatquotes.com
[2] Quoted from Dana Minassian
* Names have been changed

Chapter Seven: Healing is Circumspect

[1] Merriam-Webster Dictionary
[2] Larry Sparks, The Elijah List, January 22, 2017
[3] Paula Price, The Prophet's Dictionary: The Ultimate Guide to Supernatural Wisdom
[4] Heidi Baker, Birthing The Miraculous

Chapter Eight: Holding onto Your Healing

[1] John G. Lake on Healing, page 11
[2] John Eldridge, Waking The Dead, page 143
[3] Linda Anderson, Where Miracles Begin, page 114

Chapter Ten: Seeking Medical Attention

[1] Dr. Lilian B. Yeomans, His Healing Power
[2] John G. Lake on Healing, page 21
[3] John Hopkins, www.cancercenter.com/treatment
[4] Fred Rosner, Medicine in the Bible and the Talmud (page 13)
[5] Consumer Reports Magazine, August 2017
[6] www.biblestudytools.com/concordances/strongs-exhaustive-concordance
[7] Sir Isaac Newton, quotes.thefamouspeople.com
[8] Oswald Chambers, My Utmost For His Highest, (February 17)
[9] Consumer Reports Magazine, August 2017

Chapter Eleven: Standing on Your Feet

[1] CS Lewis, Perelandra, page 232
[2] Joy Dawson, Intimate Friendship With God, page 69

Chapter Twelve: A Sound Mind – Agreeing With God

[1] Smith Wigglesworth, Healing, page 148
[2] Francis Frangipane, The Bright Lamp of Holiness
[3] Francis Frangipane, The Three Battlegrounds, page 49
[4] Francis Frangipane, The Three Battlegrounds, p. 29
* Name changed

Chapter Thirteen: Pure Speech

[1] Is Your Tongue The Key To A Neuroscience Breakthrough? https://www.forbes.com
[2] Is Your Tongue The Key To A Neuroscience Breakthrough? https://www.forbes.com
[3] The Spirit Filled Life Bible, See Introduction to Zephaniah: The Holy Spirit At Work
* Details have been altered to protect privacy

Chapter Fourteen: The Great Exchange

[1] Peter Wagner, Prayer Shield, Regal Books 1992
[2] Derek Prince, Blessing or Curse
[3] Tony Evans, The Promise
[4] Legends of the Jews, Volume 1

Chapter Fifteen: The Redeemer of Time

[1] Kris Vallotton, Bethel Church Podcast, April 2019
[2] Arthur Burke, Plumbline Ministries
* Name changed

Chapter Sixteen: Time-Warp Healing - Heaven's Time

[1] Ted Dekker, Rise of the Mystics
[2] C.S. Lewis, Out of the Silent Planet

Chapter Seventeen: Healing Revival

* Names changed

Bible Study Questions – Chapter Eight

[1] Francis Frangipane's Eword Messages: Truth is a Person

Bible Study Questions – Chapter Twelve

[1] Oswald Chamber, My Utmost for His Highest, June 6

Bible Study Questions – Chapter Thirteen

[1] Joel Osteen, Your Best Life Now, page 122
[2] The Spirit Filled Life Bible, Kingdom Dynamics

Bible Study Questions – Chapter Fifteen

[1] The Spirit Filled Life Bible, page 526

Contact Information

His Way Ministries
1995 E Prater Way
Sparks, Nevada
89434
775.787.6259

Website and online store: www.hiswaytoday.org
Email: hwmoffice@att.net

Printed in the United States
By Bookmasters